The art of dyeing and staining marble, artificial stone, bone, horn, ivory and wood, and of imitating all sorts of wood; a practical handbook for the use of joiners, turners, manufacturers of fancy goods, stick and umbrella makers, comb makers, etc.

V H Soxhlet, Arthur Morris, Herbert Robson

THE ART OF
DYEING AND STAINING

MARBLE, ARTIFICIAL STONE,

BONE, HORN, IVORY AND WOOD

AND OF

IMITATING ALL SORTS OF WOOD

*A PRACTICAL HANDBOOK FOR THE USE OF JOINERS,
TURNERS, MANUFACTURERS OF FANCY GOODS,
STICK AND UMBRELLA MAKERS, COMB
MAKERS, ETC.*

BY

D. H SOXHLET

TECHNICAL CHEMIST

TRANSLATED FROM THE GERMAN BY

ARTHUR MORRIS AND HERBERT ROBSON, B.Sc. (LOND)

LONDON
SCOTT, GREENWOOD & SON
"THE OIL AND COLOUR TRADES JOURNAL" OFFICES
8 BROADWAY, LUDGATE HILL, E.C.

CANADA THE COPP CLARK CO., LTD., TORONTO
UNITED STATES: D VAN NOSTRAND CO., NEW YORK
1902

A·96+4+9

PREFACE.

IN recent times the dyeing and staining of wood, bone, horn and ivory, like so many other crafts, has been completely revolutionised, and has experienced a complete series of improvements. The introduction of the coal-tar colours has put at the disposal of the industry a number of dyes and stains which are now used in enormous quantities. Many dyers and stainers long remained ignorant of the very existence of these artificial dye stuffs.

In spite of the compulsory limitation of space, this manual gives an exhaustive account of the modern practice of dyeing and staining wood, bone, ivory and marble. All new processes have been tested, and have been inserted only when they have been found to be of practical utility. In this way much space has been saved for really important matter.

I have adhered strictly to my intention of giving only reliable recipes, and that in such a form that any practical worker can make use of them without further trouble. I hope, therefore, that this little work will be found of real service to the industry.

THE AUTHOR.

TABLE OF CONTENTS.

INTRODUCTION.

THE dyeing or staining of wood, ivory, bone and marble essentially consists in giving them a different colour from their natural one. It goes without saying that the process adopted must depend on the nature of the material As a general rule, the deeper the stain penetrates the more durable the resulting colour will be. Most of the dyes used are gradually bleached by exposure to light and air, so that it becomes necessary to protect them from air, light and damp by a coating of varnish.

While in the textile colouring industries we draw a distinction between dyeing (Farben) and mordanting (Beizen), and always regard the latter operation as preliminary to the former and as making the material fit to take up the dye, we do not recognise any such distinction in the branch of dyeing dealt with in this book. I should like to say that the words " Farben " and " Beizen " are here looked upon as synonymous, to prevent all risk of misapprehension

The directions given for the production of the different colours on the materials treated of are fully given in the body of the book. It has, however, been necessary to condense everything as much as possible. It need only be mentioned here that the operator will not get good results, even with the use of the best recipe, unless he understands the substances he is working with and the way in which they behave one to another.

1. MORDANTS AND STAINS.

I

ACIDS.

Sulphuric Acid.

Of all the acids which are used for our purposes sulphuric acid certainly takes the chief place. It is partly used with other stains to give them particular shades or for the solution of indigo

As a rule, two sorts of this acid are known, the difference being in the method of manufacture

The so-called English sulphuric acid is made by burning sulphur or iron pyrites in ovens with a good draught. The sulphurous acid produced passes, by a somewhat high chimney, into the so-called lead chambers. These are rectangular rooms of lead, supported by wooden framing, and arranged in series so that the gas passes through them in turn. An uninterrupted supply of air, which is necessary for the success of the operations, is introduced through a pipe leading from the last chamber to the grate of the ovens. In the first chamber the mechanical impurities of the sulphurous acid settle to the floor, and the purified gas passes into the second chamber, which contains vessels filled with nitric acid. This is reduced by the sulphurous acid, forming oxides of nitrogen, and then nitrous acid, which becomes intimately mixed with the sulphurous acid. The mixture passes into the third

1

chamber, into which steam is blown.   This, mixing with
the two gases, converts the sulphurous into sulphuric
acid, by means of oxygen from the nitrous acid.   The
dilute sulphuric acid falls in drops on to the floor of the
chamber   A fourth smaller chamber is requisite to complete this precipitation of the sulphuric acid, and into it
also steam is blown   Oxides of nitrogen escape thence
into the outer air   The sulphuric acid thus obtained is,
however, very much diluted, and must be concentrated
first in lead and then in platinum vessels.   English sulphuric acid generally has a density of 66 deg B.

The preparation of the so-called Nordhausen sulphuric
acid is quite different   Here sulphate of iron, consisting,
as is well known, of ferrous oxide, sulphuric acid and
water, is first calcined in special ovens to get rid of the
larger part of its 40 per cent of water, and then heated
more strongly in ranges of long-necked fireclay retorts
over an open fire.   As soon as white fumes (anhydrous
sulphuric acid) issue from the necks of the retorts, the
condensers are luted on, and the fire is raised till the
retorts are red-hot, and they are kept so till the condensers, which heat up at first, begin to get cool again
This is a sign that all the sulphuric acid has been distilled over, and that the process is therefore at an end
The yield is about 45 per cent of sulphuric acid, which
is at once stored in earthenware bottles   The residue
in the retorts consists principally of sesquioxide of iron,
a substance which, when ground and levigated, is known
as rouge or colcothar   This process used to be confined
almost exclusively to Nordhausen whence the acid was
sent in all directions.

These two sorts quite differently manufactured, of sulphuric acid, although agreeing in their general properties,
yet differ in many respects   Nordhausen acid emits thick
white fumes when a vessel of it is opened, and English sul-

phuric acid does not. The reason is to be found in the peculiar constitution of the Nordhausen acid While the English acid consists of equal parts of anhydrous acid and water, so that it is a hydrate of the former, the acid from Saxony consists of a compound of this hydrate with the anhydrous acid It is the escape of the anhydrous acid that causes the fumes above spoken of, when it combines with the water vapour of the atmosphere It can thus be readily seen how injurious it is to the Nordhausen acid to leave the vessel containing it open Indigo dissolves much better in the Nordhausen than in the English acid Nordhausen sulphuric acid is thick like oil, so that it deserves the name of oil of vitriol better than the English acid, which is somewhat thinner Both acids are remarkable for their extraordinary affinity for water They not only absorb enough water vapour from the air to become considerably diluted, but when added to water combine with it with much evolution of heat Two practical warnings can be deduced from these circumstances One is to keep bottles of sulphuric acid carefully stoppered, the other is never to pour water on to the acid. If this is done, so much steam will be generated that the acid will be thrown violently about It is essential always to pour the acid into water, and that slowly and with constant stirring, especially if the water is hot

Nordhausen oil of vitriol freezes at 18 deg C., the English acid at 34 deg C Both kinds of acid can be bought quite pure enough for our purposes. It is only necessary to see that the density is as high as it professes to be This can always be easily ascertained by means of a hydrometer.

HYDROCHLORIC ACID.

This substance is artificially prepared by distilling common salt with sulphuric acid To get anhydrous hydrochloric acid the vitriol must be used concentrated, but it is used diluted when it is intended to make dilute hydrochloric acid. In a state of purity hydrochloric acid is colourless.   It may be made yellow by dirt having fallen into it, or by the presence of a trace of free chlorine The white fumes which it forms in the air are formed by the hydrochloric acid gas which escapes from it condensing with atmospheric water vapour. Concentrated hydrochloric acid has a destructive action both on vegetable and on animal substances Its commonest impurities are sulphuric acid and sulphate of soda, which have been mechanically carried over by a too rapid distillation Chloride of iron, too, may be carried over if the salt used contains iron Free chlorine as an impurity in hydrochloric acid means that the oil of vitriol used in its manufacture contained nitric acid, which sets free the chlorine from some of the hydrochloric acid.

Aqua-regia is made by mixing hydrochloric acid with twice its weight of nitric acid It contains free chlorine, by means of which it exerts most of its effects

Hydrochloric acid is often used for bleaching various materials, and is much employed in producing brilliant shades in wood-dyeing

NITRIC ACID.

For our purposes, the use of nitric acid is somewhat restricted It is used mixed with other stains, or alone for the production of yellows

It is a colourless liquid, with a characteristic acid smell and taste When concentrated it emits into the air slight white fumes, which are caused by the vapour of the acid combining with moisture from the air. It absorbs moisture from the atmosphere. The commercial reddish-brown aqua-fortis is the strongest nitric acid mixed with nitrous acid. From what has been said about nitric acid, it follows that it too must be kept in carefully closed vessels

SULPHUROUS ACID.

This acid is of no interest to us, except as a bleaching agent.

Sulphurous acid is formed by direct combination when sulphur is burnt in air or in pure oxygen, and also by roasting many metallic sulphides, such as pyrites. It can be obtained chemically pure together with sulphate of copper by heating copper with concentrated sulphuric acid. Another way is to mix 24 lb. of anhydrous ferrous sulphate with 10 lb. of sulphur, and to heat the mixture in a retort provided with a wide delivery tube. The residue in the retort is sulphide of iron, which can be used for making sulphuretted hydrogen. Sulphurous acid is a colourless gas of sp gr. 2.27, and smells like burning sulphur. Its inhalation causes coughing and a feeling of suffocation. It neither burns nor supports combustion, and burning substances are at once extinguished by it. At from 15 to 20 deg C and under a pressure of three atmospheres it liquefies to a mobile fluid of sp. gr. 1.49, which produces great cold on evaporating. It is fairly soluble in water, which absorbs eighty times its own volume of the gas at 0 deg. C., and fifty times at 10 deg C The solution is colourless and acid, with a suffocating smell like that of the gas It has an unpleasant taste, and is rather unstable. The gas bleaches many dyes in the presence of water, without, however, actually destroying the colouring matter as chlorine does.

Oxalic Acid.

This acid occurs in commerce in finely formed four-sided white plates, and is used a good deal for our purposes. It is used for grading many colours, and materially assists sulphurous acid in bleaching.

Other acids, such as tartaric and citric, are not used in our business. The two just mentioned are dearer than oxalic acid, and give no better results than that acid, which is cheap and effective.

II.

ALKALIES.

Caustic Soda.

Caustic soda, or sodium hydrate, is put on the market in drums or in solutions of various strengths. It is prepared by the action of lime on a solution of carbonate of soda, when the carbonic acid is transferred to the lime. The caustic soda lye is drawn off, evaporated to the proper concentration, and then filled into iron drums in which it sets to a solid mass. The following table of caustic soda lyes (after Lunge) will be found useful:—

Specific Gravity.	Degrees Baumé.	Percentage of NaHO by volume.	Grammes NaHO per litre.
1.007	1	.61	6
1.014	2	1.2	12
1.022	3	2	21
1.029	4	2.71	28
1.036	5	3.25	35
1.045	6	4	42
1.052	7	4.64	49
1.06	8	5.29	56
1.067	9	5.87	63
1.075	10	6.55	70
1.083	11	7.31	79
1.091	12	8	87
1.1	13	8.68	95
1.108	14	9.42	104
1.116	15	10.06	112

Specific Gravity.	Degrees Baumé.	Percentage of NaHO by volume.	Grammes NaHO per litre.
1.125	16	10.97	123
1.134	17	11.84	134
1.142	18	12.64	144
1.152	19	13.55	156
1.162	20	14.37	167
1.171	21	15.13	177
1.18	22	15.91	188
1.19	23	16.77	200
1.2	24	17.67	212
1.21	25	18.58	225
1.22	26	19.58	239
1.231	27	20.59	253
1.241	21	21.42	266
1.252	29	22.64	283
1.263	30	23.67	299
1.274	31	24.81	316
1.285	32	25.8	332
1.297	33	26.83	348
1.308	34	27.8	364
1.32	35	28.83	381
1.332	36	29.93	399
1.345	37	31.22	420
1.357	38	32.47	441
1.37	39	33.69	462
1.383	40	34.96	483
1.397	41	36.25	506
1.41	42	37.47	528
1.424	43	38.8	553
1.438	44	39.99	575
1.453	45	41.41	602
1.468	46	42.83	629
1.483	47	44.38	658
1.498	48	46.15	691
1.514	49	47.6	721
1.53	50	49.02	750

The solution of caustic soda when packed in a drum is always attended with difficulty and risk, unless an apparatus is at hand for dissolving the caustic soda in the drum by means of a current of steam. This is done by placing the drum over a pan intended to catch the lye flowing from it. A suitably placed pipe leads the steam from below into an opening made at the proper spot, and the melting process begins of itself.

CARBONATE OF SODA.

Carbonate of soda, or sodium carbonate, formerly made
by burning certain sea-weeds, is now an artificial product
only.   Its manufacture may be divided into the old, or
Leblanc process (now almost obsolete), and the Solvay
process, which is now practised in all civilised countries.
It consists in saturating with carbonic acid a brine previously treated with ammonia gas, whereupon carbonate
of soda is precipitated.   The precipitate is ignited, and
the resulting mono-carbonate is sold as calcined soda.

Anhydrous calcined soda contains 58.58 per cent. of
soda, and 41.42 per cent. of carbonic acid; while the
crystallised salt contains 21.81 per cent. of soda, 15.43 per
cent. of carbonic acid, and 62.76 per cent. of water.

The following is a table of carbonate of soda solutions
after Lunge:—

Specific Gravity.	Degrees Baumé.	Weight per Cent. of Na_2CO_3.	Grammes Na_2CO_3 per litre.
1.007	1	.67	6.8
1.004	2	1.33	13.5
1.022	3	2.09	21.4
1.029	4	2.76	28.4
1.036	5	3.43	35.5
1.045	6	4.29	44.8
1.052	7	4.94	52
1.06	8	5.71	60.5
1.067	9	6.37	68
1.075	10	7.12	76.5
1.083	11	7.88	85.3
1.091	12	8.62	94
1.1	13	9.43	103.7
1.108	14	10.19	112.9
1.116	15	10.95	122.2
1.125	16	11.81	132.9
1.134	17	12.61	143
1.142	18	13.16	150.3
1.152	19	14.24	164.1

Borax.

Sodium borate or borax is a compound of soda and boric acid It has only feebly alkaline properties, but has nevertheless much dissolving and purifying action. Unfortunately it is dear, so that its use is not universal.

Waterglass.

Waterglass or silicate of soda is obtained by fusing together 100 lb. of finely powdered quartz, 60 lb. of calcined Glauber's salt and from 15 to 20 lb. of coal. It comes on the market mostly in the form of a syrup, and contains about 65 per cent of water and 27 per cent of silica

Ammonia

Liquid ammonia is a solution of ammonia gas in water, which can absorb half its own weight of the gas, thereby acquiring its characteristic smell, taste and properties. As the water increases largely in volume by absorbing the gas, the specific gravity of the solution is less than that of water In fact, the specific gravity of solutions of ammonia is the best test of their value All adulterations and impurities increase the specific gravity. Ammonia can be obtained in all sorts of different ways, for example from putrid urine, from nitrogenous animal offal such as horns, hoofs, hair, etc , but at present it is prepared solely from the so-called ammonia-liquor from gas-works.

The following table shows the percentage of ammonia in solutions of different specific gravities —

Specific Gravity.	Percentage of NH₃	Specific Gravity.	Percentage of NH₃
.8844	36	.8877	34.4
.8848	35.8	.8881	34.2
.8852	35.6	.8885	34
.8856	35.4	.8889	33.8
.886	35.2	.8894	33.6
.8864	35	.8898	33.4
.8868	34.8	.8903	33.2
.8872	34.6	.8907	33
.8911	32.8	.9021	28.2
.8916	32.6	.9026	28
.892	32.4	.9031	27.8
.8925	32.2	.9036	27.6
.8929	32	.9041	27.4
.8934	31.8	.9047	27.2
.8938	31.6	.9052	27
.8943	31.4	.9057	26.8
.8948	31.2	.9063	26.6
.8953	31	.9068	26.4
.8957	30.8	.9073	26.2
.8962	30.6	.9078	26
.8967	30.4	.9083	25.8
.8971	30.2	.9089	25.6
.8976	30	.9094	25.4
.8981	29.8	.91	25.2
.8986	29.6	.9106	25
.8991	29.4	.9111	24.8
.8996	29.2	.9116	24.6
.9001	29	.9122	24.4
.9006	28.8	.9126	24.2
.9011	28.6	.9133	24
.9016	28.4	.9139	23.8
.9145	23.6	.9245	20.2
.915	23.4	.9251	20
.9156	23.2	.9257	19.8
.9162	23	.9264	19.6
.9168	22.8	.9271	19.4
.9174	22.6	.9277	19.2
.918	22.4	.9283	19
.9185	22.2	.9289	18.8
.9191	22	.9296	18.6
.9197	21.8	.9302	18.4
.9203	21.6	.9308	18.2
.9209	21.4	.9314	18
.9215	21.2	.9321	17.8
.9221	21	.9327	17.6
.9227	20.8	.9333	17.4
.9233	20.6	.984	17.2
.9239	20.4	.9347	17

III

METALLIC SALTS.

Iron Salts.

The few iron salts used in our dyeing must be briefly described They are ferrous sulphate, ferric sulphate, nitrate of iron, ferric chloride and pyrolignite of iron

Green vitriol or ferrous sulphate is prepared artificially by exposing heaps of roasted iron pyrites to the air for a long time. Water is poured over the mass at intervals, and the liquid which runs off and contains the vitriol in solution is collected. The copper it contains is removed by means of scrap-iron, and the green vitriol is then crystallised .

Pure ferrous sulphate has a sea-green colour, and forms rhombic prisms Its taste is astringent and ink-like. It dissolves in water, forming at first a green solution, which gradually becomes reddish-yellow, with precipitation of an insoluble basic salt of the same colour Gently heated, green vitriol melts in its own water of crystallisation, and on drying out becomes a white powder At higher temperatures it is decomposed, sulphuric acid coming off and sesquioxide of iron remaining behind In warm, dry air the crystals crumble to a white powder by the loss of part of their water of crystallisation At the same time part of their ferrous oxide oxidises to sesquioxide In consequence of this the salt assumes a grass-green colour, and becomes covered with brown specks

There are different kinds of this vitriol on the market One is sea-green, and is pure ferrous sulphate Another is grass-green, a mixture of ferrous and ferric sulphates. Another is black vitriol, an impure ferrous sulphate containing free sulphuric acid, so that it is always damp, and

reddens litmus strongly. It can be purified by recrystal-
lisation, by which means a bluish-green variety is obtained.
Iron-vitriol crystals aggregate together into bunches or
else into lamellar masses The first sort can be got by
placing sticks or ropes in the crystallising pan, when the
crystals form round them.   The others are deposits on
the sides and bottoms of the crystallising pan These
crystalline masses are often met with broken to pieces.
Good green vitriol should have neither white nor brown
specks, but should consist of pure crystals with a fine
glossy lustre.

There is also on the market a variety called Salzburg
vitriol. This must be looked after, as it is very different
from ferrous sulphate, for besides that substance it contains the sulphates of copper and zinc.

Ferric sulphate is, as its name denotes, a compound of
sesquioxide of iron and sulphuric acid. It occurs combined with water in various proportions Only the pure
salt is of interest for us, as the basic compounds are all
insoluble in water.

Dry ferric sulphate is a resinous light green-yellow
powder, which is without smell, but, like its solution, has
a very harsh taste. It is deliquescent in the air, and
should dissolve in water and alcohol in all proportions
When ignited it gradually loses all its sulphuric acid, and
leaves a colcothar of a beautiful carmine red colour.
Ferric sulphate should be tested for nitric acid, ferrous
salts, copper and zinc

So-called red-burnt copperas, which consists mostly of
sesquioxide of iron, is made by heating ferrous sulphate
nearly to redness and then mixing it with one quarter
of its weight of common salt, and raising the mixture to
a full red heat. For our purposes this compound of iron
is used, but only occasionally, for the black dyeing of
certain kinds of wood.

Nitrate of iron occurs in commerce in two forms, ferrous nitrate and ferric nitrate. In the latter the iron is fully oxidised, and the salt gives blacks with tannin or gallic acid. At the same time, however, it has a very destructive effect upon woody fibre on account of the large proportion of acid it contains, so that it is not of much practical use. One usually prepares one's own nitrate of iron by mixing nitric acid with half its weight of water, and then throwing in iron filings and scraps of wire every four hours till the acid will dissolve no more. The whole process lasts about a fortnight, and the weight of iron used is about one-twelfth of that of the dilute acid. Finally the solution loses the smell of nitric acid, and is brown It is filtered through linen, and kept in the dark in well-stoppered bottles.

Tartrate of iron is a very soluble jelly-like uncrystallisable reddish-brown compound. It is used with alizarine for certain brown stains on wood It is most easily made by re-acting on chloride of iron with cream of tartar.

The so-called nitrate of iron of commerce, which, as is well known, is only oxidised sulphate, is of no use to us, as it contains far too much sulphuric acid and is very acid and sharp Used on wood, it would do nothing but harm Real nitrate of iron is much used for dyeing marble yellow.

For dyeing marble, artificial stone, horn, etc , chloride of iron is largely used; that is, the ferric chloride, for the other chloride—ferrous chloride—is comparatively seldom employed This is, however, only because we are used to the per-salt. If we accustomed ourselves to the other, we should very likely find that it gave the better results of the two.

Ferric chloride is prepared by adding nitric acid to ferrous chloride till it has assumed a dark brown colour, and then driving off the excess of acid by gentle heat.

The solution is dark brown, and will not crystallise. On evaporation it leaves a dry orange-coloured mass which is very hygroscopic and consists of 33 per cent. iron and 67 per cent chlorine Ferrous chloride is best made by saturating a mixture of hydrochloric acid of 22 deg B. and half its weight of water with clean iron filings Hydrogen is evolved, and a pale green solution remains, which can be used as liquid protochloride of iron When it is crystallised it gives a pale green salt, which is very soluble in water, and in air decomposes into ferric chloride and oxide of iron

One of the iron preparations which we most commonly use is the pyrolignite. It has the advantage over all the other iron salts that it gives up its oxide of iron more easily to the material to be stained or to the dye, and also that it is much less acid than the other salts of iron, so that it dyes our materials much better and does not injure their texture Any free acetic acid, too, which may be present soon evaporates as the goods dry after dyeing, and does not remain to act injuriously on the material

Ferrous acetate or blackstain possesses a characteristic smell and a greenish colour The iron in it remains in the ferrous state as long as an excess of iron is kept in the solution A greenish-yellow colour indicates that the sub-oxide has begun to pass into the state of sesqui-oxide It is prepared by dissolving scrap-iron in vinegar, excluding the air as much as possible, for contact with oxygen easily converts the compound into basic ferric acetate

Ferric acetate solution is not much used. It has a dark brownish-red colour, and tastes like ink. Heat decomposes it, acetic acid being evolved and a basic salt separating out in the form of a jelly and finally becoming hydrated ferric oxide.

Copper Salts.

Of these only four have any importance for us, vi^-, ordinary blue vitriol, the chloride, verdigris, and cuprate of ammonia.

Blue vitriol or sulphate of copper, otherwise bluestone, is used in large quantities by all colouring trades whenever it is a question of getting dark or black colours with logwood

Crystallised sulphate of copper is only occasionally found in nature, weathered out of copper pyrites, or in the effluent of copper-works which has dissolved sulphate of copper resulting from the oxidation of coarse metal. The salt can be obtained from this solution by merely evaporating off the water, but it is usually appropriated for the manufacture of metallic copper The salt can also be prepared by oxidising the copper and dissolving the oxide in dilute sulphuric acid. It is, however, most usually got by lixiviating copper ores which have been partially converted into sulphate by roasting.

Simple copper sulphate contains 31.79 per cent. of copper oxide, 32 14 per cent. of sulphuric acid and 16.07 per cent. of water It crystallises in rhomboid blue flat crystals, which in warm air fall to powder by the loss of their water of crystallisation After a time, however, they take back moisture from the air and become blue In damp air the crystals do not crumble, as naturally they do not lose their water to such air. At high temperatures the salt fuses and loses its colour, and finally loses its sulphuric acid, and is converted into copper oxide Sulphate of copper is soluble in five times its weight of cold, in twice its weight of hot, water, but is insoluble in alcohol It is very often contaminated with iron, and sometimes contains free sulphuric acid, especially when prepared

from solutions of copper-alloyed silver coins   The former
impurity can be recognised by the presence in the precipitate, got by adding ammonia to the dissolved salt, of
brown ferric hydrate as well as the blue hydrate of copper
The other shows itself by the crystals keeping damp,
owing to the absorption of moisture from the air by the
sulphuric acid, and also by the solution of such a blue
vitriol reddening litmus paper

The mixed vitriols usually occur in the form of bunches,
and have a bluish-green colour; the blue being less pronounced as the amount present gets less

Chloride of copper comes on the market partly in solution
(usually of 40 deg B) and partly in prismatic emerald-
green crystals. It is nothing like so much used in our
craft as copper sulphate   It contains distinctly more free
acid (hydrochloric acid) than the sulphate, so that it acts
very sharply on wood and horn   It is made by dissolving
copper oxide in hydrochloric acid. The crystals rapidly
absorb water except in well-stoppered bottles.

Verdigris is made on a large scale in many places in
Germany, Holland and England, but especially at Mont-
pellier in France   Copper plates and the freshly pressed
marc of the grape are interstratified in piles and left for
from four to six weeks   The marc (residue from the wine
press) soon ferments, becomes warm, and evolves acetic
acid, which combines with the copper which has been
oxidised by the air. When the mass cools it is a sign that
the fermentation has ceased. Then the plates are supplied
with fresh marc. Another plan is to expose the copper plates
to the fumes of arsenic or pyroligneous acid. When in any
case they have become covered with a sufficiently thick
crust of acetate of copper they are placed in earthenware
vessels and wetted with vinegar   This makes the crust blis-
ter and facilitates its removal from the metal. The salt,
which is contaminated with fragments of copper and bits of

the marc, is packed in sheepskins, kneaded with a little wine, and then put on the market

A good specimen of verdigris must not turn damp in the air, and must contain no black or white specks It should be bluish-green, have a slight smell of vinegar, and a nauseous metallic taste Proust considers that verdigris is a compound of neutral copper acetate with hydrated copper oxide and the concomitant water of crystallisation. If verdigris is treated with cold water it breaks up into three different salts—neutral acetate of copper, a soluble basic salt, and an insoluble basic salt But if warm water is used in small quantities the mass becomes dark blue, and contains a large preponderance of the insoluble basic salt, which, on cooling, settles out as an irregular blue mass without any trace of crystallisation

If verdigris is boiled in plenty of water it turns brown, and the more water is used the less heat is necessary to effect the change, which may take place even at 40 deg C. A brown hyperbasic salt precipitates, and the very dilute solution contains free acetic acid and the neutral acetate of copper.

Hence verdigris is only partly soluble in water, but in acetic acid it dissolves with the exception of traces of impurities From these it can be purified by powdering or rubbing through a sieve Intentional adulteration with chalk, gypsum, etc, can be detected by dissolving the salt in dilute sulphuric acid With either of the two impurities named present, sulphate of calcium will remain undissolved Verdigris dissolved in wax is largely used for dyeing marble.

Ammonium cuprate is only used for special purposes described below. It is made by adding caustic ammonia to sulphate of copper till the precipitate, which is first grey and then blue, has dissolved again When evaporated,

2

the solution leaves crystals which give off ammonia in the air, and crumble to a green powder

ALUMINIUM SALTS.

For us the most important of these are alum, aluminate of soda, and sulphate and acetate of aluminium

Alum has, for our purposes, a distinct advantage over aluminium acetate, because it is in a more convenient state, and can be obtained anywhere in sufficient purity Alum occurs in various crystalline forms in nature, in stalactitic rough masses efflorescing into small acicular crystals, for example in the alum-shales It also occurs in a fibrous state, as in the Island of Milo in the Grecian Archipelago, but at present the alum used in the various branches of industry is artificially prepared. One of the chief raw materials used is alum-shale. This, however, contains only two of the necessary ingredients for the formation of alum, *viz*, alumina and sulphur, and has to be roasted, weathered, and treated with alkali after the roasting. The alkali makes the mass brittle and crumbly, and facilitates its oxidation by the air. The shale is then lixiviated in wooden vessels to extract the sulphate of alumina from it. The crude lye is allowed to settle, and then put through a filter press. The clear lye is then evaporated to a certain point in pans, and then mixed with an alkaline sulphate. According to the nature of the latter we get potash-, soda-, or ammonia-alum. When the second salt is added the alum falls to the bottom of the pan in the form of a meal, so that the addition of the second salt is known as mealing The supernatant liquid is run off, and the alum is washed with cold water, and dissolved in just so much boiling water that the alum will crystallise out on cooling. The crystallisation is furthered by providing the inside of the crystallising vessels with numerous projecting rods over which the crystals form. The vessels themselves are deep, and either cylindrical or conical. The masses of tabular crystals are broken up and at once packed into casks. A similar raw material to alum-shale is alum-earth, for it contains no ingredients for alum-making beyond alumina and sulphur, and for the same reason it is treated exactly as above described in the case of alum-shale

As just mentioned, alum is, in chemical composition, a compound of neutral sulphate of alumina with neutral sulphate of potash, or soda, or ammonia. It therefore belongs to the class of double salts, as it contains two bases and an acid common to both. Its crystals are octohedral, colourless and transparent. When, however, the salt is basic, *i.e*, contains an extra quantity of alumina, the crystals are cubical. All the alums are soluble in water, and more in hot than in cold water. Their taste is sweet but astringent. Gently heated, they melt in their own water of crystallisation, and finally form a white porous mass, which is sold under the name of burnt alum (*alumen ustum*). The facility with which any one of the three alums can be made is due to the power of sulphate of alumina to form a double salt with the other sulphate, and then to crystallise out with it in a regular determinate form.

The alkaline salts, on the other hand, take one another's place to make the different alums, and must be regarded in that capacity. The alumina can also be replaced by other bases, such as the sesquioxides of chromium and iron, so that we have also chrome-alum and iron-alum Neither of these alums is used in our art, and we need take no further notice of them.

Commercial alum not infrequently contains traces of iron, which is a great drawback, especially to its use in red-dyeing. The alum can be very simply tested with a few drops of a saturated solution of ferricyanide of

potassium If this produces a blue colour at once or after a
few hours, the alum is useless for the finer kinds of dyeing.
But if, on standing throughout the night, it produces no
blue colour, or only a very faint one, the alum may be
regarded as being free from iron In the present state of
alum-manufacture it is very difficult to get the salt absolutely free from iron

Sulphate of alumina comes upon the market in the form
of white amorphous plates It readily dissolves in water,
and contains alumina free from such adjuncts as lime,
soda, or ammonia, and is therefore, when not too acid,
naturally more suitable and economical for use than alum

Sulphate of alumina is now prepared on a commercial
scale from cryolite In a furnace, cryolite is heated with
six times its weight of limestone, and while carbonic acid
escapes calcium fluoride and sodium aluminate remain
The mass is lixiviated with water, which dissolves the
aluminate from the insoluble fluoride of lime The solution is precipitated by means of the carbonic acid, which
is collected for the purpose, and forms carbonate of soda
in solution and hydrate of alumina as a precipitate The
latter is dissolved in sulphuric acid, and the sulphate of
alumina remains when the solution is evaporated to dryness.

Contamination of sulphate of alumina with ferric sulphate can be detected by adding ferrocyanide of potassium
to the solution of the sulphate In the presence of iron
a blue precipitate is formed, or if the foreign metal is
only present in traces, merely a blue colour Potassium
sulphocyanide added to solution of sulphate of alum gives
a red colour if iron is present even although its amount
may be small

Acetate of alumina contains a larger percentage of
alumina than other alumina salts It very readily gives
up the acetic acid and forms an insoluble compound richer

in alumina. Another advantage of acetate of alumina is that it will not crystallise and the affinity which it possesses for dyes, with which it forms insoluble compounds

For the preparation of acetate of alumina, until only a few years ago, alum was always used in combination with various acetates such as sugar of lead and acetate of lime or baryta, and in many cases acetate of soda. To-day, sulphate of alumina is used as a raw material. This is first converted into hydrate of alumina by precipitation with carbonate of soda. The hydrate is thoroughly washed with hot water till the washings are without action on litmus paper, and then dissolved in acetic acid. According to the proportion of the hydrate of alumina to the acid and to the dilution of the latter, we get solutions of acetate of alumina of various strengths, which behave differently on heating.

Instead of pure acetic acid pyroligneous acid has been used of late, which lessens the cost of manufacture of the acetate of alumina and makes it give fuller shades with many dyes.

For certain purposes other chemicals are mixed with acetate of alumina, such as arsenious acid, zinc chloride, common salt, sal-ammoniac and many others. Those which absorb moisture from the air, as zinc chloride does, are those mostly used.

The value of acetate of alumina is not judged of by its gravity, because the other salts present also affect the hydrometer. It stands to reason that that value depends on the proportion of alumina present in solution as basic sulphate or as acetate.

Aluminate of soda is prepared by heating cryolite with limestone in a furnace. It is soluble in water, and very easy to use.

In the preparation of aluminate of soda, alum is dissolved in water, and gradually mixed with caustic soda until the latter has completely redissolved the alumina which it at first precipitates

We are unfortunately prevented from anything like extensive use of aluminate of soda by the hyperalkalinity it so often manifests.

CHROME SALTS

The only chromates for use are those of potash and soda Among these we distinguish the neutral chromates of soda and potash, also called the yellow chromates, and the acid or double chromate of these bases, also called the red chromates.

The yellow chromates form hard lemon-yellow rhombic crystals, which, in the case of the potash salt, are permanent in the air. The bichromates crystallise in very beautiful triclinic four-sided plates which are permanent in the air. They melt when heated, have a very sharp, unpleasant taste, and are poisonous. The potash salt dissolves in from nine to ten times its weight of cold, and in from four to five times its weight of hot water The soda salt is rather more soluble.

Neutral chromate of potash or soda is prepared from chrome iron-stone (sesquioxide of chrome and protoxide of iron) This is ignited with twice its weight of saltpetre, and the chromate of soda or potash formed is extracted from the mass with water The solution is neutralised with nitric acid, filtered from the precipitated alumina and silica, and evaporated to crystallisation

Bichromate of soda or potash is prepared by decomposing a solution of the neutral salt with nitric acid, and then evaporating to crystallisation. Acetic acid can also be used instead of nitric. The yellow chromate gives up a part of its alkali to the acetic acid and the red salt settles to the bottom in the form of an orange-red powder The liquid is decanted, the powder is washed thoroughly, dissolved in hot water, and finally evaporated till it crystallises.

These chromium salts are most used, in combination with logwood, for black dyeing on all kinds of material, but they also serve for the production of the well-known chrome yellow and chrome orange. These are prepared by making chromate of potash or soda re-act in solution with acetate of lead. The double decomposition gives rise to precipitation of the insoluble pigment.

Chromic acid itself is used for black dyeing like the bichromates, especially for wood, bone and ivory. At the same time the use of chromic acid requires great care, as it is corrosive, and therefore easily injures the material to be dyed, more especially if it be wood. It also quickly destroys the brushes and makes them useless. On account of the powerful oxidising properties of chromic acid it must not be kept in wooden vessels, except those which are protected by an inside coat of a composition of resin fused with twice its weight of wax This not only preserves the wood, but saves waste of chromic acid, which, when it oxidises the wood, becomes itself changed to brown chromium chromate. The same change is produced in chromic acid by water which contains much organic matter, as river and brook water often does

The property of chromic acid to part with oxygen readily is also made use of for bleaching purposes. If, for example, cotton dyed with indigo is soaked in a solution of bichromate of potash, dried, and then printed with a dextrine thickening containing oxalic, tartaric, and a little nitric acid, those acids set free the chromic acid of the bichromate in the printed places, which become white by the destruction of the indigo. The same thing happens if chromic acid itself is printed on with the thickening, but the operation then becomes difficult on account of the trouble of finding a thickening that can resist chromic acid

To make chromic acid for ourselves we dissolve 6 oz of bichromate of soda in 30 oz. of water, and then add 64 oz of sulphuric acid free from lead, and of 60 deg B When the liquid cools, the chromic acid will crystallise out in dark red crystals, which, however, still contain some sulphuric acid. This can be partly removed by pressing the crystals between porous stones

TIN-SALT.

In our branch of dyeing the use of tin-salt for dyeing wood, ivory and bone has considerably decreased, and it is now hardly ever used except as an assistant to cochineal in scarlet dyeing.

Tin-salt is prepared by dissolving tin in warm concentrated hydrochloric acid, and then evaporating the solution till colourless prismatic or scaly crystals are formed Instead of hydrochloric acid, aqua-regia is sometimes used, and sometimes a mixture of nitric acid and sal-ammoniac, or of nitric acid and common salt Tin-salt (stannous chloride) thus prepared is hygroscopic and becomes damp in the air, turns yellowish, and deliquesces At the same time it gradually absorbs oxygen, and becomes hydrated stannic oxide. On this account the salt must not only be kept dry but in well-stoppered bottles It is decomposed by moderate heat in a still At first only pure water comes over, then water containing tin and hydrochloric acid, and a basic salt remains, which, at higher temperatures is decomposed into anhydrous stannous chloride and stannous oxide Tin-salt dissolves in a little water, but if water is added in excess turbidity results, as part of the chloride is decomposed, forming insoluble basic oxychloride, which remains suspended in the water This precipitation may be prevented by making the water first acid with hydrochloric acid, cream of tartar, tartaric acid, or oxalic acid.

Tin-salt has a disagreeable metallic taste and is very poisonous It often contains small quantities of stannic chloride, and it is then advisable to put a plate of zinc into the solution, which will throw all the stannic tin down as stannic oxide.

Stannous nitrate is also used by us, but only in special cases, *e g*, for a special shade of violet, with logwood and redwood.

Stannous nitrate is prepared by dissolving hydrated stannous nitrate in dilute nitric acid. The salt is not crystallisable, as, when its solution is evaporated, stannic hydrate is precipitated in the form of a white powder The solution is yellow

Stannic nitrate is got by dissolving in cold nitric acid stannic oxide precipitated from stannic chloride. If the acid is heated the salt separates out in white crystals.

LEAD SALT.

The only lead salt which concerns us is sugar of lead, neutral lead acetate It crystallises in four-sided prisms or needles, has an astringent taste, and is poisonous. It dissolves freely in water, and contains 58 59 per cent. of lead oxide, 26 84 per cent. of acetic acid, and 14.21 per cent of water. It is made by dissolving lead, litharge, or white-lead, in acetic or pyroligneous acid. Commercial sugar of lead usually contains basic or hyperbasic acetate, which prevents it from forming fine transparent crystals, so that this impurity is announced by the crystals being a turbid white The pure salt crystallises in transparent prisms, does not redden litmus, turns violet-syrup green, and only effloresces slightly in dry, warm air, but completely if the air is at above 40 deg. C or *in vacuo* over

sulphuric acid.   By cautious fusion in the air it loses
water and a little of its acid.   On stronger heating it
swells up, gives off acetic acid and combustible gas, leaving a mass which at still higher temperatures breaks up
into carbonic acid, water, acetic acid, and free lead and
carbon.   (

The prisms of sugar of lead when slowly formed are
large, with two wide and two narrow sides, but also in the
form of slender four-sided pyramids   The crystals possess
great lustre, and their colour is white with sometimes a
plug of yellow or red

If the colour is bluish, it is a sign that too much contamination with metallic lead exists   This is also easily
recognisable by the greater weight   A greenish colour
shows the presence of copper ; a yellowish one, that of iron,
or that yellow acid was used in making the salt.   The
presence of lead and iron may be detected by adding
sulphuric acid to a solution of the sugar of lead until
all the lead is thrown down as sulphate, and then adding
cyanide of potassium, which gives a brown with iron and
a blue with copper.   Sugar of lead dissolves in water,
but always leaves a white residue of carbonate of lead,
and which has been formed by the action of carbonic
acid in the water or in the air   If a part of the sugar
of lead will not dissolve in water it is either this carbonate
of lead or hyperbasic acetate, or it may be heavy-spar,
which is sometimes used as an adulterant of the salt.   If
it is hyperbasic acetate it will dissolve in strong acetic
or nitric acid without effervescence   If it is carbonate
of lead it will dissolve in those acids with effervescence,
giving off carbonic acid.   If it is heavy-spar, it does not
dissolve.   Sugar of lead is also adulterated with acetate of
lime, more rarely with nitrate of lime, which betrays itself
when the salt is treated with sulphuric acid, when nitrous
fumes are evolved as well as those of acetic acid.

Manganese Salts.

Of the great list of these salts the only one of importance to us is permanganate of potash or soda   The potash
salt is the one mostly used   In the textile trades it is used
in the bleaching of silk, wool, etc., but in our craft it is
only employed for brown dyeing, on wood especially. It
must be used quickly, as its aqueous solution soon destroys
the brushes. It must always be applied cold.

Permanganate of potash is made commercially by passing carbonic acid through a solution of crude potassium
manganate till the colour becomes a purple-red. It forms
larger or smaller rhombic prisms, which are black with a
metallic lustre by reflected light and a deep violet-red by
transmitted light   It dissolves in water to a deep purple-
violet solution, which, when acidulated with sulphuric
acid, has its colour discharged by sulphate of iron, sulphurous acid, hydrosulphite of sodium, or oxalic acid

Silver and Gold Salts.

Of these we use only nitrate of silver and chloride of
gold, and even these salts are only sparingly used on
account of the expense incurred.

Nitrate of silver (*lapis infernalis*) usually occurs in commerce either in white fibrous masses, or fused into sticks.
Its property of blackening organic matter under the influence of actinic rays is the reason for our using it. It must
not be forgotten, however, that it is also very destructive
to most organic substances. It dissolves in its own weight
of cold water, and in half as much hot water.

Chloride of gold is a compound of gold and chlorine,
and one of the dearest dyeing materials known   It is
largely used only in porcelain painting. It is got by dissolving gold in aqua-regia, pouring off the solution from

the precipitated silver chloride,* and evaporating it to
dryness by gentle heat on the water-bath. In this way a
chloride is got absolutely free from uncombined acid It
is dissolved in distilled water for use in dyeing. Sometimes, especially if too much heat is employed in the
evaporation, metallic gold remains undissolved, which
must be filtered off and redissolved in aqua-regia The
separation of this metallic gold shows that some of the auric
chloride was converted by overheating during the evaporation into aurous chloride, which is further decomposed with
separation of the metal on the addition of water

* The author presupposes that the gold used is a German coin in
which silver is the alloy —*Tr*.

2. DYES AND PIGMENTS.

FOR better discrimination we divide the dyes and pigments under three heads · —

1 Natural Dyes,
2 Artificial Pigments
3 Coal-tar Dyes

IV.

NATURAL DYES

REDWOOD, PERNAMBUCO WOOD, OR BRAZIL WOOD.

This is the wood of *Cesalpinia crista*, a tree indigenous to South America The tree grows to a fair size The heartwood is yellowish-red, the sapwood red The timber is hard, heavier than water, and contains a yellowish-red dye, braziline, which Chevreul isolated in 1810.

Besides Pernambuco and Brazil wood, the following other sorts are on the market : —

Sapan or Japan wood and St Marten's wood, also called Nicaragua wood, both relatively poor in colouring matter. For use in dye-works, the redwood should always be bought in the log, and rasped or ground by the purchaser, for ready-ground redwood is often adulterated with red sandalwood, or with perished and mouldy redwood

Redwood, like all other dye-woods, must be kept from sun and light as well as from damp, for all these agencies do much harm to the pigment

(29)

Decoctions of redwoods have the common property of improving by keeping in the dark, and giving softer and purer shades.

Since the introduction of the aniline dyes the use of redwood has much decreased, chiefly because warmer tints can be got with the artificial dyes, and greater fastness to light Redwood is still, however, largely used in combination with other pigments in the production of violet-reddish-brown and mode shades. But all colours so produced are inferior in fastness to light, and are rarely used except in wood-dyeing

RED SANDALWOOD.

Pterocarpus santalinus is said to be the tree from which red sandalwood is obtained Cuts in the bark of the same tree yield dragon's blood The tree is indigenous to Ceylon and the neighbouring islands, and comes to us in heavy four-cornered pieces, blackish outside and blood-red inside, which have a very characteristic fibrous texture, or else in the form of raspings. The wood has a slight smell and a feebly astringent taste The light red sort is preferred to the dark red. Four sorts of sandalwood are recognised by the trade—red, yellow, white and violet. We are concerned with the red only, as the others are never used for dyeing.

The testing of the wood for colouring power and for adulteration with logwood is best done by comparison of the colours got with others dyed with a sample known to be genuine and of excellent quality. In this way a very decisive opinion is easily formed. Adulteration with ochre is detected by incinerating the wood, previously dried at 100 deg. C. If there is a much greater percentage of ash than with genuine wood, ochre may be presumed to be present, and the conclusion may be confirmed by dissolving the ash in nitric acid, and making the solution strongly alkaline with ammonia and smelling of that substance If a flocculent brown precipitate (ferric hydrate) is formed, the presence of ochre in the sandalwood is certain.

Pelletier has shown that water hardly acts on this wood but that its colouring matter is easily extracted by alcohol, ether, acetic acid, or any alkali The fatty and essential oils, however, except lavender or rosemary oil, extract no dye from it. This behaviour of sandalwood seems to be quite distinctive.

MADDER.

Dyers' red or madder (*Rubia tinctorum*) is the root of a perennial Eastern plant, and used to be cultivated in the East and in several European countries. It dyes red saliva, water, spirit, ethereal oils, and even the bones of animals fed on it.

Many kinds of madder used to be on the market, but since the introduction of artificial alizarine one may say that the use of madder has almost entirely ceased, and hence its cultivation is a thing of the past. Exceptions may perhaps be met with in Holland.

As madder is thus of historical interest only we need say no more about it.

ORCHIL AND CUDBEAR.

These are two dyes, or really only one, which have also been almost driven off the field by the aniline colours and will soon be disused altogether as there are substitutes which are far better and cheaper.

Orchil and cudbear (the latter is dried orchil) are red substances shading off into violet, and are obtained from various kinds of lichen

The raw lichens contain no pigment, which is produced by acting on them with alkalies in the presence of air It is wine red, and turned violet by alkalies. Orchil is sold as a paste, cudbear as a powder They are only partially soluble, and leave behind more or less residue according to the quality. Many dyers like orchil to dye bluish, while others again desire a reddish shade It is, however, all the same which it is, and the chief desideratum is that the colour should be warm and lively. If it is too red, one has only to put a little lime-water or soda into the dye-bath and the desired bluish shade will result If, on the other hand, the colour is too blue, a little dilute tin-salt will put matters right.

Orchil extract is what is most used nowadays. It is a watery extract of orchil which has been evaporated to a convenient consistency It is thick-flowing and either violet-blue or red. The buyer specifies which of the two kinds he wants.

LAC DYE.

Lac dye is a red colouring matter extracted from stick lac It was first made by Stephens in India It became known in Europe in 1796 Bancroft takes the first place in calling attention to this dye, and his were the earliest recipes for using it published. The product which Stephens first put upon the market, however, was scarcely fit to dye with, and the present product is decidedly better

Lac dye comes into commerce in the form of a brownish-black dry powder, and is prepared and dissolved by treatment with boiling water and a mixture of hydrochloric and sulphuric acids.

This dye is only rarely used now as its place is better filled by many aniline dyes.

COCHINEAL.

Cochineal became known in Europe about the year 1526
It is a coleopterous insect   The dye is yielded by the
females only   These infest the nopal-plants and are collected after impregnation, leaving a few to form a second
brood   They are usually killed by bringing them into hot
rooms.

According to Pelletier and Caventon cochineal contains
a special red, carmine and various other substances.   Cochineal is not so much adulterated now as it used to be
when it was much dearer, but cochineal dust and leaves
are still mixed with the good cochineal, as well as earth,
which can be detected by levigation with water   To increase its weight, cochineal is sometimes kept in a damp
place where it becomes from 8 to 10 per cent heavier
The buyer, however, can easily detect this by the peculiar
smell which the cochineal acquires at the same time.
Cochineal must always be kept in a dry place   It used
to be much used in dyeing ivory, but to-day the cheaper
red anilines are used instead.   Carmine, however, is still
always made from cochineal.

SAFFRON.

Saffron (*Crocus sativus*) is a perennial shrub growing
wild in many Eastern countries and also in Sicily and
some parts of Italy, Spain and Turkey   It is also cultivated with much industry in fields and gardens, and made
much better than the wild kind.   It is a favourite garden
plant on account of its beauty and the constantly changing
hues of its flowers.

Saffron, as it comes upon the market, consists of threads,
twisted and entangled in all sorts of ways.   Single threads
taper from one end to the other, with three notches at the

thick end The colour is dark red or reddish-yellow, and whitish-yellow at the thin end of the threads, which are about an inch long, and lustrous. Saffron is adulterated in many ways; with safflower, long-cut pomegranate flowers, marigolds, etc. Such falsifications are known by the threads of the adulterants being whitish or only pale red or yellow, and not showing the tapering form characteristic of the threads of the genuine saffron One very crude method of adulterating saffron, *viz*, with boiled smoked beef, produces blackish threads in the sample, which, when burnt, give out the characteristic odour of burning horn. A saffron which has already been exhausted with spirit is too pale in colour and feeble in odour. Its dyeing powers are small, and the single threads are of the same colour all over Such a fraud is easily detected if the sample is compared with pure saffron, although it is not so easy when some genuine saffron has been put with the exhausted article.

ANNATTO.

Like orchil, annatto is produced by the chemical action of a sort of fermentation from the marc of the ripe seed capsules of the tree These are crushed with water, and left for weeks or even months until a violet-like smell is developed The mass is then pressed out, the annatto is allowed to settle, and the supernatant water is poured off. The annatto is then boiled with constant stirring to a thick paste, which is dried in the shade It is then packed for sale in the leaves of the tree

Good annatto has a warm red colour, occasionally brownish-red, and its colour is duller outside than inside Its smell is like that of urine, with which it is watered in the warehouses. From a solution of annatto in alkali alum precipitates the colouring matter of a dark brick-red colour, while tin-salt gives an orange precipitate, and ferric sulphate a brown one. The precipitate with acetate of lead is a pale brick-red, and that with sulphate of copper yellowish-brown. Annatto is very little used as the colours got with it are very fugitive

SAFFLOWER

We call by this name the petals of an Oriental plant which is now cultivated in Spain, France, Hungary, Germany, the East Indies, South America, etc. Its botanic name is *Carthamus tinctorius*. The petals are plucked as soon as fully grown, and mashed up to a paste with water to get out the yellow pigment from them. The yellow water is poured off, and the residue is washed several times with water, and finally pressed and dried. In this way the yellow pigment is got rid of in the main, leaving the red which is wanted The value of a sample depends upon how much of the red it contains, and is ascertained by crushing a known weight of it with water, adding carbonate of soda, and precipitating the dye on the material to be coloured by means of citric acid The value of the sample is then judged by the intensity of the colour

The red colouring matter of safflower is called carthamine, it is insoluble in water, but soluble in carbonate of soda or potash. It is only slightly soluble in alcohol to a pink solution Light rapidly destroys carthamine, so that it would never be used except for the extreme beauty of the shade it produces

FUSTIC.

This wood comes from the West and East Indies and Brazil. The tree is *Morus tinctoria*, which also grows in the Antilles, splendidly in Tabago It is a large, fairly strong tree, with a hard but brittle and easily split wood.

The wood is light or brownish-yellow and traversed by red veins, and comes on the market in chunks weighing 40 lb. and upwards. The finer the yellow of the wood and the more red veins it has the better its quality The best of all is Cuba fustic. Next come Jamaica and Porto Rico wood, and then the Brazilian sort. Rasped up fustic which has been long exposed to light and air suffers thereby just as the extract does under the same circumstances

If the wood is well boiled in water it colours it reddish-yellow, which becomes an orange-yellow on dilution with more water. Acids produce in the decoction a greenish-yellow light precipitate, which is turned to a dark reddish-yellow by alkalies or common salt Alum and tartar act nearly the same as acids, but the precipitate is of a lighter yellow Ferrous sulphate turns fustic decoction brown, and tin solutions give no yellow precipitate with it Glue-water throws out from the decoction a dirty yellow colour-ing matter, while a purer and finer yellow colour remains in solution.

The colours given by fustic with alum, tartar, tin-salt, acetate of alumina and acetate of iron, are certainly in-ferior in brightness to those produced by weld, but they are faster Fustic gives a fast Nankin yellow with chromate of potash, and olive and brown shades with acetate of iron.

FUSTET.

Fustet or young fustic is the wood of a tree growing wild in South Europe, but which is cultivated in the South of France. The wood comes from Dalmatia in barked logs which are yellow inside. The yellow colouring matter, got by evaporating the decoction, is a lustrous greenish-yellow mass with an astringent taste and soluble in alcohol and water to a greenish-yellow solution The solution is precipitated by gelatine and is turned purple by caustic potash, but the purple soon changes in the air. Alum and tin-salt deepen the colour. Acetate of lead or copper precipitates the dye in red flakes. Ferric sulphate colours the solution a light olive-green, and throws down a brown flocculent precipitate. Decoction of fustet is of a brownish-orange colour, has a feeble smell, a sweet astringent taste, and shows the following tests —

With isinglass solution	.	.	. dirty yellowish-red flakes.
„ caustic potash solution .		.	. fine red colour, but no precipitate
„ ammonia solution .		.	. yellowish-red.
„ tin-salt solution	.	.	. orange-red flakes.
„ alum solution .	.	.	. a slight yellow precipitate.
„ lead acetate solution	.		. yellowish-red flakes.
„ copper solution	.	.	chestnut-brown flakes.
„ ferric sulphate solution			. greenish-brown flakes.

QUERCITRON.

Quercitron is the bark of the black oak, *Quercus nigra*, which grows wild in North America, and has lately been introduced into France and Germany. Chevreul obtained the colouring matter of quercitron in crystals, and called it quercitrine The bark also contains a dun-coloured tannin which can be easily precipitated out of the way with lime-water or gelatine. Quercitron is even to-day one of the most important yellow colouring matters. It is richer in pigment than any other dye-wood, and produces brilliant and durable colours. As, however, in the tree the colouring matter is practically confined to the inner bark, the technical preparation consists in freeing that as well as possible from both what is outside the inner bark and what is inside it. To judge of the quality of quercitron, the colour is noted, its freedom from wood, and that its outer colour should be always pale yellow, not grey with a yellowish shade Finally, the woody parts should not be in long bast-like pieces

Like fustic, quercitron also comes on the market as an extract, both a liquid and a solid extract   Details of the extraction process will be found under logwood

Another important dye from quercitron bark is flavine It has sixteen times the colouring power of quercitron bark. It comes upon the market in the form of a fine dark yellow powder, and is dissolved in boiling water

TURMERIC.

This is the name given to the root of an East Indian plant. It contains a yellow and a brown dye, as well as gum. The yellow dye, when pure, looks yellow in small quantities, but in large masses appears cinnamon-brown or reddish-brown   It becomes damp when exposed to the air. It is only difficultly soluble in water, but readily soluble in ether, alcohol or essential oils   Hence even repeated boiling with water leaves a considerable amount of pigment still in the root

Alkalies turn turmeric to a yellowish-brown and dissolve it. Acids reprecipitate it with a lighter colour. Strong concentrated mineral acids, and also phosphoric acid, redden both the pigment and its tincture. The addition of water destroys the red and precipitates the pigment. Green or blue vitriol gives a yellowish-brown precipitate with turmeric decoction, and arsenious acid a pomegranate yellow   Tincture of turmeric gives with tin-salt a reddish-yellow, with sugar of lead a chestnut-brown, and with ferrious sulphate a dark brown precipitate.

Turmeric is unfortunately not very fast to light. Otherwise. its convenience in use would secure for it far greater employment.

WELD.

All the parts of *Reseda luteola* when boiled in water give a decoction which is yellow. and assumes a greenish cast on dilution. The plant grows wild all over Europe, and is cultivated in several parts of France, Germany and England Good weld must have a yellow or greenish-yellow colour, and have plenty of leaves and flowers The thinner the stalks are, too, the better the weld French weld is the sort most prized. Acids make weld decoction paler, while alkalies, common salt, and sal-ammoniac darken it, and, in excess, cause a dark-coloured precipitate. Decoction of weld gives with alum or tin-salt a beautiful yellow precipitate, with ferrous sulphate a blackish-grey one, and with blue vitriol a greenish-brown precipitate

A painter's colour is made from this, and also from the two preceding colours. This is done by mixing the decoction with alum, and then adding levigated chalk a little at a time till all the yellow is precipitated. The colour is much finer if the tannin is removed first of all, which can best be done with glue Various plants were formerly used as substitutes for weld, but are now disused.

PERSIAN BERRIES.

Many kinds of these are on the market. They are all very much alike and about as big as peas, angular, heart-shaped, and contain little hard seeds in several compartments The taste is bitter and unpleasant.

A decoction of Persian berries has a greenish-yellow-brown colour, is very bitter, and behaves to re-agents as follows. It gives—

With gelatine solution . . .	slight turbidity, flaky precipitate.
„ caustic potash or ammonia solution	greenish-orange, but no precipitate.
„ tin-salt solution . . .	greenish-yellow.
„ alum solution . .	weakens the colour
„ sugar of lead solution .	precipitate only after 15 minutes.
„ copper acetate solution	dirty yellow-brown precipitate.
„ ferrous sulphate solution	olive-green precipitate.

BARBERRY ROOT.

In the root of *Berberis vulgaris* is a yellow dye which has been isolated by Buchner and Herzberger and named berberine It imparts a yellow colour without any mordant, but the yellow comes out faster and more brilliant if the material is first mordanted with tin-salt   Berberine is only little used

INDIGO

The fast blue dye known as indigo was imported from Asia in the earliest times, and, since the middle of the sixteenth century when the Dutch began to bring it to Europe after the discovery of the Cape passage to the East Indies, its use has become more and more universal in spite of the prohibitions which were laid upon it by the various Governments. Indigo was thought to be a much less durable pigment than woad, which was at one time the only blue dye available

Indigo comes from *Indigofera tinctoria*, a common indigenous plant of India It has been introduced from India into the West Indies and America. To-day there are many qualities of indigo in the market, which are named some after their place of origin and some from their colour, and which have little interest for us in comparison with artificial indigo, which is one of the latest achievements of present progress Nevertheless the price of artificial indigo is still too high to enable it to drive the natural product out of the market It must be remembered that some natural indigo, such as Java indigo, contains as much as 85 per cent. of colouring matter, and that natural indigo contains other bodies, such as indigo-red, which are of great use in certain dyeing processes

Indigo comes into commerce as a dry dark blue powder,

having a violet and coppery shade. It is very fragile, and has a fine smooth uniform fracture. A very important property is that the coppery lustre is increased by rubbing with the nail Those samples which receive the most lustre by this means, have the smallest specific gravity (indigo is sometimes lighter, sometimes heavier than water) and the finest dark violet colour, are the best Accurate estimates must be obtained by dyeing tests or by titration with permanganate.

Indigo is insoluble in water, dilute sulphuric acid, hydrochloric acid, or any other acid that will not destroy it. It is also insoluble in alkalies, ether, and in volatile oils. Hot alcohol dissolves a little, according to Chevreul, to a fine blue solution On cooling, however, it gradually precipitates almost entirely.

Indigo dissolves in cold oil of vitriol to a blue solution. It is best to take four times as much vitriol (by weight) as indigo. Heat is evolved, the mass swells up, and a blackish-blue syrup is formed, which, after about ten hours, will give a blue solution in water. Nordhausen sulphuric acid dissolves indigo much more quickly and better than the ordinary acid. If the solution of indigo in the acid is neutralised with carbonate of soda or potash it remains blue, and only a part of the indigo is reprecipitated in the form of indigo-carmine. or, better, sodium or potassium sulphindigotate. Alkalies and alkaline earths will only in very small measure separate sulphuric acid from its combination with indigo. and many neutral salts will do as much, viz, sal-ammoniac, common salt, alum, etc

LOGWOOD.

The native country of this tree (*Hæmatoxylon Campeachianum*) is Mexico, and formerly especially that part of Yucatan called Campeachy, from which it derives its name.

From there it was introduced first into Jamaica, and then into other of the West Indian Islands.

The inner close-grained heavy wood is known as logwood or Campeachy wood. It is received in large masses of a yellowish-red colour inside, of rugged surface, and. owing to exposure to the air, of a blackish or blood-red colour outside Transverse sections show small dark red wavy rings. The wood is very close and firm, is difficult to cut, and is heavier than water When chewed it dyes the saliva a reddish-brown. The smell of the wood when ground or rubbed is slightly violaceous, and its taste is sweetish and slightly astringent, leaving a bitter after taste.

On boiling with water, logwood gives a deep red decoction. The colour is deepened by acids, and turned violet by alkalies and metallic oxides and their basic salts Spirit also extracts the colouring matter

Logwood is classed as splitting unevenly or evenly The former is the better kind Honduras wood is of less value, and Jamaica wood with an even surface (because it is sawn) is the worst. The logwood coming on the market in a rasped up or ground state is often adulterated with other wood or with the bark of the hæmatoxylon, and it is hence advisable to cut up one's own wood. To compare samples of logwood, they are treated in the same state of subdivision with equal quantities of water, and the colours of the infusions are compared after half an hour. That which shows the most colour shows the best wood Pure water is coloured yellow by logwood, but hard water becomes first purple-red, then violet, then blue. Acids give a red colour. finally passing to yellow.

Logwood is usually wetted with water two or three weeks before it is used so that the colouring matter can develop better. This operation is called " ageing " The rasped logwood undergoing the process must be kept in a dark place.

Logwood decoction gives:—

With alum solution	.		.	a blue precipitate.
„ tin-salt solution	.	.	.	a blue precipitate.
„ nitric acid	.	.	.	it becomes paler and yellower, and a yellow precipitate forms on standing.
„ ammonia	.	.		the colour becomes reddish-blue and dirty on standing.
„ ferric chloride	.	.	.	a dark yellowish-brown or dark violet-blue precipitate

Logwood extract is now more used than the wood itself, for it is for most purposes cheaper and better to work with. Large factories are employed in making it There is a liquid and a dry extract The former is sold in casks, the latter in cases. Ordinary extract is three times as rich in colouring matter as the wood. Besides these extracts there is another market article, the so-called hæmateine, which is the name of the colouring matter itself, but the powder known in commerce by the name is rarely more than the dry extract of the wood.

In spite of the coal-tar dyes logwood is still largely used with iron or chrome for black dyeing

CUTCH.

Cutch or catechu is an extract from decoctions of various plants. Its origin has not long been known The commercial article is of two kinds One is from *Acacia (Mimosa) catechu*, a small tree growing in Canara and Behar The tree is cut down when the flow of sap is most vigorous, and barked The wood is cut up small, and boiled in a narrow-necked vessel till half the water is evaporated. The decoction is then evaporated completely without straining in wide earthen pans The mass is left to stand a day and dried in the sun, being constantly turned over The extract is finally spread on cloths, previously plastered with ashes and cow dung, and cut into quadrangular pieces, which are fully dried in the sun.

The darker the wood is the darker should be the extract. The quadrangular pieces of extract coming on the market are of a uniform dark brown colour with an irregular fracture and a slight waxy lustre something like opium. It often contains small air bubbles. It has a burnt smell, but not very pronounced. It is gritty to the teeth. The taste is astringent. The dry powder is a dark coffee brown

The second sort of cutch comes from the catechu palm, one of the finest in the East Indies. Its fruits, the size of an acorn or small plum, are much used, with betel leaves and a little lime, for chewing. The extract is made from these nuts by decoction and evaporation.

Many sorts of cutch are recognised, but the difference is merely in the method of preparation, and chiefly depends on whether earthen or iron vessels were used

Besides the above two cutches there is a yellow kind (gambier) which consists, as a rule, of inch-long dice-shaped pieces In spite of the fact that brown cutch is usually dearer than gambier, dyers always prefer the former, which is the more remarkable as the brown kind is often made from the yellow Such cutch is called prepared cutch, and is made by simply fusing the yellow cutch over a gentle fire and adding to it 1 per cent of its weight of chromate of potash, so that the cutch is partly oxidised

A good cutch must not contain more than 3 per cent of bodies insoluble in boiling water, and must be uniformly dark brown and close in grain, with a smooth conchoidal fracture having a greasy metallic lustre. Cutch may be known from gall-tannin by being more soluble in water, and being soluble in alcohol. It gives an olive-green precipitate with iron, and its gelatine compound gradually turns brown The following reactions are shown with a 10 per cent solution of cutch :—

Colour of aqueous solution : reddish-brown.
Acids make the colour paler.
Alkalies make the colour darker.
Proto-sulphate of iron gives an olive-brown precipitate.
Ferric sulphate gives an olive-green precipitate.
Copper sulphate gives a yellowish-brown precipitate.
Aluminium chloride gives a brownish-yellow precipitate.
Bichromate of potash gives an abundant brown precipitate.
Acetate of lead gives a salmon-coloured precipitate.
Alum makes the solution paler.

GALL NUTS.

These are excrescences formed on the leaves of various oaks by the sting of an insect   Two sorts are usually distinguished in commerce, the black and the white—the Asiatic and the European.   Their chief constituent is tannin, of which the best kinds contain as much as 65 per cent   This tannin hardly changes solutions of ferrous salts, but gives a bluish-black precipitate with ferric salts.   A decoction of galls gives .—

With tin-salt . . a yellowish precipitate.
„ alum . . . a yellowish-green precipitate.
„ copper acetate . . . a chocolate-brown precipitate.
„ ferric sulphate . . . a bluish-black precipitate.
„ sulphuric acid . . . a dirty yellow precipitate.

SUMACH.

Sumach is the powder of the young twigs and leaves of a shrub which grows wild in the Levant and in South Europe, and is also cultivated   Sumach contains gallic acid, tannin, and a greenish-yellow colouring matter, probably consisting partly of chlorophyll.   A 10 per cent solution of sumach has a very strong smell, an astringent taste, and gives the following tests :—

With gelatine	. .	.	. an abundant white precipitate.
„	alkalies in excess .	.	. a greenish or reddish-white precipitate.
„	weak acids .		. a slight turbidity.
„	lime .	.	a white precipitate, turning green or red on contact with the air.
„	alum . .	.	. an abundant pale yellow precipitate.
„	ferric sulphate .		. an abundant flaky blue precipitate.
„	tin-salt .		. an abundant yellowish-white precipitate.
„	copper acetate .	.	a yellowish-brown precipitate.
„	lead acetate .	.	an abundant white precipitate.

KNOPPERN.

Knoppern or acorn galls are acorns which have become misshapen from the sting of a wasp. They have a dark brown colour and irregular shape, and enclose the eggs and pupæ of the wasp When these have escaped the galls are very light and not of much use They come from Hungary and the neighbourhood. They are richer in tannin than oak bark and equal in that respect to gall nuts.

A solid extract of them is on the market, but it is only used for tanning hides

V.

ARTIFICIAL PIGMENTS

WHITE-LEAD.

Lead oxide forms with carbonic acid a beautiful white compound known in commerce as white-lead, and prized for its pure white colour, its durability, and especially for its body, in which it exceeds all other whites. Rubbed up with oil it serves for grading other colours, and forms the basis of all mixed pigments, because it gives durability and a fine lustrous appearance. Various kinds of white-

lead are known, varying according to the method of manufacture.

There are other whites having nothing to do with white-
lead, *e.g.*, Spanish white, which is simply oxide of bismuth,
and has a brilliant white colour, but is blackened by light
and sulphuretted hydrogen Zinc white has not the fine
pure colour of white-lead, but is not so easily browned by
sulphurous fumes

Commercial white-lead is often adulterated with barytes,
gypsum, or chalk. The two former are left undissolved
on the addition of nitric acid or acetic acid The last is
detected if the concentrated solution so obtained is treated
with hydrochloric acid or solution of common salt, which
will give in the liquid, whether adulterated or not, a white
precipitate of lead chloride. Hardly any lead will be left
in the solution which is filtered off and evaporated down.
If it gives a deliquescent residue (calcium chloride), there
was chalk in the original white-lead. Another way is to
precipitate the nitric acid solution of the suspected white-
lead with ammonia The lime remains undissolved, and
can be detected by precipitation of the filtrate with carbonate of potash. Sulphuretted hydrogen can be used to
throw down the lead instead of ammonia. It is said, too,
that bone earth is sometimes mixed with white-lead. This
adulteration is detected by the ammonia used as above
for precipitating the lead remaining in solution as phosphate if bone earth was present. If the filtrate then
evaporated be ignited, a residue is left of glacial phosphoric acid. Every 40 grains of this correspond with 100
of bone earth.

Sometimes, too, it is said, sulphate of lead and chloride
of lead are substituted for white-lead, but they are at once
detected by their insolubility or difficulty of solution in
nitric acid. If the residue dissolves in hot hydrochloric
acid, it is lead sulphate.

NAPLES YELLOW.

Naples earth or Naples yellow is an antimonious lead salt, which has a light or dark yellow colour, according to the proportion between its ingredients. Passeri has given the following variations which in the order given pass from light to dark yellow —

Antimony			4,	Lead				6
„			4,	„				7
„			4,	„				5
„			4,	„				3
„			2,	„				4
„			2,	„				3

There are also additions of from 8 to 12 per cent of tartar, or 6 to 12 per cent common salt, or of 8 per cent of alum and sal-ammoniac The two metals are calcined separately and the oxides mixed, or they are alloyed together and the alloy calcined. The oxides are mixed with the other ingredients, finely powdered and sifted, and the whole is calcined in shallow vessels and then ground

Naples yellow is very valuable in the painting of glass, porcelain and earthenware For use as a water-colour on wood it is rubbed up with gum water, which gives it a more golden shade For rubbing up this pigment a very hard marble is required, and it must be worked with an ivory spatula An ordinary stone slab or an iron spatula will spoil it by making it green. Calcium tungstate has been tried as a substitute for Naples yellow. It is boiled with hydrochloric acid, and reprecipitates when cold, and is then washed with water Of late chrome yellow has replaced Naples yellow almost entirely

RED-LEAD.

Red-lead is prepared on a large scale by calcining moderately damp and finely ground and levigated massicot for

48 hours in a reverberating furnace, and constantly stirring it the while so as to bring every part into contact with the air. As soon as it has assumed the characteristic beautiful colour of red-lead, all openings are stopped, the fire is drawn, and the furnace is allowed to cool. The longer this takes, the better the red-lead will be. The cold mass is sieved through a fine hair sieve (enclosed in a box, to preserve the health of the men employed) to separate the red-lead from unchanged massicot.

Red-lead is chiefly used as a ground colour to be followed by a coat of cinnabar. For this purpose the pigment is rubbed up with drying oil. The first coat usually consists of red-lead alone, the second of equal parts of red-lead and cinnabar, and the third of cinnabar alone. It is also used as a distemper colour, and as a basis for gold or silver colouring on glass, and also for gilding and silvering other things, and also to impart drying qualities to linseed oil. In using red-lead as a pigment care must be taken not to rub it up too long with water, or it will lose all its beauty and get quite pale. Hence the pigment is best got finely divided by levigation.

The deep red of red-lead has a yellowish shade on account of unseparated massicot. When rubbed on paper with the finger it is nearly yellow. It consists of extremely minute scales, is destitute both of smell and taste, and insoluble in water. At a strong red-heat it loses oxygen and becomes litharge. Even in sunlight it blackens and loses oxygen. Heated on charcoal before the blowpipe, it is reduced to metallic lead. This is a sure way of detecting adulteration with brick dust, which remains unchanged in the process, and will not dissolve in acetic acid.

SMALTS.

Smalts or zaffre is chiefly used as a washing blue, being added to the starch, and also for colouring glass and porcelain, and as a pigment As a glazing colour for porcelain and glass cobalt oxide has now, however, the preference It is sold by the Saxony Smalts Works Smalts is an indestructible pigment used with boiled oil on wood for fresco-painting and for house-painting. It is a glass coloured blue by oxide of cobalt, and contains a little arsenic It is put on the market in fine powder It is got by fusing together sand, potash or cobalt oxide, and breaking up and levigating the resulting glass The cobalt ores are sorted, the nickeliferous ones are removed, and the rest are roasted to free them from arsenic and water, to further oxidise the cobalt and to make the substance fit for vitrification It is then ground and mixed with more or less sand It then can already be used for colouring glass blue, and is sold under the name of zaffre

Smalts is classified in a variety of tints and qualities, and these again, according to the shade and degree of fineness, are styled by various names and marks The finest marks of all are always called azure blue or king's blue, and eschel comes next Smalts is used in the many ways already mentioned If it is to be used for walls it must be rubbed up fine with spirits, and stirred up in glue-water. Ordinarily smalts should not be used with boiled oil as it then readily turns blackish. A very beautiful blue, almost equal to ultramarine, is Thenard's blue This blue, which can be used for every kind of painting, shows the greatest resistance to all manner of external influences, and of a warm colour almost surpassing the darkest ultramarine, used to be much used as a substitute for that pigment , but the ultramarine is now restored to its former position by having become cheaper. King's blue. Thenard's blue, cobalt, and ultramarine are scarcely used now except in the pottery trades, for in that artificial ultramarine cannot replace them as it cannot be fused with borax or lead glass fluxes without losing its colour from chemical change.

Stannate of cobalt (coeruleum) is hardly ever used.

ULTRAMARINE.

In describing this beautiful blue pigment we have naturally for our purposes the artificial product in view. Since success has attended the efforts to produce it on a large scale, the natural mineral is hardly ever sold, and finds room only in museums

In general, natural ultramarine has the properties and the composition of the artificial product, but shows some chemical differences from it. The principal of these is the ease with which the artificial product is decomposed by acetic acid and alum, re-agents which do not affect the natural mineral The rapid decomposition of artificial ultramarine by acetic acid is attended with the evolution of sulphuretted hydrogen

Artificial ultramarine can be used as a water-, fresco-, or oil-colour It resists the effects of air, light, water, and is not blackened by gas, but acid vapours destroy its colour. It is quite fast to alkalies

Towards acetic acid and alum the various commercial artificial ultramarines behave very differently Some are destroyed at once, while others resist for a time, especially alum. They all have one property in common, $viz.$, to absorb water from the air. Under unfavourable circumstances they may come to contain 5 per cent of water, or even more. It is by no means easy to compare two samples of ultramarine with regard to body, independently of shade, and merely by the appearance of the pigment. The best plan is to rub both to the same degree of fineness, and then to mix both with the same known proportion of gypsum Naturally the sample which requires the most gypsum to produce any given change of shade is the better of the two. Besides it has been proved that ultramarines which will bear the most admixture with alum or alumina without much change in colour are much better in other respects for certain purposes, such as paper-dyeing. Here the ultramarines rich in silica are more permanent than the poorer sorts. To detect whether a pigment is an ultramarine, treat it with hydrochloric acid, and if it is ultramarine sulphuretted hydrogen will be at once evolved.

CINNABAR.

Although cinnabar is very common in nature, it is also made artificially. It is in much use as a pigment, especially for sealing wax Holland used to be the principal seat of the manufacture of cinnabar, where it was sublimed in large pots over an open fire. Even to-day it is often made by fusing 4 lb. of sulphur in an unglazed earthen vessel, and then pouring in little by little 25 lb. of quicksilver, previously heated in a crucible or an iron spoon The two elements combine with the evolution of so much heat that the mass glows. At this point the vessel is immediately covered with a lid to exclude the air. If, however, the lid is put on before the mass glows, the arrival of that stage would cause a violent explosion which would shatter the apparatus The black non-metallic mass is finely powdered and then gently heated to drive off uncombined sulphur, and then more strongly heated to sublime the cinnabar Care must be taken to confine the fire to the bottom of the subliming vessel, or the whole of the cinnabar will escape in vapour, and if the sublimation is done in glass, the vessel may be fused. If the heating is continued for a time after the sublimation is finished the cinnabar becomes a finer red The final product is a dark red mass of a greyish-violet metallic lustre having a crystalline fracture   Finely powdered, it becomes a very deep red

Good cinnabar comes on the market in masses consisting of radiating needles of a greyish-violet metallic lustre, which give a deep red powder. The beauty of the colour ought to be distinctly increased by rubbing the cinnabar up with very dilute nitric or acetic acid.   Adulteration with dragon's blood, red-lead, or similar substances can only happen in prepared cinnabar, and is easily detected   Red-lead impairs the beauty of the red and makes it verge towards a pomegranate colour, which is made much darker when the sample is treated with nitric acid, on account of the formation of peroxide of lead   Acetic acid boiled with such adulterated cinnabar acquires a sweetish taste, and the property of giving a black precipitate with sulphuretted hydrogen. Dragon's blood causes the cinnabar to redden spirit of wine, and when the sample is thrown on the fire, produces a balsamic smell. Brick dust or red ochre makes the cinnabar colour hydrochloric acid yellow, and will not sublime   Red arsenic makes the pigment exhale a garlic-like smell when thrown on the fire.

BERLIN OR PARIS BLUE.

This blue (best known in England as Prussian blue) is much used as a brush-pigment, not on walls, but on woodwork, and combined with suitable yellows to make greens, etc

The finest sort (called in England Chinese blue) is got by dissolving a neutral pure ferric salt and adding ferrocyanide of potassium, when the Berlin blue is precipitated with its characteristic beautiful colour   It is filtered off, washed, and dried in the form of small sticks   Another very common method is to dissolve a copper-free green vitriol which has oxidised in the air, $i\,e$. a mixture of ferrous and ferric sulphates, and then to add alum The mixture is then precipitated with ferro-cyanide of potassium. As the pigment so prepared is rather of a light blue owing to the ferrous salt, and still lighter on account of the alumina precipitated with it, the precipitate must be stirred up for a long time before filtration to darken When the precipitate has fully settled it is washed on a linen filter, and brightened by rubbing up with water and boiling for a few minutes in a copper vessel with nitric acid, and then mixing it thoroughly with concentrated sulphuric acid It is then left for a day or two, and then washed, pressed, moulded into pieces, and dried, first in the shade in the open air, and then in a drying-room at from 70 to 80 deg. C. It is then allowed to cool very slowly

The purest Berlin blue is dark blue, and has a coppery lustre like indigo, a brilliant lustre, and a conchoidal fracture. If the fracture is dull and earthy or it does not easily give a full tint when rubbed on paper, it is too hard and impure Berlin blue has no smell or taste, does not moisten in the air, but is for all that very hygroscopic. It is insoluble in water or alcohol and is decomposed both by acids and by alkalies.

ORPIMENT AND REALGAR.

Although both these substances occur in nature, orpiment in crystalline plates of a beautiful lemon-yellow colour, realgar in greasily lustrous orange masses with a conchoidal fracture, yet for use in the arts they are for the most part artificially prepared. Both are much used in painting, more with oils than in water-colour, and give valued yellow and orange-red hues They are also used in the manufacture of yellow and orange-coloured varnishes.

Orpiment may be made either in the wet or in the dry way The first consists in fusing together and then sub-

liming a mixture of sulphur with seven times its weight
of white arsenic in iron vessels This sublimed product
consists of yellow crystals. The second method is carried
out by precipitating a solution of arsenious acid or an
arsenite in dilute hydrochloric acid with sulphuretted
hydrogen, when the orpiment goes down as a beautiful
yellow precipitate

Realgar is prepared by heating arsenical pyrites with
sulphur to a red heat in large earthen retorts At the
end of the operation the receivers attached to the retorts
contain a mixture of red and yellow arsenic with glassy
realgar. The last is subjected to a special refining process by remelting in cast-iron pans, and removing the
resulting slag The purified mass is made of the right
colour by adding sulphur if too dark, and by adding very
dark realgar if too light It is cast in cylindrical wrought-
iron moulds, and after it has set it is broken up and packed

Artificial realgar is brownish-red and opaque, has a
greasy lustre, and is insoluble in water or spirit It is
soluble in caustic alkalies By heating it becomes darker
and then fuses, and finally burns with a whitish-blue
flame It can be sublimed unchanged.

Orpiment made in the wet way is an amorphous powder,
but the sublimed compound consists of plates having a
subconchoidal fracture. Orpiment is also called king's
yellow It is tasteless and odourless, insoluble in water
or spirit, but dissolves in caustic potash, forming potassium
arsenite Nitric acid or aqua-regia dissolves it with decomposition

CHROME GREEN.

This is used both for an oil-colour and in the preparation of green lakes, and also for glass and porcelain The
substance is chromium sesquioxide, and is now made in a
great variety of ways, e.g., by igniting the hydrated oxide,

by heating mercurous chromate, or by treating bichromate with starch, sugar, carbon, or with a mixture of sal-ammoniac and carbonate of potash. The last process is due to Wöhler and gives a beautiful green The heat is kept up till all excess of sal-ammoniac is volatilised, and the residue of potassium chloride and chrome is lixi-viated with hot water, which dissolves out the potassium salt

Chrome is a rather dark green powder, infusible, and unchanged even by a red heat. To its power of standing heat it owes its use in making green glass and porcelain. Easily soluble in acids, it becomes insoluble by heating to redness. With water it forms a greyish-green hydrate, which loses its water at a dull red heat and forms the dark green anhydrous sesquioxide. The salts of this oxide are green and have an astringent taste Ammonia precipi-tates the hydrated oxide from their solutions

CHROME YELLOW, RED AND ORANGE.

These are used both as oil and as water colours   Accord-ing to Pubetz we have —

(a) Neutral lead chromate (chrome yellow).

(b) Basic lead chromate (chrome red)

(c) A mixture of both (chrome orange)

Chrome yellow is got in three ways .—

1 By precipitating sugar of lead with bichromate of potash.

2 By treating lead sulphate with a warm solution of yellow neutral potassium chromate

3. One hundred lb. of recently precipitated lead chloride are digested with 47 lb of lead bi-chromate.

This chrome yellow is much warmer and more beautiful than the others

Chrome red is prepared :—

1. By fusing neutral lead chromate with caustic potash or saltpetre. Half the chromic acid goes from the lead to form chromate of potash.
2. By fusing a mixture of saltpetre and nitrate of soda, and adding to the fused mass little by little neutral lead chromate. The mass is then allowed to cool, and lixiviated, and the basic lead chromate left behind is washed and dried.
3. By precipitating a solution of lead acetate with yellow potassium chromate and caustic potash

Chrome orange is made by boiling chrome yellow with milk of lime

These pigments are tasteless and odourless powders of various shades of yellow and red which resist both light and air. They are insoluble in water, slightly soluble in acids, and easily in caustic potash. Chrome yellow is not unfrequently adulterated with barytes, alumina, gypsum or lead sulphate These impurities are at once detected by the use of caustic potash, when they do not dissolve These chrome colours have, as they deserve by their beauty, durability, body, and the ease with which they can be mixed with other pigments, nearly driven out the other yellow and orange pigments

Mosaic Gold.

Mosaic gold or bronze when good and genuine is of a beautiful golden yellow, and in soft-feeling scales. Mismade specimens are in much smaller scales, and of a greenish or brownish cast. The pigment is prepared in the dry way by gradually bringing a mixture of 12 lb of tin-amalgam (one-third mercury and two-thirds tin), 5 lb. of powdered sulphur and 4 lb. of sal-ammoniac in a bolthead to a dull red heat, so that cinnabar and tin-salt sublime out. The bronze remains at the bottom as a scaly, golden shining mass.

As a rule the value of the product increases with the purity of its golden tint and with the fineness with which it is powdered. The inferior kinds are darker and brownish in colour, and are rubbed up much less fine

Bronze is insoluble in water or acid, except aqua-regia It dissolves in boiling caustic potash with partial decomposition It has a greasy feel, and easily loses its colour. At a red heat it loses half its sulphur

Mosaic gold is excellent for bronzing, and for producing gold-like ornamentation on wood, gypsum, clay, iron and copper It is largely used in making gilt paper and gilding varnishes, for which purpose it is used with a vehicle of boiled oil.

Green Mineral Pigments.

The best classification and description of these pigments is given by Gentele, but his account would be too comprehensive and diffuse for our purpose We content ourselves with a threefold classification, excepting chrome green which has already been described

1 Greens consisting of basic carbonate of copper · oil green, mountain green, and Bremen and Brunswick greens.

2 Greens consisting of arsenite of copper Scheele's green, named after its discoverer, and also called Swedish or mineral green

3 Greens consisting of arsenite and acetate of copper emerald green, otherwise called Paris green First discovered by a saddler at Schweinfurt, this is sometimes called Schweinfurt green

1. *Oil Green, Mountain Green, Bremen and Brunswick Greens.*

These pigments are either made by simply crushing natural malachite, an emerald green basic copper carbonate, or by precipitating the same substance with carbonate of potash from a solution of blue vitriol Bremen and Brunswick green are made differently. The first is prepared by precipitating carbonate of magnesia and alumina together with the basic carbonate, by adding to the copper sulphate alum and a magnesia salt before putting in the carbonate of potash Brunswick green is a mixture of basic carbonate of copper with alumina hydrate prepared by precipitating with ammonia a mixed solution of basic chloride of copper and alum   In consequence of the method of precipitation it will contain, with the copper salt, carbonate of magnesia and hydrate of alumina. Bremen green, on the other hand, contains only alumina in addition to the copper salt.

2. *Scheele's Green, Mineral or Swedish Green.*

The principle of the preparation of this pigment is precipitating with arsenious acid a solution of sulphate of copper free from iron and carbonate of potash. To this class belong also Vienna, Kirchberger and Neuwieder green, and also Imperial, Mitis, and New green, all pigments which, by numerous changes made in the methods of preparation, and to be discussed later, are made commercially in various shades

3. *Schweinfurt Green and Mineral Green (Leipzig and Paris Green).*

These pigments are obtained when arsenite of copper is treated with acetic acid and the excess of acid is distilled off, or when verdigris is dissolved in vinegar and mixed with a solution of white arsenic in the same solvent, and the mixture is gently evaporated to crystallisation These methods give, according to their nature and the details of their execution, various results, so that all Schweinfurt greens are not of the same beauty

The external appearance of these greens is very various. Sometimes they are small, shapeless lumps, *e.g*, mineral, Bremen or Neuwieder green, and sometimes occur as a more or less fine-grained powder as may be seen in the case of oil green, mountain green, and Leipzig and Schweinfurt greens The differences in colour, too, are great, as they are sometimes olive-green, sometimes bluish-green, sometimes yellowish-green, sometimes grass-green, and sometimes light and sometimes dark They are insoluble in water but soluble in the stronger acids, and unchangeable in the air, but are turned dark brown by heat, owing to the formation of oxide of copper The finest and most valuable of them is certainly Schweinfurt green It is above all the others in purity, brilliance and depth It is very fine-grained, stands exposure to the air well, and can be mixed to a uniform mass with other colours, *e.g*., white-lead, a property of great importance to the painter

OCHRES AND ROUGE.

Ochres or bloodstones are found in nature ready made Ochre may be red iron ochre, or brown iron ochre, or yellow iron ochre, but it is always hydrated ferric oxide, and occurs both in recent and in the older rocks Bloodstone occurs in red heavy masses which readily leave a mark, and consist of concentric fibres, and is commonest in the later formations.

Red ochre is an intimate mixture of red iron ochre and clay, of a more or less red colour and an earthy fracture, soft, and easily making a coloured mark This, too, is chiefly characteristic of the later rocks. The chief ochre mines are in Germany (Saxony, Hanover, Bohemia, Steiermark and Silesia), France, England and Spain

Ochre is an earthy powdery substance of various yellow shades, and the drier, more finely powdered, and deeper and brighter in shade it is, the better its quality. These remarks hold for all the ochres Powdered bloodstone has a beautiful dark red colour, the more beautiful the finer the powder. In pieces, as above remarked, it is distinguished by its regular radiating structure.

Rouge is also a powder, of very varied fineness and shade, from a pale red to a dark brownish-red Red ochre is either brownish-red or blood-red, is soft, earthy, and marks readily. The ochres are free from taste or smell, insoluble in water but readily soluble in dilute acids, unless they have been ignited. The cooled mass combines with water reproducing the hydrate. The oxide of iron is red when anhydrous, but yellow when hydrated

CADMIUM YELLOW.

Sulphide of cadmium, called cadmium yellow for short, is a beautiful warm yellow. The chief property of cadmium sulphide, however, next to its beauty is its great fastness to alkalies and soap, and, unlike chrome yellow, it is fast to sulphuretted hydrogen Chlorine only attacks it at a certain degree of concentration, and light and air only very slowly act on it

In practice various methods are employed for making cadmium sulphide It may be generally remarked that it will be purer and deeper in colour the less zinc it contains The method of manufacture is to dissolve broken cadmium in dilute sulphuric acid. It dissolves quickly with evolution of hydrogen. The cadmium must be in excess, so as to saturate all the acid. The concentrated and neutral solution is then diluted with water and completely precipitated with sulphide of sodium

It is cheaper and certainly simpler to make the pigment from cadmium nitrate, by fusing that salt with its own weight of sodium hypersulphate, a process which is largely used in the printing of textiles.

VI

COAL-TAR DYES

The aniline colours, more correctly the coal-tar dyes, are known to every reader of this book, and it is therefore superfluous to say much on a subject with which we are all acquainted.

For our purpose we will make the following classification of the aniline dyes, beginning with reds and passing therefrom through orange, yellow, blue, violet, green, brown and mixed colours to black. We also classify the single colours according to their method of production into basic, alkaline, and acid, and also into alizarine, resorcin, and benzidine dyes.

RED DYES.

The red dyes are now sold in very large numbers and answer all requirements fully, both with regard to shade and lustre, and also on the whole in reference to fastness.

Basic Reds —These are the oldest coal-tar colours We mention first fuchsine or magenta (diamond magenta) and rubine, which (as identical dyes) easily colour wood without any mordant, and, unless the bath is too concentrated, give fairly fast colours When the solution is too strong the red rubs off a good deal, and the use of tannin and Glauber's salt is necessary Rubine is said to give rather clearer shades than diamond magenta We may further mention cardinal red, safranine, safranine scarlet, garnet red, scarlet red and coralline The character of the colour is given approximately by the name

Alkaline Reds —Of these I can only mention Dahl's alkali red Whether this dye is actually used for wood-dyeing I cannot state with certainty Trials I made

myself with great care, gave quite good results when the
solution of the dye, either the R or B brand, was mixed
with waterglass, allowed to cool somewhat, and then applied
with a brush in the lukewarm state The colour produced
is fast to soap and fairly so to light and air. For cup-
boards and show-cases the dye is very suitable

Acid Reds —These are very numerous, but their fastness
is by no means always satisfactory, and the scarlets especially rub off a good deal from wood, as they have little
affinity for the fibre.

For the sake of completeness we will mention brilliant
croceine, which gives very bright hues R gives a pure
warm orange, but B, M, 3B, 5B, 7B and 9B verge towards
blue more and more, so that 9B gives a fine pale garnet
shade For full shades a little alum should be used

Similar colours are got with new red, scarlet, ponceau,
pyrotine scarlet, fast red, orchil red, and many others

Of the resorcin dyes we have the finest series of reds
They are better known as the eosines, although most of
them have other names I mention eosine pink, soluble
in water or spirit. This with lead acetate gives brilliant
bluish-pink shades Rose Bengal is still more brilliant,
and is best fixed with neutralised alum The dye is too
dear, however, for very extensive use. Similar to it is
phloxine, which is fixed in the same manner. We have
also erythrosine, and finally rhodamine The latter
answers well on wood with acetate of alumina Eosine is
often adulterated with fuchsine, coralline and safranine
To test for these falsifications the dye solution is treated
with sulphuric acid diluted with four times its volume of
water This separates eosine as an orange precipitate, and
the others remain dissolved, fuchsine and coralline yellow,
and safranine with a bluish-violet colour

The reds derived from anthracene form a group sharply
divided from all other dyes.

Of the vast number of anthiacene dyes few have any interest for us Only a few, in fact, with very special properties have attained a wide employment. During the last few years alizarine has entirely displaced madder, and extracts of madder are now only made for a few very special purposes.

Alizarine comes on the market as a yellow or brownish paste containing 20 per cent. of the dry substance We distinguish yellow and bluish shades. The former usually contain flavopurpurine, the latter alizarine

Commercial alizarine gives reds with alumina, browns with chrome, and violets with iron. All these lakes are fast to light and air. The alizarine is tested to see how much water it contains by drying it at 120 deg. C

A special class of reds is known as the benzidine dyes

These are the so-called substantive (i e , direct, dyeing without a mordant) cotton dyes, which contrast with the previously known coal-tar dyes by possessing the valuable property of dyeing vegetable fibres without a mordant This affinity with the fibre goes so far, that these dyes act as mordants for others This property can often be utilised with advantage in the dyeing of wood

With these red dyes we can get beautiful scarlet and Turkey red shades, especially with Congo red. Congo G and GR give rather yellower shades than Congo. Brilliant Congo has the advantage over Congo in fastness to acids, and shares this property with benzopurpurine 4B and deltapurpurine, but the latter is more sensitive to light. Benzopurpurine 6B is distinguished by its bluish shade, while rosazurine G and B give pure safranine tones. In small quantities these dyes give delicate pinks.

Congo corinth and Congo corinth B serve for producing full dark violet shades.

Bluish-red hues like safranine-red can also be got with Hessian purple, and the best brands are B, NG, and G

Any number of shades can be got by mixing these with other colours of the same group. All the benzidine dyes should be dissolved in at least 100 times their weight of water to be sure that nothing is left undissolved. If the water is hard it should be softened with soap or soda, and the precipitate should be removed before the dye is added. Most of these dyes require no mordant and are fairly fast to rubbing, but the dyeing is always more satisfactory with a little alkali, whether soda or potash, borax, or waterglass. Only a very little need be used, and in fact the alkaline reaction produced should be only faint. It is essential to apply the colour hot. Beautiful and easily used as the colours of this group are, they all have one great fault, and that is their want of fastness to light and acids. This is so great that a beautiful medium Congo red, for example, is quickly changed and spoiled by the carbonic acid of the air.

YELLOW AND ORANGE DYES.

The first aniline yellow was put on the market in 1864 by Simpson, Maule and Nicholson. It was a light crystalline brownish-yellow powder, but it has not been made for a long time. Before the discovery of the substantive dyes orange and yellow artificial colours were hardly used in our branch, with the exception perhaps of picric acid. We have still, however, a great choice of excellent yellow natural dyes, such as quercitron, flavine, fustic, turmeric, weld, annatto, saffron, etc., which all serve to give fairly fast colours to wood.

One of the most important and the fastest yellow anilines is undoubtedly auramine, which is of great interest to us. Used alone, it gives pure brilliant fast yellows, and it is also used in mixtures for green, red, chestnut, olive, etc., and is an excellent substitute for turmeric,

5

being much faster to light As auramine is decomposed
by boiling water, it must be dissolved in water which is
neither below 50 deg. C. nor above 80 deg. C Mineral
acids destroy the solution instantly. It dyes wood without
any mordant, but the results are better if the wood is
first mordanted with tannin.

To continue the yellows in order, we next pass to the
strongly acid nitro-dyes First of these is picric acid,
formerly the sole example of its class, and which was used
for dyeing wood, ivory, marble, etc But many defects
belong to these dyes, such as want of fastness to light,
small affinity for the material, and less or greater poisonous
qualities (especially in the case of picric acid), and have
almost entirely removed picric acid from our list, as well
as its congeners, such as naphthol yellow, naphthol yellow
S, Victoria yellow, fast yellow, acid yellow, azo acid yellow,
etc. Quinoline yellow, although not belonging to the class,
is a strongly acid dyeing body, and has the same drawbacks, and is not to be recommended. Much better results are got with tartrazine.

The orange dyes are made by mixing yellows with reds,
and there are also single orange dyes. These dyes have
only a limited use, and have not the importance of the
other dyes such as reds, blues and blacks

We may mention among basic yellows and oranges
mandarin, metanil yellow, methyl orange, chrysoidine,
phosphine, aurantia, Martius yellow, etc They are all
soluble in both water and spirit. They are used without
mordants and fixed some with Glauber's salt, some with
tannin. Phosphine, chrysoidine and aurantia are much
used in wood-dyeing, as the fastness of the colour is usually
satisfactory. Tannin is not generally used with them.

The largest number of yellows is found among the benzidines, some of which have become practically indispensable
for the production of certain shades They need only to

be applied to the wood with a brush in the state of hot aqueous solution not too concentrated.

Alkali yellow and alkali orange (Dahl) give a beautiful straw yellow, or medium orange. For the best results Glauber's salt should be used. Common salt has the same effect, but although it intensifies the colours it also makes them somewhat muddy

Fine and very fast yellow chamois shades can be produced with cresotine yellow, of which we have two brands, G and R. The results are particularly fine when the cresotine yellow is mixed with toluylene orange G Further dyes of this class are chrysamine, Hessian yellow, brilliant yellow, chrysoidine, cotton yellow, carbazol yellow, diamine yellow and thioflavine They are best fixed with Glauber's or common salt, except brilliant yellow, which is best fixed with oxalic acid. Unhappily all these dyes are loose to light, and for this reason inferior to the basic yellow and orange dyes

Primuline yellow, which is even less fast to light than the benzidines, is hardly used for our purposes The development of primuline into the so-called ingrain colours such as primuline orange, golden yellow, golden red, maroon and brown has, so far as I know, not yet been introduced into wood-dyeing

Last among the orange dyes allusion may be made to alizarine orange or nitro-alizarine It has not found the same extended use as the other alizarines, but is as fast as alizarine red It is used in the form of 20 per cent. paste on wood previously mordanted with alum free from iron.

BLUE DYES.

The number of these in use is very great We use many more blues than reds. For our purpose the following classification is the best:—

Basic dyes

Acid dyes.

Benzidine dyes.

Many blues having different names are really identical Blue dyes must be dissolved in soft water, usually in from 200 to 300 times their weight of boiling water   The solution must only be used if perfectly clear, and should be added to the dye-bath through a hair sieve, and the colour comes out much more level if the dye is put in in three or four lots

The first coal-tar blue was that of Girad and de Laire. It was made from fuchsine and called Lyons blue.   Like *bleu lumière* it is only soluble in spirit   Next came the blues soluble in water, one of the first of which was Nicholson's alkali blue, which still occupies a high place among the aniline blues

Basic Blue Dyes.—Two basic blue dyes which are only soluble in alcohol must first be mentioned   Gentiana and Humboldt blue   Both are made by the Berlin Actien-Gesellschaft.   They are said to give shades faster to light than those produced by the dyes soluble in water.

Methylene blue is a basic dye.   It is a brown powder which dissolves to a beautiful sky-blue in water, acetic acid or alcohol. Tartaric acid increases the solubility. The following are the various brands —

Methylene blue RX	.	the reddest shade
,, BX	. .	somewhat bluer.
,, BRN		the same shade.
,, BR		greener
,, X		greener still
,, R	.	reddish.
,, B		bluish.
,, G		very greenish.
,, BG		between B and G.
,, MD		a strong colour

Closely resembling methylene blue and giving exactly the same results is Oehler's ethylene blue.

Ethylene and methylene blues give very fine and fast shades, which have the merit of not rubbing. They give much deeper shades on wood if the material is first mordanted with pyrolignite of iron. The blue is applied warm after the wood has dried. Dark indigo tones of great fastness are thus obtained

Less brilliant hues can be got with the navy blues (*bleu marine*), which are, however, not so fast as methylene blue

Other blues very suitable for our purpose and satisfactory in fastness are pure blue, red blue, new blue, opal blue, Nile blue, peacock blue, night blue, Victoria blue, indazine blue, fast blue and indamine blue For getting a brilliant warm pale blue alkali blue is specially suitable I would for this purpose specially recommend ammoniacal solution of alkali blue, to which it is a great advantage to add a little Turkey-red oil. Nevertheless, the solution must not be made too alkaline or the wood may be injured The advantage of using this ammoniacal dye for wood consists in the rapidity with which the ammonia evaporates and leaves the insoluble dye behind I have found that it gives remarkably warm and lively hues to wood, and have never had any fault to find with it in the matter of fastness.

Of blue alizarines much need not be said. They are difficult to use, and it is hardly possible to make them level. This is the result of the fact that the dye has itself to be formed, which textile dyers do by long boiling or by oxidation Alizarine blue S, however, is easily used, and gives level shades

Other blue alizarines, the so-called alizarine cyanines, are hardly suitable for our purpose, although they cause no risk of want of uniformity

Blue Benzidine Dyes.—We must first mention azo blue

benzoazurine, of which there are various brands The peculiarity of these dyes is that they look reddish during dyeing, and only become quite blue later Benzoazurine gives very full indigo shades when mixed with half per cent. of its weight of chrysamine. The mixture is dissolved in boiling water with a little soda, and the solution is used hot. Although the benzidines have multiplied greatly of late their use has not extended, probably because the basic and acid blues are more brilliant in shade, faster to light and more easily used

Finally, as regards the artificial indigo of the B A. and S F. Indigo pure (indigo rein) comes on the market in the form of powder or paste. It is in no way different from refined natural indigo and, like it, contains 97 or 98 per cent of indigotine. Pure indigo, like natural indigo, is dissolved in sulphuric acid and then diluted with water for dyeing purposes I would, however, decidedly recommend that when indigo carmine is wanted that it should be bought One is then sure of a carefully made article. Home preparation is very difficult and easily goes wrong ; the indigo is not fully dissolved, and unlevel and dull shades are the result

Violet Dyes.

The first prepared artificial violet was mauveine or Perkin's violet, and was also called aniline violet, aniline purple and indisine Perkin was the first chemist to make an aniline dye on a large scale for industrial purposes, and his provisional specification was obtained as early as 1856. His English and French patents expired in 1857 and 1858 He is said to have discovered mauveine by chance in attempting to synthesise quinine

Mauveine is obtained by oxidising aniline containing toluidine with sulphuric acid and bichromate of potash.

The free base is a black crystalline powder, soluble in alcohol to a bluish-violet solution, and forming with acids a series of salts which are coloured like those of safranine and behave like them chemically. Although mauveine is very fast it is not much used now by dyers

There followed then various other violets such as dahlia, primula, Hofmann's violet, Dorothea and Paris violet, which were all abandoned later, when makers learned to make violets far exceeding them in beauty and fastness.

Basic Violet Dyes—The chief representative of these is methyl violet

This is the violet that is of all the most used for our purposes. It comes into commerce in so many shades that all possible violets can be produced with it. It can be applied on wood without any mordant, but if absolutely clear and non-rubbing colour is wanted it is advisable to mix the solution before use with a little sulphurous acid or bisulphide of soda

Ethyl violet and crystal violet behave just like methyl violet. The other dyes of this class, gentiana violet, ruby violet and new violet, are less suitable for our use.

Of the acid violet dyes only the acid violets need be mentioned, and of them only the marks 4BN, 6BN and 8B These are largely used. Care must be taken in dissolving them as they are somewhat difficultly soluble, and any undissolved particles cause unlevel dyeing.

Of the alizarine violets galleine is the one most used, and, to a less extent, anthracene violet The others are scarcely or not at all employed because they are difficult to handle. Although all these dyes are fast they are not easily fixed on wood

We only need to mention a few of the benzidine violets as suitable for us. The same objections apply as in the case of the blue benzidines Only azo violet, Hessian purple and heliotrope are occasionally used. After dyeing the wood must be carefully cleaned with solution of soda to prevent the colour from rubbing

GREEN ANILINE DYES.

Before green artificial dyes had been hit on dyers had to make greens by mixing blues and yellows. A beautiful green was thus made from indigo.

The first aniline green, aldehyde green, came out in 1862. The discoverer was Cherpin, a Frenchman   Later appeared iodine green, also called Hofmann's green   The interest of these is now historical merely. Methyl green, which has almost been abandoned for wood-dyeing, is got by heating methyl chloride with methyl violet.   The soluble dye thus obtained is even less stable than malachite green.

When methyl green is in solution in water a part of it is apt to resinify. In consequence only cold water must be used for making the solution, and alcohol should be mixed with it. Temperatures above 80 deg. C reconvert the dye into methyl violet

Malachite green, bitter-almond oil green, or fast green is a very beautiful green. It occurs in yellowish and bluish shades, and in powder or in crystals. It can be used on wood without a mordant, or with acetate of alumina or with a mixture of chromium acetate and magnesia.

Brilliant green, new Victoria green and diamond green are new dyes which can be shaded yellow with auramine. The Berlin Actien-Gesellschaft sells a mark of ethyl green and another of olive-green which are closely allied to those already mentioned in the way they are used.

Other beautiful greens are China green and the Elberfeld light green. Specially fine shades are got with acid green, which fixes itself on wood easily and uniformly with a little acetic acid. Very dark green shades always rub a little, and the wood must always be first mordanted with tannin solution. We have no suitable dye among the benzo dyes Benzo green cannot compare with the basic greens in brilliancy and beauty.

Anthracene green, usually called coeruleine, an alizarine dye, has only a very limited use in our industry, because it will only give dull shades although they are very fast Shaded with Persian berries or quercitron, it produces mode shades which may on occasion be extremely useful

Till very lately coeruleine was sold as a brown 11 per cent. paste, but it is now obtainable as a powder soluble in water (the bisulphide compound). It is best fixed on wood with chromium acetate, and after dyeing the wood is thoroughly washed with weak solution of soda.

BROWN DYES.

The first brown coal-tar dyes were made from the waste by-products of fuchsine manufacture, and some of them, maroon for example, are still made. One of the first proper browns to be discovered was the phenylene brown of Roberts, Dale & Company, Manchester. The most important brown now used is unquestionably Bismarck brown, of which there are two marks, G (yellowish) and R (reddish). Bismarck brown is obtained by fusing hydrochloride of aniline with fuchsine. It dissolves in water or spirit, and the solution dyes wood alone, but better when applied mixed with a little acetic acid. Years passed before Bismarck brown was followed by other artificial browns, but there are now several, of which we may mention Berlin brown, Philadelphia brown and mode brown, which are basic and much like Bismarck brown We have also fast brown and excelsior brown, which are fixed with a little alum. Vesuvin is, however, better fixed on wood with tannin

The brown alizarines are numerous and give very fast colours We can use —

    1 Anthracene brown with acetate of chromium
    2 Alizarine orange with nitrate and acetate of chrome
    3. Alizarine red with acetate of alumina

Of the benzo dyes I must first mention the benzo brown of the Elberfeld Farbenfabriken. It fixes easily and uniformly, and the wood requires no special washing afterwards to give a pure clear shade Very beautiful and fast chestnut browns are also easily got with toluylene brown. The colour produced stands soda and soap well and is faster to light than most benzo-browns Its fastness to acids is also satisfactory If it has to be used with other benzo dyes that require soda, that base is best used in the form of Glauber's salt Alkali brown, however, is best used with soda, but it is more difficult to get level shades with it than with benzo brown Of late some sulphur browns, such as thiocatechin, have been put on the market, which are on trial as regards their use on wood So far they have not been very satisfactory. The hot solutions have an evil smell owing to the evolution of fumes which, in small rooms, will bleach any already dyed articles that may be there

GRAY AND BLACK DYES.

, Much need not be said about the gray dyes, for most grays are got by diluting black with white The well-known nigrosine, which is sold in a form soluble either in water or spirit, can hardly be looked on as a gray dye For our purposes the spirit-dye is always preferable

More claim to be called gray may be conceded to new gray (Elberfeld) This gives very pleasing grays on wood

Real black dyes have only been introduced quite recently. At first, blacks were always got by combinations, using logwood, fustic, sumach, ferrous sulphate, bichromate of potash, blue vitriol and other ingredients, so that the black was first produced when they came into contact with the fibre. Even aniline black is no true black dye. Our description of it comes in the chapter on the black-dyeing of wood

The most suitable real black dye for our purpose is Cassella's naphthol black. It is sold as a bluish-black powder, and gives a deep violet solution in boiling water. It fixes best on wood when applied very hot, and best of all with a little bisulphate of soda To get a deep black it should be mixed with a little yellow We recommend for this purpose naphthol yellow or fast yellow

Another black dye suitable for wood-dyeing is jet black (Bayer) It is one of the newer basic dyes, which dyes wood without the use of acids or alkalies. The addition, however, of a little common salt is advisable

The mark R gives bluish-black shades of great permanence in the air, while jet black G gives a strong dead black

Finally, there is alizarine black, the fastest known black dye, which is also quite fast to acids. It is best fixed with dilute sulphuric acid.

The various benzidine blacks have no interest for us as they are not suited to our purposes

As an appendix to the aniline dyes we give a short account of the anilines soluble in fat, and also of aniline lakes, which are largely used for dyeing marble and stone and for dyeing and varnishing wood

Aniline Dyes Soluble in Fat.

Most aniline dyes are insoluble in neutral oils and fats Methyl violet is an exception, and many processes enable us to prepare dyes soluble in fats For example, most anilines dissolve in organic liquids of high boiling point such as nitrobenzole, aniline oil, fusel oil and carbolic acid. For dyeing oils the dye is generally dissolved in aniline oil Aniline oil dyes are largely made by precipitating the colour bases from the dye solutions with caustic soda and then combining them with warm oleic or stearic acid The oleates and stearates so obtained have the colour of the base, and as they will dissolve in fats will dye them Another method is to precipitate a solution of a basic dye with soap, which also gives compounds of the dye base with fatty acids For example, if fuchsine, which is hydrochloride of rosaniline, is so treated with a soda soap, we get chloride of sodium and stearate of rosaniline

Another method of dyeing fats is to dissolve the dye first in sulphoricinoleic acid neutralised with soda or ammonia so as to form the well-known sulpho soap The soap used to dissolve the dye must be as nearly neutral as possible, as free acid or alkali in it might change the colour of the dye. Of course only fatty bodies can be dyed by any process which has no action on the dye which it is proposed to use They must, for example, be free from lead

A very different method for getting anilines soluble in fat, which he calls resinate colours, is due to Müller-Jacobs, and shall be briefly described. The discoverer had observed that the precipitates formed by metallic salts in solutions of rosin-soaps would combine with all basic aniline dyes to form distinct compounds These coloured lakes have been introduced into commerce by the name of resinate colours They are made as follows 100 lb. of pale colophony, 10 lb. of dry caustic soda (96 per cent.) and 33 lb. of crystal soda are boiled with constant stirring in 100 gals. of water for an hour. The liquid is then brought down to about 50 deg. C by the addition of 100 gals of cold water To this rosin soap solution is added a filtered solution of a basic dye such as fuchsine, methyl violet brilliant green, safranine, chrysoidine, auramine, methylene blue, rhodamine, etc, using, according to the colour wanted, from 5 to 10 lb of the dye. If the temperature is too low, or the concentration of the soap solution too great, the operation will fail as the colour bases will be precipitated as abietates. To the solution of soap and dye is next added a dilute solution of a metallic salt, little by little, with constant stirring, till precipitation is complete. This point is known by dipping a strip of filter paper into the liquid. A slight excess of metallic salt facilitates the subsequent filtration and washing For precipitation with zinc I use about 55 lb of zinc sulphate for every 100 lb. colophony, previously dissolved in 100 gallons of water It must be remarked that the mechanical properties of the precipitate depend largely on the quantity of water used The precipitate is now filtered off, best in a filter-press, and thoroughly washed. The resulting hard cakes contain from 18 to 25 per cent. of resinate colour. Unless made from very dilute solutions the magnesium resinate lakes cake together instead of, like the others, being finely divided, and in their mechanical properties they are resinous They must therefore be washed in filter bags, and dried at as high temperatures as possible

The lakes, if not to be sold as paste, are dried at from 40 to 50 deg. C., but at 70 deg. for magnesium lakes, until they cease to lose weight.

These lakes when dry are extremely light, and in either lumps or soft powder, and have unusual freshness and beauty of colour. They electrify on rubbing more than colophony itself. Air and damp affect them in no way They yield no quantity of their colouring matter worth mentioning either to cold or to warm water Weak alkalies or acids have no action on them, and even strong solutions of hypochlorites only attack them exceedingly slowly, provided they have not previously been exposed to light, in which case oxidising agents destroy them readily. In alcohol they are all more or less soluble, according to the metal used. Resinates of aluminium, beryllium, iron, nickel and manganese, whether coloured or not, are almost insoluble in spirit; while those of zinc, lead, cadmium and silver are fairly soluble; those of the alkaline earth metals still more so, and that of magnesium most of all. The dry lakes dissolve easily in their own weight of benzole and its homologues, of ether, chloroform, acetol and many essential oils. The solutions dry when painted on a flat surface to a hard, transparent, lustrous-coloured varnish which however, unfortunately, soon cracks and flakes off. The durability of the coat depends largely upon the metal present. The lakes are also readily soluble in alcohol, benzole and turpentine varnishes, in fused wax, in resins, in palmitic or stearic acid, in oleic acid and its homologues, in rancid fats and boiled oil. The solubility decreases as the amount of dye increases, and that amount must not exceed 20 lb. for every 100 lb. of colophony used in the manufacture. In oil of turpentine and the hydrocarbons of the mineral oil series ($C_{10}H_6$) the lakes are quite insoluble. Some of the metallic resinates, that of aluminium for example, quickly decompose in solution, even in the dark, precipitating the metallic oxide, while others, e g., of zinc, lead, calcium and magnesium, will keep unchanged indefinitely. Heated rather above 100 deg C., the lakes fuse without decomposition, but break up at higher temperatures. In an open fire they burn, and, like colophony, with a smoky flame, leaving the metal as oxide. The resinate lakes stand light fairly well, much better indeed than the combinations of fatty acid with aniline bases dissolved in benzole. The worst lakes are made by brilliant green, no matter what the metal is. On the other hand methyl violet, safranine, chrysoidine, auramine and rhodamine make good lakes whatever the metal. Rhodamine probably makes the best and most brilliant lakes of all. The aluminium and chromium lakes usually bleach more easily than those made with zinc or magnesium. By exposure to light, especially in thin coats, the colours lose their solubility in benzole completely, behaving exactly like a resin, asphalt in particular. We may infer that the light decomposes the lake into free dye and metallic resinate first, and that the latter is further changed subsequently. The dye set free can be completely extracted by any solvent that will act on it when it is by itself, or can be acted on by hypochlorites or other oxidising agents. If, for example, a piece of paper is painted over with a resinate varnish and exposed under a negative, a print can be made on it, as dilute alcohol or *eau de Javel* will afterwards dissolve the varnish where it has not been protected by the negative. The lakes which are soluble in alcohol exhibit this property much better than those which are insoluble, although the optical properties of the dye have a great influence on the result which is obtained.

As can be gathered from the above description of the properties of these bodies, they can be used for all sorts of purposes, whether dry or in the form of paste. In making transparent oil or benzine varnishes the resinate colour is either added to the boiled oil in the necessary quantity or first dissolved in benzole. This at once enhances the body of the varnish. I generally use for this purpose the resinate of zinc, iron, copper, or magnesium, containing not more than 8 to 12 lb. of dye per 100 lb. of colophony. By adding solution of india-rubber or gutta-percha the elasticity and durability of the varnish is materially increased. Such a composition of special value, which can be used alone or mixed with other varnishes, is made by dissolving 30 lb. of magnesium resinate lake in

80 lb of benzole and 200 lb chloroform, and then adding 150 lb of a $1\frac{1}{2}$ per cent solution of india-rubber in carbon bisulphide and benzole and clarified by heat Such varnishes are excellent for decorating bright metallic surfaces, or wood, paper, leather, glass, etc In many cases, e g., in painting on wood, the resinate lakes of iron, chromium, copper and manganese, combined with Bismarck brown, are to be preferred, on the one hand for economy, and also for the sake of greater fastness to light Very pretty dark brown or black shades are obtained with suitable mixtures of fuchsine resinate, green or blue, chrysoidine or auramine, and these do well for printing and lithographic inks, and for boot blacking, etc. Besides, textiles can be dyed in one bath with single or mixed resinate lakes in dilute solution in benzole Unfortunately this form of dyeing only gives delicate light shades, but for these it is already largely used for silk, satin and artificial flowers, where the dye must not rub off, both on a household and on a commercial scale. The lakes are also good for printing and dyeing india-rubber and india-rubber goods, celluloid, oilcloth and linoleum, and for colouring mineral whites.

In the form of paste they are excellent for making coloured pencils, and when thickened with tragacanth, albumen, dextrine or starch, for carpet printing. It should be mentioned that the lakes when acted on by the vapours of their solvents pass into a dissolved transparent state, in which they will adhere to any surface like a varnish

Aniline Colour Lakes.

The methods of making lakes from coal-tar dyes are the same in their essential features as those already described, i.e., they are precipitated mechanically or chemically, or in both ways at once, on to a white base We shall here confine ourselves to short descriptions of the most important of them

Red Lakes.—The darkest ones and those most like cochineal and carmine lakes are made by the action of tannate of fuchsine on starch and alum mixed with solution of soda. The whole of the colour is precipitated, and the lake will yield none of it to water.

By mixing paste Paris blue with this brilliant violet lakes are got, which, with oil as a vehicle, appear very beautiful and permanent The other coal-tar reds have no interest for us, not even the alizarine lakes

Violet Lakes are made like red lakes, but are hardly used, except those of methyl violet.

Blue Lakes.—The most beautiful aniline blue lake is decidedly that of alkali blue A mixture of starch and chalk is digested in alum solution, and solution of alkali blue is then added till the desired intensity is attained. The alum precipitates the blue completely on the chalk and starch. Alkali blue will answer for green lakes but not perfectly. Lakes made with Lyons blue and its allies have no particular beauty, and are rarely used

Yellow Lakes—Few aniline yellows are used for lakes. The only one giving an intense colour is picric acid on alumina and zinc oxide. It occurs in commerce as an orange-yellow powder under the name of golden yellow. According to Gentele the colour is chiefly due to dinitrocresol. Of other aniline yellows such as Manchester yellow, dinitronaphthol, naphthylamine yellow, naphthol yellow and Martius yellow, only the last is really fit for making yellow lakes The lake is sold usually as a lime salt, but occasionally as a soda salt, and is also sometimes precipitated with alum

Green Lakes.—The most important green lake is that of methyl green It is mixed with extract of quercitron or picric acid. The white basis is kaolin or alum, gypsum or sugar of lead These quercitron lakes are very brilliant.

6

The quercitron may be replaced by a decoction of Persian berries.

Brown Lakes.—Under this collective name many aniline lakes are sold of very different composition They are made from aniline brown, Bismarck brown, cinnamon brown, garnet, Havana brown, phenyl brown, vesuvin, alizarine brown, etc.

Black Lakes —The only one we need consider is nigrosine lake, although for the same results it comes much dearer than logwood lake Black lake made from aniline salt or oil is hardly ever used

3. DYEING MARBLE AND ARTIFICIAL STONE.

VII.

DYEING MARBLE.

THE art of dyeing marble has been well understood since the days of ancient Greece, for various statues of that period showing that they have been dyed are preserved.

The dyeing of marble is to-day very fashionable in Italy, and much money is thereby earned with little labour, for no particular qualification except some manual dexterity is required We may be sure that we still use the same dyes employed by the ancient Greeks, adding, perhaps, cochineal and the dye-woods. On the scientific side, the dyeing and imitation of marble has made very little progress, and as in all purely empirical arts, where ancient recipes are jealously preserved secret, innovations are invariably kept at arm's length

The result is that the work is usually done with very few colours, chiefly verdigris, gamboge, dragon's blood, cochineal, redwood and logwood Greens are always made by mixing yellows and blues Nevertheless nearly all vegetable dyes are suitable, and many of the coal-tar colours, if properly used, give very fast and beautiful colours to marble. For all dyes it is essential to use their solutions in alcohol or ether, and of anilines only those soluble in fat may be employed. If these rules are broken, the results will be bad. The preliminary treatment of the marble has also to be considered . in what weather the dyeing is done, whether the dye solution is to be hot or cold, whether the marble has to be warmed before or after the application of the dye   The dye tinctures penetrate the deeper into the stone the warmer it is   The marble is usually warmed by heating an iron plate red-hot, and passing it over the place to be dyed until the marble is hot enough   In many cases the marble is heated after dyeing.

As in all dyeing, the intensity of the colour is regulated by the concentration of the dye solution.   That is a different thing from saying that strong dye solutions penetrate more deeply.   This depends on the nature of the dye alone.   As a general rule, aqueous solutions penetrate the marble least, tinctures better, and solutions of the dye in wax best of all.

It is unnecessary to lay stress on the fact that only well-polished marble can be dyed   The quality of the marble is also of importance   It should be fine grained and neither too hard nor too soft.   We must also remember that on marble, being a carbonate, acid dyes cannot possibly be used, for they will not only injure the marble but will themselves be totally changed.   We shall consider the different colours in order, and we have already described the dyes and their methods of preparation

RED

Very warm reds can be produced with cochineal.   The cochineal is put into strong warm spirit, closely stoppered, and allowed to stand for three or four days in a warm place   The solution can then be used.   If too dark it is diluted with spirit, and is applied warm to the stone   The marble then assumes a beautiful and durable scarlet-red colour.

Equally permanent reds, but of somewhat different hue can be got as below :—

Warm tincture of annatto gives a brilliant red.

A solution of dragon's blood in alcohol as hot as possible gives a lustrous red which can be made much faster by subsequently heating the marble, and which then also penetrates much more deeply

A very fast dark red, which also penetrates very deeply, is given by nitrate of silver, but the colour blackens in time with many marbles.

Reds of somewhat bluish shade are got with hot tinctures of redwood. One of these, however, sandalwood, gives yellowish reds.

I wish to mention among anilines only fuchsine soluble in fat. Carefully mixed with hot wax it gives brilliant magenta shades, but too concentrated solutions cause much bronzing and the colour easily rubs off.

Violet.

Violets are chiefly got with tinctures of redwood alone, or mixed with logwood tincture Alum alters the shade.

Warm tincture of alkanet or of mallow, too, gives beautiful violets, but of less fastness than the preceding

A fairly fast purple violet can be got with chloride of gold, but the colour hardly penetrates the stone and is very expensive.

Among anilines I place methyl violet first, and next geranium violet. The first is used in oil or wax, the latter as a tincture, and both are applied warm Methyl violet in hot wax penetrates deeper than geranium violet, but the latter colour has the advantage on the score of fastness

Blue.

It is hardly practicable to colour marble blue. The assertion that it can be done with solution of copper sulphate is erroneous, and seems to have been made by some

theorist and afterwards accepted as gospel. I am unable
that way to get any colour having any pretension to be
called blue Attempts with ammonium cuprate, too, were
failures.

Blue anilines soluble in fat and tincture of Lyons blue
certainly give a blue, but the colour does not suit the
stone, and is only used when absolutely necessary. Solution of the aniline in wax penetrates deeper than the tincture of Lyons blue but is less fast to light.

GREEN.

This colour is produced with verdigris almost exclusively.
Alcoholic verdigris solution gives a pale bright green, but
a compound of verdigris and fused wax gives a fuller and
an emerald green, which also penetrates the marble much
better, reaching a depth of two-fifths of an inch, or twice as
far as the alcoholic liquid.

The colour can be shaded with yellow by adding to the
alcoholic verdigris a little tincture of gamboge

Although there are aniline greens soluble in fat they
have not yet been used for marble, as they give in no way
the results which might have been expected.

YELLOW.

For marble this is the colour most used and most sought
after Hence its production is the most advanced branch
of marble-dyeing, several chemists having made improvements of which we will inform our readers without delay.

One of the most usual dyes is gamboge, carefully dissolved in spirit, and applied warm with a brush. The
marble must be warmed after dyeing. A very beautiful
dark yellow is produced by tincture of saffron. The stone
simply requires painting with the warm solution

Less usual is the employment of orpiment in spite of the

very fine results it produces It is only necessary to brush over the marble with a solution of the pigment in ammonia. As the solvent evaporates, the beauty of the colour comes out. Orpiment is very poisonous

We now come to the process of Dr. Weber of Berlin, which solved the problem of dyeing white marble durably with any shade of yellow, and uniformly, with a penetration of at least a twelfth of an inch, and without altering the nature of the marble

This process is based on the little known fact that ferric salts are not precipitated from solution in strong alcohol by calcium carbonate, which does precipitate their aqueous solutions Such alcoholic solutions also penetrate the marble better. The physical effect of the marble on the dye solution has also to be taken into consideration. When the strong tincture meets the surface of the marble where there is an angle we can observe in the resulting transparency of the stone how deep the alcohol penetrates The soaked part has not the same shade as the solution as the alcohol penetrates further than the dye, leaving the latter near the surface. Dr Weber observed that heat altered this effect by diminishing the absorptive power of the marble for the dissolved iron salt; for, while the dye penetrates less deeply into the cold marble, it does not merely remain on the surface when the marble is moderately heated but easily penetrates a twelfth of an inch and upwards If the dry marble is subsequently wetted with water the iron salt inside the stone is decomposed by the carbonate of lime, and finely divided oxide of iron separates out in a state mechanically inseparable from the marble. The reaction can be watched by observing the change of colour.

The iron salt used is neutral ferric chloride. It is dissolved in 85 to 90 per cent. spirit and applied warm to the warm marble with a brush or by pouring. The concentration of the tincture to be used depends on the depth of colour wanted, and experience of the temperatures required is necessary It is best to make repeated applications of a very dilute solution, especially for light shades

When dyed and dried, the marble is wetted with water or exposed to damp air. When the decomposition of the iron salt has taken place the process is finished. The surface can then be polished, or if it was polished before it must be well rubbed with a wet cloth. The marble does not suffer in hardness or in power of taking a polish by the dyeing.

Many sorts of marble have an irregular texture, soft in one place and hard in another, and may contain enclosures of foreign matter Even those which appear whitest and most uniform to the eye are not of the same texture throughout, and the variations often cause the artist much trouble. They naturally make the different parts of the stone behave differently to dyes According to Weber this is particularly the case when considerable penetration has been produced by heating, and less when little colour is used and when the penetration is slight.

Marbles which, when dyed to some depth below the surface, show unlevel shades will, nevertheless, always take delicate shades uniformly if painted over with the tincture of iron when only slightly warmed Although in this case the colour does not penetrate so deeply, repeated wetting and drying and polishing with a wet cloth will give a quite sufficient colouring to the stone Even the most homogeneous marble should not be dyed till the sculptor has done with it.

If veined and naturally coloured marbles are treated hot by Weber's process specially mottled effects can be produced which are often very valuable, especially in close-grained stone

The best concentration of the iron tincture depends on

the depth and nature of the shade required Tinctures weak in iron give more yellowish shades, while those strong in iron give reddish hues The shade can be graded by adding a little manganous chloride to the iron solution. If that salt is to be used, the marble when dry after dyeing should be treated with alcohol containing a little ammonia before being wetted with water. Experiments seem to have shown that this process is applicable to other dyes besides iron. It has also been found that when the marble is wetted with aqueous solutions of salts having no chemical action on it they have very varied degrees of penetration. Ferrous salts, for example, penetrate very slightly, but permanganate of potash colours slabs half an inch thick right through in twenty-four hours

Few of the vast number of aniline yellows are used by us. Picric acid is less used than formerly, while auramine, in the form of a resinate lake, is finding increased employment. Its use, however, gives rather a harsh colour, and at a greater cost than Weber's process.

ORANGE.

These are usually produced with mixtures of red and yellow. Tincture of saffron gives a reddish-yellow, Weber's process as described above with the manganous chloride gives marble an orange hue. The colour, however, like brown, is in no great demand

BROWN.

For this tincture of cutch is used in various strengths Only yellow cutch or gambier must be used, and for certain shades this is combined with annatto Or the marble after dyeing with the gambier can be well rubbed with annatto in oil.

Anilines, *e g*, Bismarck brown, give unsatisfactory results as regards beauty and fastness, although many attempts have been made to use solution of the dye in spirit   The dyes soluble in fat answer better, but none can be compared to gambier.

BLACK.

Although marble is often dyed black, and oftener than people believe, especially when unsuccessful attempts have been made to dye it another colour, the recipes are still kept secret   Nevertheless, tincture of nigrosine, or better still, nigrosine and wax, will, according to its concentration, give every possible shade up to the deepest and fullest black.

PRODUCTION OF PARTI-COLOURED DESIGNS

If various colours are to be applied to marble so as to produce a sharp design, sundry precautions have to be taken which we now proceed to relate

Too many colours must not be put side by side. two or three at most, or they will not look well and will probably run.   Again, it is not indifferent which colour is applied first.   Those should go on first which want the most after-heating to make them penetrate

If, for example, a red, yellow and green pattern is wanted, the yellow is applied to the marble first, then the dragon's blood, and finally the wax and verdigris.   All colours used with wax must be put on last, and with great care, as they readily spread as soon as the stone is warmed For all colours applied with oil of turpentine or spirit, the stone must be first heated   With tinctures of dragon's blood or gamboge the stone is not heated till after dyeing. This is done by passing a red-hot iron repeatedly close to the stone   This is a better plan than holding the stone over glowing coal.

The only point remaining to be mentioned is that the marble to be dyed must be carved, cleaned and polished, for it is obvious that no work can be done on it with chisel or file after it has been dyed.

VIII.

DYEING ARTIFICIAL STONE

The processes for dyeing artificial stone are analogous to those employed for marble, but are easier of execution, and the more porous the stone the deeper the colour will sink into it The same dyes are used as for marble, but water-soluble anilines will here give beautiful and fast effects.

Generally, however, artificial stones are dyed during their manufacture The same is the case with the so-called gypsum marble, etc This manufacture does not come strictly within our province, but as the dyeing is bound up in it we must discuss its chief features.

For a red, a combination of gypsum and cinnabar is exclusively employed It is a good plan to make three mixtures containing different proportions of cinnabar, by using which any hue from light to dark may be produced The shade may be intensified and yet made vaguer by mixing in soot Soot can be so used with all colours to advantage.

For yellow orpiment and gypsum in various proportions are generally used A little cinnabar can also be added to give variety of shade

For green I have used chrome with the best results, obtaining much better effects than with the usual complicated mixtures of orpiment, light ochres and chrome yellow, with indigo or artificial ultramarine. They certainly give greens suitable for many purposes, but not a pure, fine colour. Guignet's green gives very good results

For blue I have used only ultramarine and gypsum, which give a very beautiful and bright result

Special effects can be got by adding to the coloured gypsum various shining bodies, such as filings of brass, tin or copper, little bits of eggshell, etc

Moulding, polishing, etc , do not come within the scope of this book.

4. DYEING AND IMITATION OF BONE, HORN AND IVORY.

IX

BLEACHING AND DYEING BONE.

Bleaching Bone.

BONE can be bleached by processes to be described under horn and ivory The bone should first, however, be boiled for from two to four hours in water containing salt and soda, to free it from particles of flesh, marrow and sinew On removal from the pan the bone is wiped clean with cloths, and rinsed in water

For bleaching we may use sulphurous acid, bisulphite of soda, chloride of lime or peroxide of hydrogen or sodium

Hedinger gives the following method The bones are steeped for ten hours in turpentine in tightly closed iron drums. They are then removed, and boiled in water for three hours with a little soft soap, skimming frequently At the end of the operation cold water is added, and the bones are taken out and allowed to dry on pine shelves, but without exposure to the sun In a few days they will be quite white.

Another method is to do the boiling with dilute caustic potash and then to dry on shelves as above.

Bones intended for keyboards can be bleached by simply leaving them for ten or twelve weeks in running water To get the highest possible degree of whiteness they can be treated with sulphurous acid afterwards.

(93)

If the bones are freed from fat by slow boiling, they will bleach quicker in running water, but exposure to the sun and treatment with sulphurous acid are still quicker.

Schmeisser recommends that sulphurous acid should never be used in the gaseous state, as it fills the bones with cracks This effect is still more pronounced with ivory

To bleach with chloride of lime prepare a solution of fresh bleach in four times its weight of water, and leave the bones or ivory in it for a few days; then rinse and allow to dry

Angenstein's process consists in boiling bones or ivory in a concentrated solution of alum for an hour, and then brushing them thoroughly They are then put into damp sawdust to prevent cracking

Bones can also be bleached with a mixture of unslaked lime, bran and water In this they are boiled till white.

Bleaching with urine and lime should be discarded, as, when worked afterwards, the bones make a lot of dust, full of ammonia and lime, which is very injurious to the health

Another method is steeping in hot oil of turpentine for ten to twelve hours, then boiling in soap-boilers' lye, and finally exposing the bones to the sun This gives a very good white

Even very yellow bone or ivory is rapidly and perfectly bleached by peroxide of hydrogen The bone or ivory is first dipped into benzine, then rubbed with a woollen cloth, and then placed in the peroxide till quite white.

When bones are wanted very white, it is important to begin with them as fresh as possible. The bleaching is then much more effectual

Dyeing Bone.

The dyeing of bones, like their bleaching, is much like that of ivory. The same dyes with few variations are used for both, and also for horn. Here we shall describe the new processes for bone, but for ivory the older ones, which, although more troublesome, are much more certain. For horn special recipes are given which have stood the test of much experience.

The dyeing can be done direct with most dyes, but it is best to soak the bones for a long time first in very dilute nitric and tartaric acids mixed, so that some of the phosphate of lime is removed from them. The mordant used is tin-salt or stannous sulphate (made by acting on 4 lb. of tin with a mixture of 6 lb. of hydrochloric acid, 3 lb. of sulphuric acid and 6 lb. of water). For many colours the preliminary treatment with nitric acid must be omitted or the colours will be destroyed.

Black.

The usual process is to employ logwood decoction or a solution of the extract in one of the two following ways —

(1) *With Bichromate.*—The bones are first treated for ten hours in a 10 per cent. solution of bichromate of potash or soda, and then put straight into a hot solution of logwood extract   The purer and more concentrated this is, the fuller and deeper the black will be   Fustic should only be used sparingly. The shade got is apt to turn somewhat green.

(2) *With Pyrolignite of Iron* —This does not give such a fine black as bichromate, but one faster to light   After staying for five or seven hours in hot logwood the bones are taken out when the liquid has cooled and put at once into a 10 deg. B. solution of the pyrolignite. This black

can be shaded by adding acetate of alumina or alum, which makes the black brighter and gives it a violet cast, to the logwood bath. Fustic, on the other hand, deadens the black.

Bones are most easily dyed black with anilines, especially with the spirit-soluble nigrosines No mordanting whatever is required A fairly concentrated solution of the nigrosine is made in methylated spirit and the bones are soaked in it as long as necessary.

Many water-soluble anilines can also be used with advantage, such as jet black, wool black, Biebrich patent black, naphthol black and many others. The process consists in giving the bones a preliminary bath of strong acetic acid for a few hours and then steeping them in the hot dye.

Black dye may be formed in the bone by means of aniline hydrochloride. Dr. Godeffroy of Vienna recommends this process, and gives the following recipe.—

Soak the bones for one hour in a solution of 20 oz. of the hydrochloride and 2 oz copper chloride in 300 oz of water, and then transfer to 10 per cent. bichromate till a deep black.

A still better process than this somewhat troublesome one is to soak the bones first in a solution of—

Hydrochloride of aniline	20 oz.
Sulphate of copper	6 ,,
Common salt	8 ,,
Water	150 ,,

and to transfer them thence to a solution of pyrolignite of iron Both processes give full blacks, fast to light, alkalies and acids

The same advantages can be secured even more simply in a single bath without heat and in less than an hour and a half. The bones are simply placed in the following solution till finished —

Hydrochloride of aniline	.	.	.	.	.	.	20 oz.
Bichromate of soda	.	.	.	.	.	.	10 ,,
Sulphate of copper	.	.	.	.	.	.	15 ,,
Sal-ammoniac	.	.	.	.	.	.	8 ,,
Sulphuric acid	.	.	.	.	.	.	5 ,,
Water .	.	.	.	.	.	.	200 ,,

The black can be given a reddish cast by subsequent treatment with soap, and a greenish one by the action of strong acetic acid.

RED.

A beautiful red is got by treating bones first mordanted with nitric acid in a decoction of cochineal or a solution of carmine in ammonia. With the cochineal, alum and a little tartar are added to the bath. Deep red is produced by a solution of 30 oz carmine and 10 oz crystal soda in 50 oz. of water, made slightly acid with acetic acid. In this the bones are boiled to shade   More about this coal-tar dyeing, however, will be found under ivory-dyeing

At present bones are almost solely dyed red with the coal-tar dyes, of which we have a large number at our service. The bones are first mordanted, usually with tin-salt, and then dyed with a basic dye, or are dyed direct in a single acid bath with an acid dye. The spirit-soluble anilines are the most easily fixed.

Among them we may mention fuchsine, extra ponceau, cardinal, amaranth, cerise, ruby S, eosine, rose Bengal, coralline, safranine and scarlet. For dissolving the spirit-soluble dyes they are heated with the spirit in a still with an upward condenser, or better in a strong closed vessel of copper or enamelled iron. The dyes require from ten to 100 times their weight of alcohol (90-95 per cent.).

Bluish-reds are best got with fuchsine, ruby S, cerise, cardinal and amaranth, all of which are soluble in spirit, and any shade can be got by suitable concentration of the dye

For delicate pink shades, eosine, rose Bengal and safranine are specially suitable   Scarlets are got without difficulty with extra ponceau, scarlet and coralline.   Bones may be dyed direct or after mordanting with tin-salt.

Of the water-soluble acid reds I may mention brilliant croceine, ponceau R, pyritine RRO, scarlet, etc   All these require previous mordanting of the bones with tin-salt or hydrochloric acid

According to the experience I have gained from many experiments the dilute acid alone is a sufficient mordant not only for reds but for other acid anilines   It is a decidedly cheaper mordant than citric or tartaric acid Nitric acid is to be avoided entirely for reds as it impairs their brilliancy   After a sufficient time in the acid, the bones are transferred to the dye solution at about 50 deg. C   The acid dyes give more or less scarlet-reds, partly brick and partly crab reds   In any case the acid reds will soon be the only mediums used to produce that colour in bone

YELLOW.

The best mordant in this case is nitric acid, but dilute hydrochloric gives very good results

The oldest and best known dyeing process is to soak the bones first in a hot solution of bichromate of potash and then in a similar one of lead acetate

It is, however, much easier to dye bones with a tincture of picric acid, which gives a beautiful deep yellow which can easily be shaded at pleasure by mixing the tincture with tincture of safranine

The use of turmeric, fustic, weld and saffron is now nearly obsolete

BLUE.

Until recently commercial indigo carmine and the extract were the only substances used for the blue-dyeing of bones. The use of ferrocyanide of potash was too troublesome, and never gave good results

With commercial indigo carmine the process is extremely simple The bones are soaked in a strong solution of it in hot water. Many of the spirit-soluble anilines can be used just as easily, *e g.*, methylene blue, navy blue, fast blue, peacock blue, and benzyl blue, and also *bleu lumière*

In dyeing with indigo carmine mordanting with acid is indispensable, but with the spirit-soluble anilines it is at the option of the dyer Indigo extract and carmine give characteristic blues, but the anilines usually give much brighter and warmer shades.

Violets are easily got with suitable mixtures of red and blue anilines A common but not very warm violet is got by mordanting with tin-salt and then dyeing the bones in a hot logwood bath. All the spirit-soluble aniline violets give brilliant hues just as easily, especially Hofmann's violet, ruby violet, Gentiana violet and Regina violet.

Greens are usually dyed with mixtures of blues and yellows in various proportions according to the shade wanted

Ordinary green is got by first dyeing the bone with indigo carmine or an aniline, and then in a bath of fustic, quercitron, picric acid or weld Here again, however, we have numerous spirit-soluble anilines, which give much warmer greens, especially malachite, ethyl, methyl and iodine greens The bones are mordanted in dilute hydrochloric acid, rinsed, and dyed in the dye tincture Malachite green is undoubtedly the best

Grays and browns are now produced exclusively with anilines

Permanganate of potash although lately strongly recommended, is strictly to be avoided, as the colour obtained although beautiful enough at first is very loose, especially in the lighter shades. Acid fumes in the air at once destroy it, and the least contact of the bones with dilute vinegar will make it disappear like magic.

To obtain a fine gray I specially recommend the use of spirit-soluble nigrosine This unquestionably gives the best results.

A pretty and very fast brown can be dyed quite easily and conveniently with spirit-soluble Bismarck brown The following dyes also give good browns, though with various reddish and yellowish casts: resorcin brown, Philadelphia brown, Berlin brown, mode brown. With the last three the colour can be shaded by adding a little bichromate to the bath.

X.

HORN.

BLEACHING AND WHITENING.

Real bleaching of horn, which is always more or less darkly coloured, is impracticable without injuring the horn, as many experts have shown. We therefore content ourselves with whitening it.

To dye horn white it is first stained brown with red-lead and then dipped in hydrochloric acid free from arsenic and iron This converts the lead sulphide into chloride which remains as a white precipitate on the horn and gives it a milky white opalescent appearance. The horn must not stay too long in the lead stain, which is made by stirring up 5 lb. of caustic lime and 3 lb of red-lead with caustic potash lye, or it will become brittle. It must not stay too long in the acid either, or some of the lead chloride will be dissolved out and the whitening partly undone If care is taken satisfactory results are certain. If the horn is exceptionally pale at first the solutions should be used weaker.

DYEING HORN BLACK.

By Wagner's Process.—As is well known comb-makers dye pale or speckled horn to make an imitation of buffalo horn. This is done with the red-lead stain already described. The combs are left entirely immersed in it for twelve to twenty-four hours, taken out, washed with water (usually mixed with a little vinegar), dried and polished. They thus acquire a fine black colour

The theory of the process is simple. Horn contains sulphur, which forms calcium sulphide with the caustic lime. This sulphide dissolves and re-acts in the pores of the horn with the lead which has also penetrated in the form of calcium plumbate, and forms black lead sulphide Hence the horn is dyed black to some depth below the surface This method is very cheap and usually gives good results. It has, however, the great drawback that the lime often causes the finer teeth of the comb to lose their parallelism The whole comb may be twisted if thin. There is yet another and greater disadvantage, *viz.*, that if damp gets to the combs dyed in this way while they are in stock, a few months sees them covered with a white crust which can only be removed with difficulty by polishing, and always returns again. This makes the combs unsightly and unsaleable. The cause is the formation of white sulphate of lead, and the harm is particularly likely to occur while exported combs are on the sea.

Dr. Wagner gives the following account of his attempts to devise a process free from these drawbacks Logwood or galls are not to be recommended as they are difficult to use cold, and heat spoils the horn Logwood and bichromate give a good black at a temperature that the comb will stand, but the black is not fast to even dilute alkalies It was therefore necessary to find a mineral stain free from the disadvantages of the red-lead mixture. The only ones which were found not to oxidise in damp air were the sulphides of bismuth, mercury and silver. Sulphide of silver is barred by economic considerations. Bismuth was tried in many ways with the most discouraging results

Mercury oxide made into a paste with slaked lime and water does not blacken horn, probably because no soluble mercury compound is formed, so that the mercury does not come into contact with the sulphur in the horn Dr. Wagner, however, supplanted it by soaking the horn first in a solution of a mercury salt and then in one of potassium sulphide He found that the nitrate was the mercury salt which gave the best results, and best of all in the form of Millon's re-agent for albumen

To prepare the mercury solution dissolve 2 oz of mercury in 5 oz of cold concentrated nitric acid, and then dilute with 50 oz of water In this solution leave the combs over night, then rinse them quite free from acid They are now red, and very much like tortoise-shell They are next placed for one hour, or two hours at most, in a dilute solution of potassium sulphide The blackened combs are rinsed first with vinegar then with pure water, dried and polished. They have then, according to experts, the exact appearance of buffalo horn Care must be taken in the polish as although the colour is very fast it does not go in very far

Numerous experts have shown that very small quantities of the mercury solution suffice for the reddening, so that the process is to be preferred even on the score of expense.

There are still various other methods for blackening horn, which we will describe briefly

Boil the horn in—

Domingo logwood	30 oz.
Acetate of alumina	3 ,,
Water	220 ,,

for half an hour, dry well, and steep in a 10 per cent. solution of nitrate of copper.

According to Andés a very fine black is got by boiling the horn in concentrated solution of sugar of lead The blackening takes place from a reaction between the lead and the sulphur of the horn, forming black lead sulphide The horn is boiled for from a half to one and a half hours, and carefully rinsed with vinegar and water A deeper black is got if the horn is mordanted first with sulphide of potassium

Several experiments in dyeing horn with hydrochloride of aniline and bichromate gave very good results, but the dye does not penetrate sufficiently

Aniline Black in the Cold--Mix together the following two solutions —

1. Aniline oil	.	12 oz.
Hydrochloric acid (19 deg. B.) . . .	.	14 ,,
Water		25 ,,
2. Bichromate of potash . .	.	18 oz.
Sulphuric acid	.	20 ,,
Water	.	35 ,,

Steep the horn in the mixture for from an hour to an hour and a half, then soak in a strong soap bath, dry and polish. Equally good results are got by the following, another cold process.

Fast Aniline Black—Mix together the following solutions :—

1. Aniline hydrochloride . . . . . 15 oz.
      ,,   oil . . . . . . 3 ,,
   Water . . . . 30 ,,
2. Bichromate of potash . . . . . 20 oz.
   Concentrated sulphuric acid . . . . 20 ,,
   Nitrate of iron (45 deg B) . . . . 5 ,,
   Water . . . . . . 35 ,,

Steep the horn in the mixture for from an hour to an hour and a half, wash, dry and polish.

GRAY.

This colour is got by analogous methods to black, merely using diluter baths All the above directions for black dyeing will then give good results

A beautiful gray is obtained by first dyeing the horn white and then staining it in ferric chloride solution to shade. If the chloride solution is strong the gray will be yellowish, but bluish if it is dilute.

BROWN.

To produce browns, blues, greens, violets and reds the horn must first be dyed white, and then dyed by simple immersion in the tincture of the proper aniline dye. For brown the best dyes are Bismarck brown and resorcin brown.

BLUE.

For this use Lyons blue or navy blue It economises dye to mordant the whitened horn in a strong alum bath before dyeing it, and in this case a solution of indigo carmine answers perfectly, and gives a characteristic blue with a greenish shade.

GREEN.

This is best got by combining blues and yellows, for example, the tinctures of picric acid and indigo carmine or of malachite green. The whitened horn is simply placed in a mixture of the concentrated tinctures.

Violets are now dyed with methyl violet almost exclusively. The tincture of this dye certainly gives the brightest and most beautiful colours, which shimmer splendidly on the horn.

Mixtures of blue and red give results which are far from being successful

RED.

We wish, before giving any practical recipes, to describe two processes · that of Burnig of Stuttgart, and that of Lindner of Berlin

French Method of giving Horn a Beautiful Red Colour.— The usual stain by which the comb-makers make horn look like tortoise-shell is a mixture of soda, quicklime and white-lead, which causes brown specks on acting for fifteen or twenty minutes Longer exposure to the stain makes the specks dirty-looking and spoils the effect. The French imitations are noted for their fiery red marks, which make them look very well, especially by transmitted light On this ground Lindner had requests from many quarters to make a red stain for horn Close study of the nature of horn and comparison of it with wool soon showed that the brown specks consisted of sulphide of lead in a finely divided state Lindner determined to decompose the brown matter in the horn and convert it into oxide of lead by adding caustic soda to the red dye-baths. He had found by his own experiments, as empirical experience had previously shown, that they were of no use on the horn with the brown marks, even after treatment with various metallic oxides On adding caustic soda, however, he succeeded completely and obtained the very finest red colours both with redwood and with orchil Perhaps, too, the caustic soda has the additional advantage of dissolving the fat out of horn.

Lindner's method, which is now universally used in Berlin, is as follows.—

The horn is first prepared in a mixture of nitric acid with three times its weight of water at a temperature of 30 to 37 deg C It is then mordanted with the usual mixture of freshly burnt lime with its own weight of white-lead, and twice its weight of soda. This second operation lasts ten to fifteen minutes, so that the specks only appear yellowish-brown The horn is then rinsed and wiped, and brought into a bath of caustic soda lye of 20 deg B. mixed with four times its weight of redwood decoction. The horn is finally rinsed, pressed, and after thirteen or sixteen hours polished. The decoction can be made by boiling Pernambuco wood with three times its weight of water If zinc oxide is used in the mordant together with the white-lead, bluer shades are got Tin-salts make the red more like a scarlet.

Tortoise-shell Imitation with Fuchsine—The French are the best imitators of tortoise-shell, and distinguish themselves above other makers by the fiery red marks they produce. All the various processes used for this production depend on combining the sulphur of the horn with oxides or salts of lead. Burnig of Stuttgart has published a method he has discovered for getting this red marking It has this distinct difference from its predecessors that it is independent of the sulphur in the horn, and fixes a pure dye on the material He places the horn in solution of caustic potash, where it remains from five to sixty minutes, according to the strength of the lye and the nature of the

horn The horn will then combine with fuchsine without
further preparation. The dye is then applied to the parts
to be marked in a thick paste, so that it will not run,
but without any thickening. As soon as the fuchsine has
dried enough at ordinary temperatures to show its usual
bronzy appearance, it is removed with a wooden spatula,
the dry paste is softened with spirit and again applied
It is impossible to prevent the colour spreading somewhat,
but the parts which should not be dyed can afterwards be
whitened again mechanically by polishing with soft soap
or tripoli. The parts covered with fuchsine have a dark
red colour which looks particularly fine by transmitted
light, and are quite as warm in hue as in the Parisian-made
horn. Exceptionally light horn alone makes them appear
somewhat too blue They stand both light and damp, an
important advantage for this method, in addition to the
ease and certainty with which it can be carried out.

Horn can be dyed with anilines in the ways already
described for other colours. If water-soluble anilines are
used the horn requires a preliminary treatment with
caustic soda or potash lye, or with strong soap solution
Spirit-soluble anilines, however, require no mordanting

YELLOW.

These can be got with aniline yellow after mordanting
with caustic soda lye, or just as well by immersing
whitened horn in about a $1\frac{1}{2}$ per cent solution of bichromate of potash until the desired shade is produced, which
may be from a sulphur to a deep yellow.

We now proceed to the methods of giving horn a metallic
appearance. The horn is prepared as usual without giving
any colour The application of chloride of zinc, by immersion or brushing, gives a yellow bronze colour, zinc chromate a green, chloride of copper a black, copper chromate

a brown bronze Potash reddens all these bronzes. The bronzed articles are dried at about 68 deg. C., or in the open air in fine summer weather. When dry they are rubbed with a composition which gives them a beautiful appearance, and is made by heating together 16 oz. of tin amalgam (made by heating 5 oz of quicksilver with 11 oz of tin), 3 oz of sulphur and 5 oz. of sal-ammoniac, all in fine powder till the quicksilver has evaporated, leaving a yellow mass

HORN BUTTONS.

We finally quote from the *Industrie Zeitung* an account of the manufacture and dyeing of horn buttons

For black-dyeing it is best to use nitrate of mercury and potassium sulphide.

Dissolve 13 oz of mercury in 13 oz of cold concentrated nitric acid and dilute with about 100 oz of water, and leave the horn in the solution over night Then wash it, first with water, then with dilute vinegar, and then with water again. The button-shapes are now cut out by machinery The rim produced by the stamping is removed by children Each button is then smoothed at the edges, and polished by means of a brush with a composition of which the main ingredient is wax The buttons are then wrapped in paper by girls.

The waste horn from button manufacture is either used as manure or by heating and moulding is made into buttons of an inferior and less durable kind

We shall here also briefly describe the process of Leopold Müller of Berlin for dyeing stone-nut buttons.

The nut or vegetable ivory as it is often called is the fruit of a palmaceous shrub which grows in the equatorial part of South America Of late the plant has been regularly cultivated. The fruit, like that of a horse-chestnut, has a rough spiny outer skin, which is removed before the nut is exported. Under it is the solid shell containing normally two, but sometimes more kernels, sometimes, too, only one. The chief shipping ports are Cartagena and Maracaibo. On breaking the shell the kernel, which is the part used, is seen, of the appearance and size of a potato. It is so hard that only steel tools will cut it It contains under a thin brown surface layer a white compact mass closely resembling ivory

Even fifteen years ago the value of this nut, which was used for ballast, was unrecognised, but since it has been used for making buttons there has been a great demand for it. The kernels are sawn by a circular saw into pieces of the proper size, which are then turned in a lathe.

The buttons are dyed before being polished, just as they come from the lathe. To certain dyes they behave peculiarly, and they will stand no acid They differ very widely from the textile fibres in their affinities for dyes, and require specially prepared baths as they cannot be mordanted That process would prevent the subsequent polishing.

Müller reports as follows on vegetable ivory dyeing No exact recipes can be given for the dyeing of vegetable ivory buttons, as they are only dyed to order, and not for the purpose of being kept in stock Again, the ivory shows, according to the place and time of year at which it was gathered, such varieties of structure and affinity for dye that no precise rules can be given Nearly every parcel requires different treatment Beautiful shades of all colours can be got by very gradual addition of dye to the bath, steady boiling, and keeping the bath always clear and bright. The buttons must always be perfectly clean and free from all fat When they are in this state a short boil in a weak soap bath greatly increases the richness of the colour. Yellowish buttons are sorted out from the rest, and reserved for dyeing black or at least dark shades.

Red is usually dyed with anilines alone The buttons are put with water into a small pan, and the dye is dissolved separately in boiling water and put slowly through a filter into the pan with the buttons a little at a time The bath is kept boiling all the time, stirring up the buttons with a stick till the proper shade is reached. The buttons are then taken out and allowed to dry on a sieve. They are then polished and bored.

A fine magenta is got with diamond magenta, a cherry red with cerise, and other reds with the corresponding anilines

Yellow, especially straw yellow, is dyed with picric acid. A dark yellow is got by simply putting the buttons into a warm solution of bichromate. It has to be borne in mind that the colour deepens afterwards, so that the buttons must be dyed somewhat lighter than sample

Green is dyed with malachite green The powdered dye is dissolved in luke-warm water, and the solution gradually added to the buttons immersed in water In the meantime the water is gradually heated, but not above 50 deg. C, and the colour is shaded during the progress of the dyeing by adding picric acid. If, however quite a pale green is wanted, the picric acid is used first by itself Green can also be dyed cold without any mordant with malachite green The process only takes longer. Dark and Russian greens are got with a blue dye and picric acid

Violet is dyed with reddish or bluish water-soluble methyl violet, used like fuchsine. Fine lilacs and mode grays are also dyed with it, of course using the dye in very small quantities.

Blue can be dyed either with aniline blue or alkali blue. The buttons are put into a soap bath and boiled, after adding concentrated solution of the dye, for at least two hours, then rinsed slightly and put into cold, weak acetic acid to develop the colour If alkali blue is used some borax should be put into the soap bath. For blue-dyeing only the whitest buttons should be chosen so as to get pure shades

Brown is got either with aniline brown, which may be shaded if required with fuchsine, methyl violet, malachite green, orange, etc , or with cutch. This being cheaper is more commonly used. After cutch-dyeing treatment with a hot bath of ferrous sulphate, bichromate of potash or bluestone is needed, according to the shade wanted

Orange is dyed with anilines only, fixed like fuchsine

Gray can be got capitally with sumach, boiling for a longer or shorter time according to shade, and then fixing with hot solution of green vitriol A bluish gray is got by using galls in exactly the same way.

Water-soluble nigrosine gives a fine blue-black

Black is dyed with logwood and bichromate The buttons are boiled for at least half an hour in a strong logwood bath, and are then entered into a cold bichromate bath for ten minutes. They are then rinsed, and the whole process is repeated until the desired colour is obtained.

Aniline black obtained with aniline salt or oil in the usual way never answers well

XI

IVORY

New ivory need not be bleached, as it can be bought white enough, but old ivory which has become yellow with age is bleached exactly as described for bones Ivory articles must be polished before dyeing, and the various methods of doing this must be acquired by practical experience The dyeing of ivory is exactly analogous to that of bone, and any deficiency in the following account may be supplemented by referring back to that of bone-dyeing

I wish to mention here specially that the colourist cannot fail to be amused, when he peruses the literature of the subject, to find that the dyes stated as being requisite for ivory-dyeing are all vegetable colouring matters, knowing as he does that the finest and purest shades are got with spirit-soluble anilines. Hardly an author mentions these, but weld, fustic, redwood, logwood, turmeric and cochineal are always quoted as *the* dyes employed. We follow here the same order as for bones, and begin with black

BLACK ON IVORY.

The most expensive black, which, however, according to my experience, is not utilised in practice, is that obtained with nitrate of silver. There is no objection, nevertheless, to the process except its expense. I quote now one of the latest recipes for the black-dyeing of ivory

Boil 20 lb. of logwood extract wrapped in a linen bag in 20 gallons of water for two hours. This will dissolve the colouring matter, and the insoluble residue in the bag is then removed. Then put in 2 lb. of calcined soda, and boil and stir till it is dissolved, removing all scum with a ladle. The ivory is stained in the liquid for two or three hours, and is then put into a bath of bichromate dissolved in fifteen times its weight of water

Another recipe is to boil 20 lb of crushed galls and 80 lb. of powdered verdigris in 60 gallons of water. Then filter, and boil up the clear solution with the ivory. Later the ivory is transferred to a bath of—

Logwood extract	20 lb.
Ferric acetate	10 ,,
Gum-arabic	2 ,,
Water	24 gals

This bath is first boiled for an hour, and filtered.

The very full black, which may be shaded with aniline yellow, can be got on ivory with spirit-soluble nigrosine If the ivory is first mordanted for two or three hours in very dilute acetic acid the black is deeper and more velvety.

Another black answering every requirement is got by steeping in a cold solution of aniline oil, water, hydrochloric acid, bichromate and blue vitriol, until the ivory has assumed the proper colour

RED.

Here the chief part is played by cochineal. Various anilines are also used but mostly give less satisfactory colours Prechtl gives the following antiquated recipe · Mordant for a few minutes in very diluted tin-salt solution, and then place in a decoction of Brazil wood. The red is much better if a little cochineal is added to this. The addition of fustic makes the red more of a scarlet. If the ivory is treated with weak carbonate of potash after dyeing it becomes a cherry red.

We quote another process from a New York technical paper Scarlet cloth-cuttings are boiled in water, adding carbonate of potash little by little till all the colour is extracted. The decoction is then cleared with a little alum and filtered through linen. The ivory, previously mordanted with aqua-fortis, is placed in the filtrate till the desired shade is reached The aqua-fortis must not be too strong nor may the ivory stay in it too long The moment the least roughening appears the ivory must be transferred to the dye solution This should be luke-warm, but not hot. A little practice will enable the dyer to get any desired shade If part of the ivory is to be left undyed, it is protected by a coating of wax or paraffin. In this way any writing or design can be executed The same use of wax or paraffin can, of course, be made with any dye The method given by the New York paper is really good, and gives excellent results if the cloth used has been dyed with cochineal, which is now rarely the case

Andés recommends the following Boil finely powdered cochineal in thirteen times its weight of water for three hours, and paint the ivory several times with the solution When dry apply a mordant of tin-salt and tartaric acid The result is a rich red. If the cochineal is boiled in a decoction of quercitron (one of bark to sixteen of water) instead of in plain water, all shades can be made, from yellowish to scarlet-red. The same author recommends for a permanent red on ivory Pernambuco wood in combination with tin-salt. It can hardly be supposed, however, that now when so many splendid aniline reds are at hand any one would use redwood, as the colour can be got with the anilines just as fast and far more easily I can mention as very suitable the tinctures of fuchsine, extra ponceau, Russian red, cardinal, amaranth, camellia, cerise, rubine S, acid fuchsine, garnet S, the rubine, phosphine and methyl cosine, erythrosine, safranine, rose Bengal, phloxine and coccinin. These colours are equally soluble in water.

The ivory must be cleaned and bleached if necessary, and then steeped in the tincture, or the latter can be applied with a brush. If the solution of the dye in water is used, the ivory must be first mordanted with dilute nitric acid While the dyeing is very easy with a tincture, the other method is difficult, for experience is requisite to judge the right strength for the nitric acid mordant. Instead of nitric acid, hydrochloric, acetic or tartaric acid is much used, and which to use must be decided according to which aniline dye is to follow As water-soluble anilines which give rich reds we may mention fast red, orchil red, ponceau, scarlet GR, azorubine, Victoria scarlet, brilliant scarlet, Bordeaux, etc

For dissolving the dye-stuff soft water must be used at the boil, and in such quantities as to make from $\frac{1}{2}$ to $\frac{1}{3}$ per cent. solutions. Stir till solution is complete If rubine solution has to be kept for some time, it must be preserved by the addition of spirit or part of the dye will precipitate To dissolve one of the above-mentioned spirit-dyes in water make the bath alkaline first with a little soda, and filter before use Ponceau, croceine and Bordeaux dissolve easily in eighty times their weight of water There are so very many aniline reds that they enable us to produce every conceivable shade in the easiest possible manner. In spite of this we must not omit to mention that we can shade our reds at pleasure with aniline yellows and violets; in the first case towards orange, and in the second towards lilac.

YELLOW.

Yellows are got with anilines on ivory exactly like reds The most commonly used dye is certainly picric acid in spirit or water, spirit solution giving the best results. The solution should be filtered before use as a precaution. Of other yellow anilines soluble in water or spirit we may mention phosphine, aurantia, curcumine, Philadelphia yellow, Martius yellow, chrysophenine, brilliant yellow, chrysoidine, auramine, mandarin, methyl orange and metanil yellow Special and very pure greenish-yellows can be got with quinoline yellow, which, however, is only soluble in spirit

To return to the old processes, we will first again quote Prechtl. The ivory is first mordanted for a few minutes in dilute sulphate of tin. It goes straight from this to warm decoction of fustic, or of fustic and redwood for orange. Another process is to boil the ivory first in alum, and then to steep it for half an hour in an aqueous infusion of turmeric. Another beautiful yellow is got by using the turmeric in the form of tincture.

Andés describes the following method of producing a

chrome yellow direct on the ivory Steep the ivory for a few hours in a 5 per cent solution of bichromate of potash. Then transfer to a solution of sugar of lead in five times its weight of distilled water till done By altering the proportions, or by adding a little lime, all sorts of shades can be got up to the deepest orange.

BLUE.

The favourite blue was formerly indigo carmine only, the ivory being first mordanted with hydrochloric acid Or the ivory was left overnight in an acetate of alumina solution of 4 deg. B . and dyed next day with indigo carmine These were at one time the only known processes worth having, for the American process with verdigris only gives greenish-blue or rather bluish-green shades. It consists in first dyeing the ivory articles green in a solution of verdigris in dilute nitric acid, and then converting the green into blue with a strong solution of carbonate of potash or soda Naturally these colours, and also those obtained with soluble indigo, will bear no comparison with those got with the aniline blues

The following dyes soluble in water and spirit have to be mentioned methylene blue, navy blue, peacock blue and benzyl blue. Of those soluble in spirit only the most important for us are Humboldt blue, aniline blue, king's blue and Gentiana blue Less valuable, and soluble only in water, are water blue, capri blue, brilliant blue, alkali blue, China blue, black blue and many others, including the blue benzidines, none of which give specially good results in ivory-dyeing Many experiments have shown that decidedly the most fast and beautiful colours are got with the spirit-soluble aniline blues Kayser recommends, in order to secure the greatest possible penetration of the dye, that the ivory should undergo a preliminary treatment with a dilute nitric acid, and should then be thoroughly rinsed with plenty of water, and, after dyeing in the tincture, dried, and finally rubbed with soft flannel to get a fine polish. Used in this manner the above-named water-soluble aniline blues are also well fixed. With alkali blue, however, a subsequent short fixing with very dilute sulphuric acid is to be recommended to bring out the full beauty of the colour.

VIOLETS.

Violets are rarely required alone, and are always then produced with tincture of methyl violet Of this dye there are so many marks from the reddest to the bluest that it is hardly possible to be ever under the necessity of using any other. We may mention as a historical curiosity that alkanet used at one time to be used The root was macerated in alcohol for a long time and the tincture was filtered, and the ivory steeped in or painted with it. The resulting colour is very beautiful but, unfortunately, very loose, especially if exposed to the sun

GREEN.

Until the aniline dyes were discovered there was no direct green, and the colour was always got by combining blue and yellow The only exception was the verdigris green already described. Ivory was generally dyed blue with indigo carmine, put for a few minutes in very dilute tin-salt, and then dyed to shade in hot decoction of turmeric or fustic

The present aniline greens far surpass these greens in lustre and richness. Most of them dissolve in either water or alcohol Of these we may mention iodine green, methyl green, ethyl green and malachite green Guinea green and olive green are only water-soluble. I, however, recommend that only tinctures should here be used. If the colour is too bluish add a little tincture of picric acid.

With this any desired yellow cast can be given to the green.

GRAY.

Most gray shades are got like blacks, using, of course, only very dilute solutions Andés recommends the following gray mordant as giving a very fine and fast gray, but it looks rather too expensive . Dissolve pyrogallic acid in twenty times its weight of water and steep the ivory in the solution for about twenty minutes Then dry well, and put into a solution of ferrous sulphate in twenty-five times its weight of water The gray can be made lighter by using still weaker baths, and strengthened and made more bluish by using them more concentrated

Instead of pyrogallic acid we can use logwood decoction, or better, solution of hemolin, and the green vitriol may be replaced by pyrolignite of iron of 7 deg B This gives a brighter and more bluish gray, but the shade may be varied at will by altering the strength of the baths. By adding fustic the grays can be shaded with green.

The gray anilines are, of course, much used, partly because the processes are so simple, and partly because the results are so brilliant Only two spirit grays need be mentioned, *viz*, nigrosine and aniline grays, although the water-soluble silver gray is to be recommended for a few special purposes.

BROWN.

Browns are often required on ivory, whether all over or only on parts Partial dyeing is best done with permanganate, which, however, must be used with certain special precautions. The articles must first be absolutely free from fat, which is best effected by treating them with ordinary or with petrol ether. It must be remembered that the use of either of these involves considerable danger of fire, and should never be carried out in the same room with a naked flame. When free from fat the ivory is steeped for from five to fifteen minutes in hydrochloric acid diluted with twenty-five times its weight of water, then well rinsed and placed in a half per cent. solution of permanganate of potash. Care must be taken no undissolved permanganate is left in the bath The salt dissolves very slowly, and the solution is so dark that undissolved particles are very apt to escape detection They will cause unlevel and speckled dyeing The solution must be used cold, and the time of exposure to it depends on the shade wanted, as a matter of course As soon as the dyeing is over, rinse, dry and polish the ivory as usual. For special and redder browns the ivory, after being polished, should have a bath of grenadine or fuchsine (a 1 per cent solution). According to the length of stay herein the brown will be more or less toned with red. In using permanganate it must not be forgotten that the browns it produces are highly sensitive to sulphurous acid in any form. Even a weak solution of sodium sulphite destroys them, and makes the article perfectly white.

Cutch is another brown ivory-dye, but is now hardly at all used.

Among anilines the following (soluble both in water and spirit) may be used: Bismarck brown, mode brown, Berlin brown, and also (water-soluble only) fast brown, acid brown and nacarat S

DESIGNS ON IVORY.

If it is a question of making black or coloured designs on ivory, it is best done by etching. Rub 6 oz tear mastic and 3 oz. asphalt separately to fine powder. Then fuse 6 oz of wax, and put in the powders a little at a time, first the mastic and then the asphalt. When a homogeneous mixture has been got by stirring it is poured into lukewarm water, and, while cooling, shaped with the hand into sticks or pellets. Mastic is rather dear and can be replaced by clear colophony, which answers nearly as well In this case the best proportions are 12 oz. asphalt, 6 oz. colophony and 3 oz wax

This composition is painted over the ivory which is first warmed and must show a well-polished surface All along the edge of the wax coating make a raised border of wax so as to make a little bath with a wax bottom, in which the design is drawn, laying bare the parts of the ivory to be etched. The wax bath is now filled with concentrated sulphuric acid, which may be slightly warmed first to hasten matters The exposed parts of the ivory are blackened by the acid If the design need not be very sharp, wax alone can be used without any asphalt, mastic or colophony If instead of sulphuric acid we use a solution of nitrate of silver and afterwards expose the ivory to the sun we get a very durable black pattern, and with gold chloride a purple-red one. When the etching is finished rinse in water and remove the wax with turpentine

To make white stripes on a coloured ground on billiard balls, the balls are wrapped in a waxed strip of cloth so as to protect the parts to be white from the dye, and then dyed The strip may be fixed securely with thread Should the white colour have run into white streaks, which it is very apt to do, the colour is removed by careful scraping. It must be mentioned that all colours are much faster on unpolished than on polished ivory, so the dyeing should be done before polishing. The polishing is done by rubbing with soap and Vienna chalk with the bare hand. In dyeing, the ivory must not be boiled too long, or it will crack As soon as it is taken out it should be quickly cooled by being thrown into cold water. To silver ivory it should be put into a weak solution of nitrate of silver till it is a dark yellow and then exposed in water to the direct rays of the sun After about three hours the ivory will be quite black, and when dried and rubbed with a soft leather will assume a splendid silvery lustre

Ivory shares with bone the property of being softened by dilute acids This can be utilised to mould it. Soak the ivory for three or four days in a mixture of 2 oz of nitric acid and 5 oz. of water. It will then be soft enough to be dented by the fingers The softened ivory is then dyed if desired, and shaped by being pressed into metal moulds When taken therefrom it is buried in very dry common salt, whereby it recovers its former hardness Phosphoric acid can also be used for softening ivory, and is used in a solution of 1 13 sp gr Laid in this the ivory partially loses its opacity. When it is soft enough it is washed with cold water, and is then restored to its former hardness and opacity by steeping in hot water

Batonnier and Michel of Paris have patented a process for fixing several colours at once on bone, ivory or horn, without allowing them to run into one another. Meal is made into a thin paste which is spread on a sheet of paper On this again the colours are placed in the form of powder or thick paste and the sheet is then applied to the surface to be dyed, naturally with the coated side next to it. To ensure perfect contact a metal plate is applied to the back of the paper, and the whole is placed in a suitable press The whole arrangement is then brought into a steam chamber, or placed in boiling water The colour then fixes on the surface of the ivory, etc. Finally, the paper is removed and the dyed surface is washed and dried in the shade

Painting and inlaid work is imitated by C Spatz (German patent No. 34) in the following manner Transfers are laid upon a sheet of gelatine and more gelatine is then poured over them, so as to enclose them. The result will have a different appearance from either ivory or tortoise-shell.

5. WOOD-DYEING AND IMITATING FANCY WOODS.

XII

DYEING AND STAINING WOOD

THIS industry is not yet practised on a large scale in factories, except in very isolated cases. For a long time, unfortunately, the art had no secure foundations. To make the matter clearer I may mention that practical men do not speak of dyeing at all but of staining wood, however the colour may be produced. A distinction should be drawn between dyeing and staining in the common interests of all concerned, and we shall here restrict the term dyeing to the use of coloured dyes, and the term staining to the use of colourless liquids which cause the wood to assume particular colours, such as salts, acids, and alkalies

The art of wood-dyeing consists of imparting colours to cheap home-grown woods which are not natural to them, without the application of pigments, and also of bringing out and beautifying the various veins and markings in the wood.

The commonest woods selected for dyeing are lime, pear-tree, walnut, acacia, elm, horse-chestnut, fir, pine, ash, maple, beech and plane.

The wood to be dyed must be first carefully planed and smoothed with a file, or with fishskin, pumice or glass paper, so that nothing has to be done after dyeing but to bring out certain parts. The deeper the dye penetrates the more durable the colour. Most of the shades produced

(122)

are very loose to light and require a protecting varnish to shield them from the effects of air, sun and damp. The varnishing, which will be more fully described later, has also the aim of increasing the beauty of the appearance of the work.

The art of varnish-making consists in dissolving by the aid of heat one or more resins in a liquid, so that the resins unite well with it and with one another. The solvent used must evaporate quickly after the varnish has been applied, and leave the resin behind as a transparent coat which must not crack or flake off. Few solvents fulfil all these requirements, and, in fact, there are only three sorts of varnish, pale or spirit varnishes, fat or oil varnishes, and turpentine varnishes. Most varnishes contain turpentine with the object of making the resin less brittle. The preparation of the varnish must vary according to the nature of the body to be varnished, such as wood, metal, gypsum, bone, etc.

We now return to dyeing. This is done sometimes warm, sometimes cold, according to the kind of wood, and to the desired intensity of colour. A cold dye never penetrates a given wood so deeply as a warm one, especially if the latter is applied more than once, or the wood is left a long time immersed in it. Each case must be treated individually in the following pages as no general rules are possible.

We now proceed to describe the latest dyeing processes, and shall pass afterwards to the more important special processes.

BLACK.

Although we have now countless methods for dyeing wood black proposed, yet the chrome logwood process is the only one adopted. The well-polished wood should be rubbed with alum-water as a preliminary   Logwood always has to be used in combination with a metallic mordant, which may be iron, copper, chromium, vanadium or cerium

Black with Logwood and Chrome.

The best and easiest black-dyeing process is with log-wood decoction or a solution of the extract and bichromate of potash   The potash salt and the logwood are not mixed but applied alternately, and each coat is allowed to dry thoroughly before the next is put on   The first coat is usually of logwood. Chromate is sometimes substituted for bichromate but, in my opinion, with less success

The alternate coats succeed one another till the desired shade is obtained   Hauboldt recommends a black dye which can be used without any mordant and will keep per-fectly well. It is made by dissolving 40 lb of logwood extract in 12 gallons of boiling water, filtering, and then adding 2 lb. of yellow chromate of potash first dissolved in water. It has a fine violet-blue colour, which soon becomes a deep black on wood

Instead of this dye I would recommend as more suitable the well-known indigo substitute (hemolin, a logwood pre-paration)   This dissolves in 1 per cent acetic acid quickly and completely, and gives a brilliant blue-black to wood immediately

Black with Logwood and Iron or Copper.

This is dyed as above with the exception that an iron or copper salt is substituted for the chromium compounds. The cheapest black is that with green vitriol, but that with nitrate of iron gives distinctly fuller and finer results Copper-blacks, especially that with copper nitrate have always a somewhat greenish hue. I will give a recipe, which although old, gives a black which is much superior to those produced by the new processes. I possess articles dyed by means of it sixty years ago which have a most brilliant appearance The wood is first mordanted in lukewarm solution of alum for half an hour, and logwood raspings having been boiled with water till the volume of the decoction is reduced by one-half, the colour is painted over the mordanted wood A little indigo carmine with the logwood improves the colour

The first coat gives a violet hue and is followed by two others, drying each time The wood is finally, when dry after the last logwood coat, painted over with a solution of verdigris in hot vinegar. It is finally polished with an oiled brush. The appearance is improved by subsequent varnishing.

Ebony Blacks with Galls.

I here give another antiquated process which gives very excellent results, as is proved by articles dyed by it. The process may be varied by using commercial calcined sulphate of iron, or by substituting for the galls one quarter of their weight of tannin I give here the original recipe in full as I received it

Twenty-five oz of coarsely crushed gall nuts are steeped in 100 oz of water in a glazed vessel. In another 18 oz. of calcined sulphate of iron and 75 oz of iron filings are digested for 24 hours in 25 oz. of strong vinegar.

The vitriol is calcined by placing it in powder on an iron plate kept nearly red hot, and letting it remain till it ceases to bubble up. The wood is first painted with the iron solution and, when dry, with the gall infusion, and so on alternately three or four times. One or two coats of soot and brandy are next put on The wood when dry after this is polished with tripoli and a wet rag, and finally dried and polished with a dry cloth.

Black by Berger's Method.

A solution of vanadic and nitric acid is mixed with ammonia to a clear green solution. The application of this to wood first mordanted with a 2 per cent solution of tannin gives a greenish-black. Vanadate of ammonia gives better results on the mordanted wood however. It is used as a 2 per cent. solution. To get deep full shades the tannin mordant must be applied several times In many cases a solution of logwood extract can be advantageously substituted for the tannin.

Black with Pyrogallic Acid.

This black is rather too dear for ordinary use, but the black is very fine and velvety, and if such an one is required no better process can be used. It is to be noted that the pyrogallic acid must not be too weak, and that two or three applications of it must follow each painting over with iron salt Pyroliguite of iron gives distinctly the best results, but ferrous sulphate will do.

Aniline Black by Godeffroy's Method.

The use of aniline oil or hydrochloride (aniline salt) in textile dyeing induced Dr. Godeffroy to try it for wood He dissolves 100 oz of the hydrochloride in 1,500 oz. of water, adds 2 oz of copper chloride and paints the wood with the hot solution When dry again it is painted over with a 5 per cent. solution of bichromate, and then when dry is of a beautiful black The colour is fast to light and remains so It never turns green, and neither acids nor chlorine affect it.

Paris Ebony " Stain ".

Under this name a dye is put on the market made from the following recipe · 60 oz. of logwood extract solution of 6 deg B are mixed with 20 oz of solution of wax in concentrated carbonate of potash, and 20 oz of the decanted solution from 9 oz. iron filings and 30 oz. of nitric acid. To this mixture add 2½ oz. of gum-arabic and the same weight of common glue. The stain is then ready for use, and is said to give excellent results.

It only remains now to speak of the coal-tar dyes, but we can refer the reader to our previous description of their action on wood Only those soluble in water are used for that material, and they can be employed cheaply and effectively.

GRAY.

Till very recently these were got with a stain and a dye combined, but now gray or black aniline dye solutions of suitable concentration are largely used. By varying the nature and the ingredients according to the wood all sorts of shades can be obtained The following table gives the chief examples . —

Reddish pale gray, on maple	. Chrome alum, 10 deg. B., or ferrous sulphate solution.
Mouse gray, on acacia .	. Bichromate solution.
Mouse gray, on apple . .	. Solution of iron pyrolignite.
Mouse gray, on pear . .	. Solution of iron pyrolignite.
Mouse gray, on birch . .	Chrome alum solution.
Dark medium gray, on oak .	. Copper nitrate solution.
Pearl gray, on oak .	. Chromic acid solution.
Pearl gray, on alder .	Solution of ferrous sulphate.
Pearl gray, on cherry . .	. Solution of ferrous sulphate.
Pearl gray, on lime . .	. Acidulated solution of bichromate.
Pearl gray, on elm . .	. Acidulated solution of bichromate.

Brighter grays are easily got with any basic gray or blue aniline. The first coat is applied warm, but always very dilute. After drying apply a 10 per cent. solution of tartar emetic, which will make the colour much faster.

Fine grays can, of course, be obtained with logwood and metallic mordants as for black, adding also, if desired, tannin and pyrogallic acid Vegetable matters containing tannin can be used instead of tannin itself, for instance acorn-galls, gall nuts, sumach or divi-divi All that has to be remembered is that dye and mordant must invariably be applied separately, drying after every coat Only in this way can handsome fast colours be obtained

I conclude with an old recipe for gray on wood : Dissolve 6 oz alum and 25 oz of ferrous sulphate in 100 oz. of boiling water. Stir in a little tincture of galls, and apply with a brush

One of the most important colours for wood is a fine fast brown We will begin with some recipes, which, if old, nevertheless give excellent results

BROWN.

Quicklime is slaked with urine, and the wood is painted over with the mixture The wood is then washed with tanners' waste liquor It then becomes green. Both processes are repeated till the colour changes to brown The alkaline solution can be replaced by one of caustic soda, and the tanners' waste by a solution of tannin

Another method is to mordant with alum and ferrous sulphate, and dye in logwood

A third method is to boil dry green walnut-husks with alum, and paint wood with the decoction Mouldy roots of the tree can be used instead of the husks The husks, however, answer better, but they should be gathered in the autumn and left in heaps for at least two months to mould They are then crushed and boiled with twice their weight of water and a little alum This liquid gives a splendid and very cheap brown The roots are stamped and boiled in the same way

Brown with Bismarck Brown.

Dyeing with this and other basic anilines is perfectly simple, and consists simply in applying a warm solution in water. If it is desired to get fine clear shades it is very much better to apply a weak dye solution several times than to try to use a stronger dye with a single application Let each coat dry before the next is laid on

Brown with Permanganate.

Browns got on wood with permanganate of potash are of no special beauty, but they are very cheap and fairly fast Here again it is essential not to work with too concentrated a solution. This, especially if hot, destroys the brushes, and will never give level colours.

The following table gives the browns got on the various woods with the dyes and stains indicated —

Reddish pale brown on white beech	. Nitric acid and 4 times its weight of water.
Reddish medium brown on white beech	. Solution of carbonate of potash.
Reddish dark brown on white beech	. Solution of chromic acid.
Yellowish pale brown on elm	. Nitric acid and 4 times its weight of water.
Yellowish pale brown on pine	. Nitric acid and 4 times its weight of water.
Yellowish pale brown on maple	Nitric acid and 4 times its weight of water.
Dark brown on maple . .	. Solution of chromic acid.
Pale brown on maple . .	. Solution of carbonate of potash.
Full yellowish-brown on cherry	. Solution of cutch and bichromate.
Full brown on cherry . .	. Solution of potassium ferrocyanide and acetate of magnesia.
Full reddish-brown on ash .	. Solution of cutch and bichromate.
Medium brown on alder .	. Solution of chrome alum.

9

Medium brown on maple	.	. Hydrochloric acid.
Medium brown on acacia		. Solution of carbonate of potash.
Yellowish medium brown on apple	. . . .	. Solution of potassium ferrocyanide and acetate of magnesia.

In combination with alizarine red, yellow or brown, using a copper or chrome mordant, many browns can be got which have the advantage of being more or less fast to all external influences

A remarkable mahogany dye is said by Schmidt to consist of aloes and hydrochloric acid. Mr. Schmidt, however, has evidently made a mistake; he must mean nitric acid, for the former acid gives no red fumes with aloes If we boil aloes with six times its weight of nitric acid of 36 deg. B red fumes are evolved, and when they have passed off, which soon happens, the dye is ready, and is applied to the wood after dilution with three times its weight of soft water. This dye has the advantage that the colour darkens after application and also the drawback that the nitric acid attacks the wood and prevents the subsequent polish from lasting.

If the acidity were the only fault of this dye it would be possible to avoid it by nearly neutralising, best with chalk.

According to the same author the following brown " stain " is used in imitating antique wood . 2 lb. of coffee substitute (from the residues of sugar manufacture), which has a shiny fracture, are boiled in from 6 to 8 lb. of water, and articles carved out of Indian walnut wood are painted with it, or with a mixture of soot and five times its weight of very dilute spirit In this way a very ancient appearance is imparted to the carvings.

We now give some recipes due to Leo of Benstein, and given by him to the trades' unions of Hesse. They may be of interest and value to many of our readers

Pale Walnut Dye.

Dissolve permanganate of potash in thirty times its weight of water, and paint the wood twice with the solution. After five minutes wash with water, dry, oil and polish The solution should be fresh Cost—2½d per sq. yard.

Dark Walnut or Palisander.

The same solution is used, but after the washing the dark veins are brought out by painting with pyrolignite of iron. Dry, oil and polish as before. Same cost.

Dark Mahogany.

Digest 3 oz. chopped alkanet, 6 oz. powdered aloes and 6 oz powdered dragon's blood for three or four days in 100 oz. of 95 per cent spirit in a closed flask, in a warm place, shaking frequently Mordant the wood with nitric acid, dry, and apply one or more coats of the tincture till the desired colour is attained. Then dry, oil and polish. This recipe is also suitable for floors

Pale Mahogany.

As above, but applying one coat only A skilled hand can imitate the veining of the genuine wood by means of a brush filled with pyrolignite of iron This, too, is suitable for floors, and costs 2½d. per sq yard

These preparations can be bought ready-made mixed with oil.

VIOLET.

Violets are at the present day produced almost exclusively with coal-tar dyes. According to circumstances alizarine red or methyl violet is used, but the demand for violet-dyed wood is very small We here give three old recipes for violet-dyeing which can often be adopted on wood with the most excellent results.

Dissolve litmus in water and paint the wood with the filtered solution. If the colour comes out too dark give a second coat with a weaker solution. When the colour is right dry and polish

Another process is to make a decoction of 15 oz of redwood and 33 oz of logwood adding 8 oz of acetate of alumina.

A third process is to dye the wood red, dry it, and then paint with solution of indigo. Or the wood may be first dyed blue and then painted over with a red dye

A full violet is prepared by mixing indigo substitute with carmine red (oxidised redwood extract) in various proportions. For example, 3 oz indigo substitute and 2 oz. of the red in 50 oz of water acidulated with 1 oz of acetic acid give very beautiful violet shades, which can be made even more brilliant with 1 to 2 per cent. of methyl violet (on the combined weights of the carmine and indigo substitute)

Stubenrauch's Violet.

Paint the wood with, or immerse it in, a solution of 2 oz tree oil and 2 oz. calcined soda in a pint of boiling water. When the wood is dry paint it over with solution of fuchsine, or better, with solution of methyl violet in twenty-five times its weight of spirit. Parma or Victoria violet will do as well. The shade may be varied at pleasure with tinctures of different strengths, and the colour is equalled in brilliancy by hardly any other wood-dye.

Dull Violets.

The lively and rich violets are not as a rule great favourites, especially for furniture. Finer and duller shades can be got with alizarine or benzopurpurine. Alizarine red and acetate of alumina on pear give a dull reddish-violet, while the same dye with sulphate of copper gives a bluish shade on birch. Medium subdued violet on birch is got with benzopurpurine solution of 4 deg. B

Blue.

Here as with violets the anilines are fast making the natural dyes obsolete. Water-soluble fast blue is largely used with a tannin mordant. Very brilliant staring pale blues are got with spirit-soluble water blue, Lyons blue, *bleu lumière* and light blue. These dyes, however, only answer for white wood and for special purposes.

Logwood extract is now hardly ever used for dyeing wood blue. The following recipe once much used is now practically abandoned.

Boil litmus with sixteen times its weight of lime-water for half an hour, and apply several coats of the solution to the wood.

Stubenrauch's Blue.

Mordant first with solution of acetate of alumina of 1 deg. B. This is prepared by mixing a solution of 2 oz. of lead acetate in fifteen times its weight of water with one of 8 oz. of iron-free alum in 40 oz. of water, and adding a pinch of soda crystals. When the mixture has cleared, decant from the precipitate of lead sulphate and dilute with water to 1 deg. B. The mordanted wood is then dyed a beautiful blue by a solution of indigo carmine, of strength proportionate to the shade desired.

Blue alizarines, although very fast to light, are difficult to use, and are hence rather neglected. Indigo substitute gives a reddish-blue.

RED.

Most reds, especially for furniture, are desired in dull subdued shades, but some are wanted bright and lively. In the second case the aniline-reds are mostly used as they alone will give really rich shades. For bright pale reds the wood must be first bleached. This is done with bleaching powder and a little soda, and the wood must be as pale as possible naturally   To remove the last traces of bleach from the whitened wood, rinse thoroughly several times, and then apply a solution of antichlor. Some old recipes which follow are to my knowledge still largely adopted.

Red on Wood.

First mordant for a few hours in a solution of alum in thirty times its weight of water. Then steep to shade in decoction of redwood   The colour can be made somewhat darker with a little saffron. If the decoction is made with vinegar instead of water, the red comes out much warmer, especially on soft wood   It makes the colour much faster if a little isinglass solution is added to the redwood decoction   In that case, however, the dye must be applied warm to warm wood.

Second Recipe.

Dissolve dragon's blood in vinegar or spirit, and paint on the mordanted wood till the colour is as wished.

Third Recipe.

This is a strange enough recipe, but is said to give very good results   The chief part in the process is played by hippuric acid.

Place a hamper full of horse-dung over a tub to receive the drippings from it. The moisture and the fermentation of the dung must be promoted by watering it with horse-stale The liquid collected will in one or two coats give a very durable colour to wood.

It has been discovered that this process does not answer equally well with all woods. The difference has been ascribed to differences in the porosity of the wood. It has also been asserted that it answers better on wood grown in damp places than that grown on heights and in very dry soils The process dyes some woods purple-red and some pink-red. Veiny fir for example receives a marbled, wavy colouring. Old wood, too, assumes a different tint from freshly cut stuff, so that experience is necessary in using the method.

Red on Wood.

Take 12 oz of coarse Pernambuco wood sawdust and cover completely in a wide-mouthed vessel with spirit Warm gently for forty-eight hours, and filter the tincture The residual sawdust is treated for another forty-eight hours with warm water. The two solutions are mixed and applied to the wood.

Deep Cochineal Red (Stubenrauch).

Boil 4 oz of powdered cochineal in 32 oz of water for three hours, and paint the wood with the decoction. When dry, give a coat of dilute tin-salt containing a little tartaric acid. The best proportions are 4 oz. of tin-salt and 2 oz. of tartaric acid in 64 oz. of water. If the cochineal is boiled in a decoction of quercitron bark in sixteen times its weight of water instead of in water, the use of the tin-salt enables all shades from yellow and orange to a deep scarlet-red to be produced

Monier's Pink.

Place maple in a solution of iodide of potassium in twelve times its weight of water for a few hours and then steep in a solution of sublimate of mercury in 40 times its weight of water. A very fine pink is the result.

We now come to modern red-dyeing, *i.e*, to the use of aniline dyes For light rich reds and pinks the various marks of brilliant croceine are decidedly our most useful colours

Benzopurpurine, too, gives on white wood very good results, but not on all woods. For example, it gives a beautiful pink in alder, but on ash, cherry or elm it gives a brick-red. The following are some other examples of the effects of benzopurpurine —

> On pink a dirty reddish-brown.
> On maple a dirty reddish-brown.
> On lime a dirty reddish-brown
> On oak a dirty pink-brown.
> On acacia a dirty reddish-brown.

The alizarines are also much used for dyeing wood, and have the advantage of being very fast to light. For light shades the wood should be first treated with a $7\frac{1}{2}$ per cent solution of Turkey red oil and then dyed with a 10 to 20 per cent solution of alizarine red. The following table shows the effect of different mordants on the colour got with alizarine red : —

> Acetate of alumina gives brownish-red.
> Alum gives brownish-red
> Chrome salts and chrome alum give browner red.
> Iron salts and iron alum give violet.
> Tin-salt gives rich scarlet
> Nitrate of tin gives yellowish-brown.
> Perchloride of tin gives yellowish-brown.
> Bichromate and sulphuric acid give reddish-violet.

We must repeat here that aniline dyes must never be used too strong or the colour will never be clear and pure

YELLOW.

Here, as usual, we give the old recipes first.

Old Recipe with Turmeric.

The wood is first mordanted for a few hours in alum dissolved in thirty times its weight of water, and then painted over with turmeric decoction. When the shade is reached, the wood is placed for some hours in cold water and then dried. Fustic gives too dark and dirty a yellow. It is better to use tincture of turmeric than the decoction.

A solution of annatto in warm spirit also gives a beautiful yellow.

A Beautiful Yellow with Saffron.

Digest 3 oz. of fine-cut saffron in 25 oz. of 95 per cent. spirit for an hour with occasional shaking. Then add about 100 oz. more of the spirit, and heat the digesting vessel in warm water. With the tincture two coats are applied to the wood, and give it a very beautiful golden-yellow colour which can be deepened by further applications. When dry after dyeing, the wood is soaked in glue-water, again dried, and finally polished or varnished.

Yellow with Persian Berries.

These give a bright lively yellow. The berries are crushed and boiled for about half an hour in weak solution of alum. The solution is filtered, and painted on the wood. It may be kept for use in well-corked bottles, shaking well before application. This dye can be mixed with the saffron solution mentioned above for getting a deeper yellow.

Gamboge.

This should never be used for toys, for it is one of the most poisonous substances in its effects on the animal organism.

Chrome Yellow.

This can be produced cheaply and easily, by applying a solution of bichromate to the wood with a brush or sponge Chrome compounds, however, must not be used on oak or walnut or other woods rich in tannin.

Yellow with Picric Acid.

A beautiful and very pure yellow is got with picric acid either in alcoholic or in aqueous solution. In either case it is simply applied warm with a brush. Other anilines are used in the same way, especially acid yellow, fast yellow and Victoria yellow

Yellow Staining with Nitric Acid.

One of the cheapest and fastest yellows is obtained by the use of this acid, but it will not do for every kind of wood We give some examples The acid gives—

On white beech	a reddish-yellow.
On elm	a pale medium yellow.
On pine	a brownish medium yellow.
On maple	a brownish medium yellow.
On acacia	a bright medium yellow.

Nitro-alizarine yellow, too, gives a yellow very fast to light. We now conclude with green

GREEN.

Most greens are now produced exclusively with aniline dyes. We begin as usual with the older recipes.

Mixed Green.

It is well known that all shades of green can be got by mixing blues and yellows in various proportions. Very rich greens are got, for example, with indigo carmine and picric acid, but unfortunately they are rather loose to light.

Green with Acetate of Copper.

A very pleasing but poisonous green is got on wood by fixing a solution of verdigris in acetic acid with a sharp alkaline lye. Dissolve separately, each in 70 oz of hot water, 25 oz. of sulphate of copper, and 30 oz of sugar of lead. Then mix and filter, or decant the clear liquid after settling The precipitate of lead sulphate is thrown away. The liquid is used as above directed

Another Recipe.

Rub up powdered verdigris with strong vinegar, adding little by little green sulphate of iron. Then boil the whole in water for half an hour Then paint the wood to shade with the solution

Green with Anilines.

The following aniline greens are used without any mordant: iodine green, brilliant green, malachite green, acid green and Guinea green The last, however, is often fixed with alum.

XIII.

IMITATION WOODS.

We have already described the production of special colours. We proceed now to describe more closely the processes for imitating various woods.

We must first consider the researches of Dr. Bergers, who was the first to describe the use of alizarine for the purpose, and to introduce it to practical use. We give his more important recipes

The alizarine solution is made by diluting commercial alizarine red paste (20 per cent of alizarine) with twenty times its weight of water, and gradually stirring in ammonia till the liquid smells strongly of it. This ammoniacal liquor costs about 3d. per quart.

1 Two applications of it on dried wood give—

With pine . . .	yellowish-brown,
With maple	reddish-brown,
With oak	yellowish-brown,

at a cost of $1\frac{1}{2}$d per sq. yard.

2 Dissolve crystallised chloride of barium in 100 times its weight of hot water, and use as a mordant before applying the alizarine   We then get—

On pine	a brown,
On oak	a brown,
On maple	a dark brown,

at a cost of $1\frac{3}{4}$d per sq. yard   The mordant costs 1d a gallon.

3. A mordant of chloride of calcium of the same strength as the barium solution costs the same, and gives with the alizarine—

On pine	a brown (like burnt Sienna),
On oak . .	a reddish-brown,
On maple	a dark brown,

at a cost of $1\frac{3}{4}$d. per sq. yard

4 A mordant of 2 per cent. sulphate of magnesia costs 1d. a gallon, and gives—

On pine	dark brown,
On oak	dark brown,
On maple	dark violet-brown,

at a cost of $1\frac{3}{4}$d per sq yard.

These four recipes are specially good for imitating old oak.

5 A mordant of 3 per cent. solution of alum costs 1d. a gallon, and gives—

On pine	deep red,
On maple	deep red,
On elm	dark red,
On oak	blood red,

at a cost of $1\frac{3}{4}$d. per sq yard.

A 2.6 per cent. solution of sulphate of alumina is better than the alum, and barely dearer

6. A mordant of 3 per cent. solution of chrome alum costs 3d per gallon, and gives—

On elm	reddish-brown,
On maple	reddish-brown,
On pine	reddish-violet,
On oak	Havana brown,

at a cost of $1\frac{3}{4}$d. per square yard

7 A mordant of $2\frac{1}{2}$ per cent solution of sulphate of manganese costs 9d. per gallon, and gives—

On pine	dark violet-brown,
On elm	dark violet-brown,
On maple	dark violet-brown,
On oak	dark walnut-brown,

at a cost of $2\frac{1}{2}$d per sq. yard

8. A mordant of 1.6 per cent. ferric chloride costs 1d a gallon, and gives—

On elm	yellowish-black,
On oak	yellowish-black,
On pine	dark yellowish-brown,
On maple	a smoke brown,

at a cost of $1\frac{3}{4}$d. per sq. yard

9. A mordant of 2 per cent solution of crystals of green vitriol costs 1d. a gallon, and gives—

On pine	reddish-black,
On elm	reddish-black,
On maple	reddish-black,
On oak	black,

at a cost of $1\frac{3}{4}$d per sq. yard

10   A mordant of $2\frac{1}{2}$ per cent. solution of crystallised cobalt sulphate costs 3s per gallon, and gives—

On elm	dark brown,
On oak . .	dark walnut-brown,
On pine . . .	lilac,
On maple	amethyst,

at a cost of 5d. per sq. yard

11. A mordant of $2\frac{1}{2}$ per cent solution of crystallised nickel sulphate costs 10d per gallon, and gives—

On pine	lilac,
On maple	lilac,
On oak . . .	dark reddish-brown,
On elm . .	dark reddish-violet,

at a cost of $2\frac{1}{2}$d. per sq. yard

12   A mordant of $2\frac{1}{2}$ per cent solution of crystallised zinc sulphate costs $2\frac{1}{2}$d. per gallon, and gives—

On pine .	dark cherry-red,
On elm .	dark cherry-red,
On maple . . .	dark cherry-red,
On oak	dark reddish-brown,

at a cost of 2d per sq yard.

13   A mordant of $2\frac{1}{2}$ per cent solution of crystallised cadmium sulphate costs 2s. per gallon, and gives—

On pine	reddish coffee-brown,
On oak	coffee-brown,
On maple . . .	reddish-coffee-brown,
On elm	coffee-brown,

at a cost of $4\frac{1}{4}$d. per sq. yard

14. A mordant of $3\frac{1}{2}$ per cent. solution of crystallised lead acetate costs $3\frac{1}{2}$d per gallon, and gives—

On pine							reddish-violet,
On elm							reddish-violet,
On maple							reddish-violet,
On oak							Bordeaux violet,

at a cost of 2d. per sq. yard

15. A mordant of 2 9 per cent. solution of crystallised sublimate costs 9d. per gallon, and gives—

On pine						reddish-brown,
On maple						reddish-brown,
On elm						brown,
On oak						coffee-brown,

at a cost of 2½d. per sq. yard.

16 A mordant of 2 per cent solution of copper sulphate costs 2d per gallon, and gives—

On pine						reddish-violet,
On elm						reddish-violet,
On oak						brownish-violet,
On maple						cherry-red,

at a cost of 2d. per sq. yard.

17. A mordant of 2 per cent. solution of crystallised tin-salt and enough hydrochloric acid to make the liquid clear costs 3½d per gallon, and gives—

On pine			the appearance of Pernambuco wood,
On elm			brown,
On oak			reddish-brown,
On maple			wine-red,

at a cost of 2d. per sq yard.

18. A mordant of 2 per cent. solution of tartar emetic costs 4d. per gallon, and gives—

On pine							orange-red,
On maple							orange-red,
On oak							coffee-brown,
On elm							dark brown,

at a cost of 2¼d per sq yard

19. A mordant of 1½ per cent. solution of nitrate of bismuth and enough nitric acid to make the liquid clear costs 1s. 6d. per gallon, and gives—

On pine	.		.	.		.	reddish-brown,
On elm	.	.	.	.		.	dark brown,
On oak	.	.	.	.	.	.	dark nut-brown,
On maple		.	.	.			dark cherry-red,

at a cost of 4d. per sq. yard.

The last three mordants require the application of ammonia to the wood after the alizarine or the free acid present will prevent the development of the colour

The process with all these nineteen mordants is to apply the metallic salt with a brush, hot, and to let the wood dry before the alizarine is applied If the colour is not strong enough both applications are repeated in the same order If this is not observed, or the intermediate dryings are omitted, or the various solutions are used too strong, the colour will be streaky and wanting in uniformity.

Besides all these recipes Dr. Berger has tried ferrocyanide of potassium with many other metallic salts, and thereby got very successful results upon wood. Some of these are given below as examples, and show those which can be recommended for practical use

1. A mordant of 6 8 per cent solution of sulphate of manganese gives on pine, maple or oak a light drab

2. A mordant of 6 5 per cent solution of crystallised ferrous sulphate gives—

On pine	.		.	.		dark blue.
On oak	.	.	.	.	.	.	bluish-black.
On elm	.		.	.		indigo-blue.

3. A mordant of 6 5 per cent solution of crystallised cobalt sulphate gives a light violet-brown on maple, pine or oak.

It will be of even greater interest to give the following table of the action of most mordants with the natural dyes This table is taken from Andés, and is of the greatest importance for every wood-dyer.

Mordant	Colour with			
	Logwood Decoction.	Fustic Decoction.	Redwood Extract.	Persian Berry Decoction.
Dilute hydrochloric acid.	reddish.	yellowish-brown.	pale red.	pink.
„ nitric acid.	red.	brown.	„ „	yellow.
„ sulphuric acid.	„	brownish-red	purple.	„
Sulphuretted hydrogen	yellowish-brown.	dark yellow.	pale red	dark olive green.
Nitrate of iron.	black.	dark greyish-green.	dark violet.	brownish-yellow.
Bichromate of potash.	„	„ „	brownish-red.	dark yellow.
Tin-salt.	violet.	yellow.	pale red.	white.
Tartaric acid	greyish-brown.	„ „	reddish-yellow.	greenish-yellow.
Sulphate of copper.	dark green.	orange.	dark red.	„
Tannin	yellowish-red.	light yellow.	red.	„ „
Sal-ammoniac	yellow.	dark yellow.	dark red.	„ „
Verdigris.	dark brown.	„ „	„ „	dark yellow.
Sugar of lead.	grayish-brown.	yellow.	yellowish-red.	pale
Ferrocyanide of potash.	yellowish-brown.	„	„ „	„ „
Permanganate of potash.	pale brown.	brownish-yellow.	dark carmine.	yellow.
Carbonate of potash.	dark red	yellow.	„ „	„
Pyrogallic acid.	„ „	„	dark violet.	pale yellow.
Ferrous sulphate.	black.	„	„ „	„ „
Alum.	dark red	„	„ red.	„ „
Sulphide of ammonia.	„ „	dark yellow.	„ „	„ „

10

The experiments are made by preparing a concentrated solution or decoction of the dye in water. This is painted on to slips of wood about 6 by 4 in., on both sides. When dry the slips are labelled. The mordants are prepared in solutions of three strengths, and painted over the slips, each of which has then the name and strength of the mordant used placed on the label where is already the name of the dye.

A patent which was taken out by a man named Thimm, and has now expired, protects a process in which wood was first painted over with solutions of metallic salts by means of a brush, dried completely, and then exposed in closed chambers to the action of gases such as ammonia, sulphuretted hydrogen, etc In this way with the latter gas we get the following colours ·—

With bismuth nitrate . . .	brown.
With cadmium sulphate . . .	yellow.
With tin chloride . .	golden yellow.
With lead acetate . .	iron-brown.
With chromic acid	green.
With antimony salts	red.

The expense of the process is said to be very slight, but the principle is a wrong one, just as it is in textile-dyeing, and prevents all possibility of uniformity. For this reason Thimm's process was a failure.

It will also be of great interest to record how the different woods colour with the various dyes, and we give the following examples :—

Redwood decoction, prepared by boiling the wood for an hour with twenty times its weight of water, gave—

(a) With oak, plane and red beech . .	a ripe cherry colour.
(b) With maple, lime and white beech .	an old mahogany colour.
(c) With walnut wood	a red mahogany colour.

If these woods are soaked in a decoction of madder containing 20 per cent. of alizarine, they all take a uniform chestnut-brown, which comes out best on plane and white beech.

Soaked with turmeric extract they become a pale yellow, which is very beautiful on plane and red beech, and best of all on maple which thus becomes like American satin-wood.

With aqueous solution of gamboge we get—

With poplar	.	.	.	a wax yellow.
With acacia		.	.	a lustrous dark lemon-yellow.
With walnut		.	.	a fine lustrous brown.
With pear	.	.	.	a fine lustrous brown
With chestnut	.		.	an old mahogany colour.

Extract of saffron gives dark yellow on ash and chestnut, and a darker, more brownish-yellow on pear and walnut.

All the woods are polished before dyeing, and also dried for forty-eight hours at 40 deg. C to open the pores and evaporate the sap. An old boiler is often used as a drying-chamber, and afterwards as a dyeing-vat in which the wood is soaked till the dye has penetrated about half an inch.

We now return to the imitations of various woods. These need only be spoken of briefly, for, as Hauboldt very justly says, it is not merely necessary to imitate colour and texture, but also weight and other physical properties Hence it is futile to give processes for making fir or pine imitate a heavy wood as it is too light and has also a betraying texture which cannot be concealed The chief requisite for the imitator is a skilful hand for using the brush, and the art cannot be learned from books, but by practice alone.

MAHOGANY IMITATION.

The other wood properly chosen is well polished and stained with dilute nitric acid It is finely varnished with properly tinted shellac varnish

DARK WALNUT IMITATION.

For this a not too concentrated solution of permanganate of potash is the best

OAK IMITATION.

First apply an oil ground with pale ochre and a little white-lead Apply two coats of this, the second only when the first is dry and has been polished with sand-paper. So far the process is the same in all cases, and in the following recipes it must be understood that this ground has been applied Rub burnt sienna and Cassel brown fine with vinegar and apply with a brush, but not in too thin a state. Grain in the dark spots afterwards with Cassel brown, and then put in the veins with a proper broad flat brush, used by grainers for the purpose, with downward strokes Another and stiffer brush used from below upwards serves for representing the pores of the oakwood Naturally, the previous applications, *e g*, the veins, must have been allowed to dry or this process will smudge and destroy them The medullary rays are then put in with the use of a stencil and a wet sponge, but not too wet, or the wet will get under the stencil plate Oakwood knots are done with Cassel brown after applying the vinegar colour, and the year rings of the knots are put in with the sharply pointed side of a feather The surroundings of the knots are done with a feather cut zig-zag, and the pores and veins of the knot in the same way as those of the wood itself To imitate nature thoroughly the characteristic wavy marks are imitated on the proper places, while they are still wet, with a brush 5 inches wide and with hairs at least $3\frac{1}{2}$ inches long, dipped in vinegar, and finished and scumbled in the usual way

Birch Bark Imitation.

The oil pigment ground is made several shades lighter than for oak imitation. The vinegar colour is burnt sienna, put on rather pale Light-coloured parts are then put in with a damp sponge, and after the scumbling and other usual treatment of these the long pale marks are put in with a leather roller. The little knots are imitated by marks made with the tips of the fingers wetted with vinegar For the dark ones Cassel brown is put on the finger-tips.

Alder Marquetry Imitation.

The oil ground is somewhat darker than for oak. A vinegar colour of unburnt sienna is first applied, and then, after grinding and sand-papering, a few red spots are put in with burnt sienna and darker ones with Cassel brown. The knots are done as above described

Walnut Imitation.

The ground is still darker than it is for alder The vinegar colour is Cassel brown, applied rather dark The darker parts are now imitated with more brown, especially in the knots. The year rings of the knots are put in as described for oak, and the whole is scumbled in the usual way

As soon as the colour is quite dry the wood is gone over lightly with Cassel brown, leaving out the dark spots, the characteristic year rings are put in, and the whole is scumbled once more.

Walnut Marquetry Imitation

Here the oil ground must be still darker. The special grain is marked out with still darker Cassel brown, mixed

with a little black for the darkest places. The paler places
are done first, and then the darker. Finally the whole is
scumbled lightly but thoroughly.

MAHOGANY.

The oil ground is the same as for walnut marquetry.
For ordinary mahogany we apply burnt sienna, using more
colour for the darker places, and also a little Cassel brown
The pale places are worked in with a sponge. We then
scumble and do the pores as for oak   For very dark wood
(Spanish mahogany) the surface must be gone over again
with more sienna, repeating all the operations.

SPANISH MAHOGANY IMITATION.

Paint on burnt sienna, putting in the places where the
pyramids are to come somewhat darker   Then give the
grain with a sponge and also the smooth places by the
sides of the pyramids   The long streaks which occur in
the pyramids themselves are done with a stiff card or
leather.   The whole is then scumbled and, when dry, gone
over once more with burnt sienna   The veins which run
over the pyramids are either done with the jagged edge of a
card or with a proper brush, and the pores as usual   A
final slight scumbling completes the work.

PALISANDER OR ROSEWOOD IMITATION.

The oil ground is a mixture of English red and ochre,
the vinegar colour is Cassel brown.   This is applied thicker
to imitate the dark places, and the darkest of all are
done with black.   Veins are put in with the brush and the
grain with a feather, as above described.

TORTOISE-SHELL IMITATION.

The oil ground for light tortoise-shell is chrome yellow
white-lead and pale ochre, that for dark tortoise-shell is

Prussian blue, ochre, white-lead and a little black; the vinegar colour is burnt sienna. With this the lighter places are first made on the oil ground and scumbled When these are dry the streaks are put in with a stencil plate with more burnt sienna, not too wet. The places are then scumbled with the stencil still in place. Then allow to dry, replace the stencil, not quite in the same place, and go over the streaks so as to make them darker, and again scumble Apply the Cassel brown a third time, but only here and there. When this is dry, varnish the wood, and let the varnish dry till it is only just sticky Then let the smoke of a lamp come upon the dark places. Allow to dry completely and varnish again. The varnish to be used is good, quick-drying copal. When the varnish is quite dry polish with finely powdered bone earth, and finally with leather. The copal will then have a durable lustre equal to that of the best shellac.

Oak Imitation.

The articles, the wood of which is to imitate oak, are exposed to the fumes of ammonia in an air-tight chamber till finished.

Ebony Imitation.

For this we refer to our description of black-dyeing The best woods for ebony imitation are pear, maple and white beech.

To Give the Appearance of Wavy Pearwood.

Make freshly burnt quicklime to a thin paste with dilute ammonia. Make the wavy marks with a brush full of this, wash them when dry, stain or dye at pleasure, and then varnish or polish the wood. Another way is to sprinkle the wood with the lime paste, whereby it receives a fine speckled appearance.

Real Mahogany Imitation (without Oil Ground).

Make a very concentrated decoction of real mahogany sawdust and paint the white wood several times over with it After drying and polishing it will ha   the lustre and colour of real mahogany.

XIV.

DYEING WHOLE BLOCKS OF WOOD WITH A PENETRATING DYE

This is a very useful process, for in many branches of woodwork wood dyed through and through is required, and that which is bought is rarely sufficiently penetrated The few processes so far known will be here exactly described, and one worked out by the author, which has given results which, for some wood-trades such as the walking-stick business, are extremely satisfactory.

The use of steam is essential to ensure the penetration of the colour, both during and after the black-dyeing, and full success depends upon that and upon the choice of a proper dye.

We will treat first of Andés' apparatus. This consists of a boiler and a dye-box, by means of which wood $1\frac{1}{2}$ in thick can be dyed through in twelve hours, and wood $2\frac{1}{2}$ in thick in fourteen hours, and so on in proportion. The wood is first thoroughly steamed in the dye-box till all its sap has been extracted and the condensed water runs bright and clear. The box is then exhausted with an air pump, and the hot dye solution is admitted. This is forced into the cells of the wood by the external atmospheric pressure and in time penetrates it completely.

Similar, but with a few variations, is the process of Gottheil and Auffermann of Berlin They enclose the wood in air-tight cylinders, pump out the air from them, and then drive in the dye solution under a pressure of about thirty atmospheres. With ordinary thickness, from thirty to sixty minutes will finish the process, but very thick woods of course take longer

A rather different method is that of Riefenbichler, which is said to give the very best results The apparatus consists of a boiler and a cylinder to receive the wood, which, however, is heated by a worm so that the steam does not touch the wood The boiler contains a stirrer capable of both rotatory and up-and-down motion so as to produce perfect reaction between the contents of the boiler. In working this cylinder is filled two-thirds full of the dye solution mixed with waterglass, the wood is introduced, and the cover closed air-tight. When the air has been driven out by the heat of the worm through a valve the external pressure begins to force the dye into the wood. What is further asserted with regard to the facilitation of the penetration of the dye to the interior of the wood by boring holes in it before treatment will hardly be taken seriously, even by people who are only very imperfectly acquainted with the subject

Here, as well as in the above process, the black is got with logwood and a subsequent treatment with pyrolignite of iron. This method may be modified by reversing it and using the iron salt first

Borton Jenks has investigated this dyeing system very thoroughly, and we append his chief results He obtained—

      Light warm grey with nitrate of iron.
      Dark warm grey with nitrate of iron and paraffin
      Pale colder grey with ferrous sulphate.
      Darker colder grey with ferrous sulphate and paraffin.

Pale or dark colder grey with various strengths logwood and green vitriol.

Dark warm grey with ferrous sulphate, logwood and paraffin

Paler yellowish-grey with chromate of potash.

Dark yellowish-grey with bichromate of potash.

Fine yellowish-grey with bichromate of potash and paraffin

Pale orange with logwood.

Dark orange with logwood and paraffin.

Slate blue with aniline blue.

Dark slate blue with aniline blue and paraffin.

Yellowish-violet with aniline red.

Dark yellowish-violet with aniline red and paraffin

Purple with fuchsine.

Dark purple-red with fuchsine and paraffin

The process is carried out by first steaming the wood, then making a vacuum in the steam chest and then admitting the dye, which is at once sucked up by the empty cells. The heightening of the shade is afterwards done with fused paraffin. The method has given admirable results on a large scale

My own researches on the dyeing of large masses of wood were carried out for black through-dyeing in the apparatus as above described. The novelty which I introduced was the use of certain chemicals which make the wood still more ready to take up the dye through great thicknesses, but which will not injure the material or the wood, or alter the structure

I have found the best reagent to use for this purpose to be a strongly alkaline solution of 75 per cent. soda Turkey-red oil   Although the beauty of the colour was not much improved, the penetration was made very much greater The logs were first steamed without pressure and then dyed with a mixture of the Turkey-red salt and logwood decoction. The second treatment, with pyrolignite of iron, is preceded by another steaming For some purposes the iron salt can be replaced by a solution of nitrate of copper of 36 deg. B. This also gives a very beautiful black, and the choice between iron and copper is simply a matter of taste.

XV.

VARNISHES AND POLISHES

Varnish is a name usually employed to denote any kind of application intended to produce a level and shining surface. They are commonly used for giving a brilliant appearance to pigments For our purposes we sometimes use oil varnishes. These are made of vegetable oils, which dry naturally and are increased in their siccative properties by artificial treatment This at the same time makes the varnish more brilliant. The non-fatty varnishes made with mastic, sandarach, benzole, copal and amber, and asphalt are, however, of more importance to us.

The art of making varnishes consists in dissolving the resins in suitable solvents and getting a perfect combination of all the ingredients The solvents used must be such as will evaporate quickly after the varnish has left the brush, and the resin must be left as a transparent coat, elastic enough to keep whole and unbroken. We think we shall best meet the wishes of the reader by proceeding at once to give the best recipes.

ENGLISH POLISH.

The so-called English polish is of remarkable durability when made according to the English recipe and with good copal. That made in Germany is usually its equal in appearance, but far inferior to it in durability.

Take of—

Shellac	25 oz.
Copal	6 ,,
Dragon's blood	6 ,,
Very strong spirit	50 ,,

If light wood is to be polished the dragon's blood is omitted   It is a great improvement, however, for dark wood.   The shellac and dragon's blood dissolve in the spirit without difficulty, but the copal requires a preliminary treatment before it will do so.   This consists in mixing it in powder with three times its weight of finely powdered glass or chalk   It is then put by itself with half the 50 oz of spirit in a flask on the sand-bath and kept warm   The flask should be frequently shaken.   When the spirit has assumed a dark yellow colour and a few drops of it turn water milky it is decanted and replaced by the other half of the spirit   The second extract is, of course, weaker and paler   The two lots of spirit are finally mixed and used to dissolve the other ingredients with the aid of gentle heat   It is rare not to get perfect solution when this method is employed

A polish thus prepared will endure considerable heat without losing its lustre, and lasts well on furniture in constant use   But if made wrongly, or with inferior copal, the results will be very different, and articles polished with it will soon lose their lustre in the sun or near a fire.   At the same time it will get soft and collect dust, which will quite spoil its appearance and can only be removed by removing the polish itself.

This method of preparation has naturally the advantage over one consisting of a mere digestion of the resins with spirit   The surface of contact offered by the copal to the spirit is increased by the admixture of chalk or glass, and if the spirit is not quite strong enough, the chalk extracts part of its water   If the polish is to be made in large quantities a large green glass flask should be kept handy and should be thin, so as to be less likely to crack.   To avoid the same danger it should be gradually heated, and put on the sand-bath before the heating of the latter is begun.   The flask can then be heated to boiling without risk.   The sand used must be sifted, as the presence of stones causes unequal heating, and probably the cracking of the glass The flask must not be filled too full, but room for the expansion of the contents allowed, and so as to permit of the contents being shaken.

Experience has shown that soft wood wants thicker polish than hard wood. If too thick, the polish is diluted with spirit; if too thin, it is thickened with a solution of shellac in spirit The addition of sandarach or mastic increases neither the lustre nor the durability The polish must never be applied till the surface has been carefully smoothed by the usual processes, using last of all soft pumice steeped in oil The oil is removed and the last finish given to the polish by means of a rubbing with brickdust. The polish can then be laid on This is done by soaking a pad of several folds of woollen cloth in the liquid and then enclosing it in a piece of calico first oiled with linseed oil. The whole is held in the hand by the corners of the calico and applied to the work with a circular movement till the whole surface has been done Fresh oil must be put on the calico if it begins to stick to the wood, but the polish is only renewed when the first supply is exhausted. Before the pad is put away after use it must be well cleaned with spirit. When the proper lustre is produced the surface is dried and freed from oil by the light application of a cotton cloth The oil is necessary to keep the pad in proper condition, but as too much of it interferes with the polishing it must be used with discretion.

Although the application of furniture polish may seem easy, it nevertheless requires great experience, and even very skilled workmen often have great difficulty with very soft wood It is a good plan to give such wood a preliminary soaking in glue-water to stop up the pores The polish must be applied, too, in considerable quantity after the glue is dry and the wood has been smoothed as above directed. The first application of the polish is then made without reference to lustre, and is followed by a second polishing, first with pumice and water, and then with pumice powder and oil, and finally with the brick-dust. A second and slight application of the polish will then suffice to give the desired result.

Turned goods are polished in nearly the way we have described. The whole process is carried out on the lathe itself. After smoothing with fine glass paper, followed by the use of powdered pumice and oil on a woollen rag, the superfluous oil is removed with tripoli or burnt hartshorn, and the polish is applied with the pad Small articles which would lose their sharp edges under the action of powdered pumice are smoothed with pieces of pumice-stone cut into the proper shapes Care must be taken to move the pad to and fro horizontally, or the wood being heated by the friction will soften the polish, and so cause the pad to remove it again. This also hinders the proper action of the pad, as it clogs the rag and prevents the free exudation of the polish. While the pad is being rotated with one hand a finger of the other should be applied to the wood just opposite to it The friction against the skin increases the lustre, and the feel tells the workman whether he is applying too much or too little pressure with the pad or rubber, and the removal of superfluous oil is facilitated After the drying of the polish the last lustre is given with a new application of pumice and oil In this way as good a lustre can be obtained as with any copal or amber varnish, although naturally the polish is not so durable as that given by those varnishes.

With regard to the means of preserving the lustre of a polished article and keeping it from injury, it must be remembered that it owes its beauty to the smoothness and closeness of its surface, whereby it reflects most of the light which falls upon it These properties are produced by the polish, which fills up all inequalities and presents a smooth compact exterior Hence all liquids capable of acting on the polish must be kept away, such as spirits of all kinds If such a liquid is spilt on a polished surface it dissolves some of the polish, and the water it contains precipitates the resins from the solution causing a whitish mark Water alone does no harm, unless it is applied to the surface when the latter is warm through exposure to the sun or a fire It is then liable to injure the lustre and cause a more or less opalescent or coloured appearance. The reason of this is that the heat opens the pores of the polish and enables them to admit the water Hence the surface no longer reflects the rays of light uniformly One must, therefore, be very careful when polished furniture is brought from a cold into a hot room not to wipe off water which condenses on it, but to allow it to evaporate. If polished wood has to be cleaned with a wet cloth it must never be rubbed or the heat developed by friction will open the pores and admit the water, and also make the surface apt to collect dust.

A simple solution of shellac is often passed off as English furniture-polish It is simply made by making a solution of the shellac of the desired strength by warming with spirit. It is much less durable than the genuine article.

AMBER VARNISH.

Amber has long been used for varnish-making, but eighty years ago few possessed the recipe, and these charged very high prices for the varnish. The varnish must only be applied to a perfectly uniform and smooth surface. All cracks and small holes must be carefully stopped with a priming, and when that is perfectly dry the now uniform surface must be made quite smooth with pumice, etc The best results are got by circular rubbing with pumice, etc, in a dry and very finely powdered state. The surface is then wiped clean with a damp sponge and carefully dried with a soft cloth. If a very superfine smoothing is desired, a rubbing with starch powder may be given last before the application of the sponge. The wood is then gone over with glue-water, or with a body colour of white-lead and glue, and is then, when dry, ready for the varnish

The best recipe for amber varnish is—

Amber	10 oz.
Pure oil of turpentine	15 „
Boiled oil	5 „

The coarsely powdered amber is wetted with some of the turpentine in a glazed vessel and left covered over for a few hours. The vessel is then moderately heated over a fire, and its contents are stirred with an iron spatula till thoroughly fused. It is then allowed to cool partially, and the rest of the turpentine, first made hot, is stirred in The vessel is then returned to the fire, and allowed to froth up once or twice, when the linseed oil is slowly added boiling hot The finished varnish is filtered while still warm through a plug of tow.

The wood, after smoothing and soaking in glue, receives two coats of the varnish, and thereby acquires a beautiful lustre The varnish coat can, however, not be further polished. If the wood is light in colour varnish must be used for it made of the finest and palest amber, but for darker woods varnish made with the darker kinds of amber will do perfectly well.

Much depends on the purity of the ingredients of the varnish. The amber in particular must be cleaned from all dirt and impurities before solution as they cannot be thoroughly got rid of afterwards It should be washed in lukewarm water, and dried in the sun in places free from dust and fumes, because amber absorbs them

The amber may also be melted in a copper vessel. The clearness of the varnish usually depends on that of the linseed oil used, so that the oil must be carefully examined first. Linseed oil adulterated with rape oil is also to be avoided, as the varnish made with it dries much too slowly. If the opportunity presents itself of buying a really good oil, a large stock should be laid in, for the oil improves greatly by keeping, and old oil makes by far the best varnish On keeping it deposits its mucilaginous and coloured particles, and becomes much paler and of far superior quality. The oil should be drawn off every year into a fresh vessel, and the sediment left behind in the old cask cleaned out and thrown away, or better, used mixed with lard for cart-grease, or for painting over coarse wood-work exposed to the weather. The gain in the quality of oil by keeping makes up for the loss of the weight of the sediment twice over. Boiled oil from freshly pressed raw oil is hardly ever clear, and amber varnish made with it is useless with light colours, as it darkens them and gives them a dirty yellow hue

The boiled oil used in making amber varnish must be made from genuine crude oil. The oil may be purified to a large extent before boiling it by churning it with water for an hour The water and oil are then allowed to separate, and the dirty water is run off. The whole process is repeated with more water as long as it is obvious that the water is removing dirt.

The boiling is done with litharge, sugar of lead, or white vitriol. Although raw oil is used for coarse work in the open, it is quite unsuitable for making amber varnish, partly because it dries so slowly and partly because it does not go so far.

COPAL OIL VARNISH.

Take of—

Coarsely powdered copal	24 lb
Pure oil of turpentine	26 „
Boiled oil	36 „

The copal is wetted with some of the turps in a glazed earthen vessel, and put over a fire to melt. As soon as fusion begins it is stirred with an iron rod till it is complete. Then the oil is put in boiling hot, a little at a time, and the fire is increased to make the varnish boil up once or twice. The vessel is then taken from the fire, and when it has cooled enough the rest of the oil of turpentine is stirred in Then strain into a warm barrel. Before this varnish is applied, the wood is soaked with weak glue-water or with boiled oil, and when this priming is quite dry the varnish is put on with a brush One coat is usually enough. If a second is necessary, it must not be applied till the first is dry When the varnish is dry the surface is smoothed and polished.

COMPOSITION FOR PRESERVING FURNITURE

Take small pieces of wax, white or yellow, and add to it as much oil of turpentine as will make a thick pasty solution. Rub the furniture with this and then polish with a woollen rag This process will restore articles of walnut, marble or varnished metal to their pristine brilliancy. If it is to be used on red articles, the turpentine must be dyed deep violet with alkanet before the wax is mixed with it. The alkanet is simply soaked in the oil till the desired colour is produced. For mahogany this colour must not be too pronounced, because the wood itself browns with time. Cherry wood does not, however, so that the turpentine must be strongly dyed when used for making composition for this wood

Only a small piece of the composition, about the size of a bean, should be used at a time, or very long rubbing is necessary It is best to repeat the operations of rubbing with composition and with the woollen cloth, as a better lustre is then got A final rubbing with a bit of old soft linen is to be recommended after the woollen rag has been used The composition can be bought ready made.

THE END.

INDEX.

(165)

Special Technical Books

FOR
MANUFACTURERS, TECHNICAL STUDENTS AND WORKERS, SCHOOLS, COLLEGES, ETC.
BY EXPERT WRITERS

INDEX TO SUBJECTS.

PUBLISHED BY
SCOTT, GREENWOOD & SON,
8 BROADWAY, LUDGATE HILL,
LONDON, E.C.

Inks.

THE CHEMISTRY OF PIGMENTS. By ERNEST J. PARRY, B.Sc (Lond.), F.I.C., F.C.S., and J. H. COSTE, F.I.C., F.C.S. Demy 8vo. Five Illustrations. 285 pp. Price 10s. 6d. net. (Post free, 10s. 10d. home, 11s. 3d. abroad)

Contents.

Introductory. Light—White Light—The Spectrum—The Invisible Spectrum—Normal Spectrum—Simple Nature of Pure Spectral Colour—The Recomposition of White Light—Primary and Complementary Colours—Coloured Bodies—Absorption Spectra—**The Application of Pigments.** Uses of Pigments. Artistic, Decorative, Protective—Methods of Application of Pigments : Pastels and Crayons, Water Colour, Tempera Painting, Fresco, Encaustic Painting, Oil-colour Painting, Keramic Art, Enamel, Stained and Painted Glass, Mosaic—**Inorganic Pigments.** White Lead—Zinc White—Enamel White—Whitening—Red Lead—Litharge—Vermilion—Royal Scarlet—The Chromium Greens—Chromates of Lead, Zinc, Silver and Mercury—Brunswick Green—The Ochres—Indian Red—Venetian Red—Siennas and Umbers—Light Red—Cappagh Brown—Red Oxides—Mars Colours—Terre Verte—Prussian Brown—Cobalt Colours—Cœruleum—Smalt—Copper Pigments—Malachite—Bremen Green—Scheele's Green—Emerald Green—Verdigris—Brunswick Green—Non-arsenical Greens—Copper Blues—Ultramarine—Carbon Pigments—Ivory Black—Lamp Black—Bistre—Naples Yellow—Arsenic Sulphides Orpiment, Realgar—Cadmium Yellow—Vandyck Brown—**Organic Pigments.** Prussian Blue—Natural Lakes—Cochineal—Carmine—Crimson — Lac Dye — Scarlet — Madder — Alizarin—Campeachy—Quercitron—Rhamous—Brazil Wood—Alkanet—Santal Wood—Archil—Coal-tar Lakes—Red Lakes—Alizarin Compounds—Orange and Yellow Lakes—Green and Blue Lakes—Indigo—Dragon's Blood—Gamboge—Sepia—Indian Yellow, Puree—Bitumen, Asphaltum, Mummy—**Index.**

THE MANUFACTURE OF PAINT. A Practical Handbook for Paint Manufacturers, Merchants and Painters. By J. CRUICKSHANK SMITH, B.Sc. Demy 8vo. 200 pp. Sixty Illustrations and One Large Diagram. Price 7s. 6d. net (Post free, 7s. 10d. home ; 8s. abroad.)

Contents.

Preparation of Raw Material—Storing of Raw Material—Testing and Valuation of Raw Material—Paint Plant and Machinery—The Grinding of White Lead—Grinding of White Zinc—Grinding of other White Pigments—Grinding of Oxide Paints—Grinding of Staining Colours—Grinding of Black Paints—Grinding of Chemical Colours—Yellows—Grinding of Chemical Colours—Blues—Grinding Greens—Grinding Reds—Grinding Lakes—Grinding Colours in Water—Grinding Colours in Turpentine—The Uses of Paint—Testing and Matching Paints—Economic Considerations—Index.

DICTIONARY OF CHEMICALS AND RAW PRODUCTS USED IN THE MANUFACTURE OF PAINTS, COLOURS, VARNISHES AND ALLIED PREPARATIONS. By GEORGE H. HURST, F.C.S. Demy 8vo. 380 pp. Price 7s. 6d. net. (Post free, 8s. home, 8s. 6d. abroad.)

THE MANUFACTURE OF LAKE PIGMENTS FROM ARTIFICIAL COLOURS. By FRANCIS H. JENNISON, F.I.C., F.C.S. **Sixteen Coloured Plates, showing Specimens of Eighty-nine Colours, specially prepared from the Recipes given in the Book.** 136 pp. Demy 8vo. Price 7s 6d. net. (Post free, 7s 10d. home, 8s. abroad.)

Contents.

The Groups of the Artificial Colouring Matters—The Nature and Manipulation of Artificial Colours—Lake-forming Bodies for Acid Colours—Lake-forming Bodies' Basic Colours—Lake Bases—The Principles of Lake Formation—Red Lakes—Orange, Yellow, Green, Blue, Violet and Black Lakes—The Production of Insoluble Azo Colours in the Form of Pigments—The General Properties of Lakes Produced from Artificial Colours—Washing, Filtering and Finishing—Matching and Testing Lake Pigments—Index.

THE MANUFACTURE OF MINERAL AND LAKE PIGMENTS.
Containing Directions for the Manufacture of all Artificial, Artists and Painters' Colours, Enamel, Soot and Metallic Pigments. A Text-book for Manufacturers, Merchants, Artists and Painters. By Dr. JOSEF BERSCH. Translated by A. C. WRIGHT, M.A. (Oxon.), B.Sc. (Lond.). Forty-three Illustrations. 476 pp., demy 8vo. Price 12s. 6d. net. (Post free, 13s. home; 13s. 6d. abroad.)

RECIPES FOR THE COLOUR, PAINT, VARNISH, OIL, SOAP AND DRYSALTERY TRADES.
Compiled by AN ANALYTICAL CHEMIST. 350 pp. Demy 8vo. Price 7s. 6d net. (Post free, 8s. home; 8s. 3d. abroad.)

OIL COLOURS AND PRINTERS' INKS.
By LOUIS EDGAR ANDÉS. Translated from the German 215 pp. Crown 8vo. 56 Illustrations. Price 5s net. (Post free, 5s. 4d. home; 5s. 6d. abroad.)

Contents.
Linseed Oil—Poppy Oil—Mechanical Purification of Linseed Oil—Chemical Purification of Linseed Oil—Bleaching Linseed Oil—Oxidizing Agents for Boiling Linseed Oil—Theory of Oil Boiling—Manufacture of Boiled Oil—Adulterations of Boiled Oil—Chinese Drying Oil and Other Specialities—Pigments for House and Artistic Painting and Inks—Pigment for Printers' Black Inks—Substitutes for Lampblack—Machinery for Colour Grinding and Rubbing—Machines for mixing Pigments with the Vehicle—Paint Mills—Manufacture of House Oil Paints—Ship Paints—Luminous Paint—Artists' Colours—Printers' Inks.—VEHICLES—Printers' Inks—PIGMENTS and MANUFACTURE—Index

MODERN PRINTING INKS.
A Practical Handbook for Printing Ink Manufacturers and Printers. By ALFRED SEYMOUR. Demy 8vo. Six Illustrations. 90 pages. Price 5s. net. (Post free, 5s. 4d. home, 5s. 6d. abroad.) [*Just published.*

Contents.
Introduction.—Division of Labour—A Separate Industry—Choice of Materials—Skilful Manipulation—Some Important Factors—The Medium—Ink and Colour Mixing—A Justification. Linseed Oil.—Extraction of the Oil—Classification—Mechanical Purification—Adulteration—Boiled Oil—Preparation of Boiled Oil—An Alternative Process. Varnish.—A Vehicle and Essential Component—A Reference to Lithography—Baltic Oil—Preparation of Varnish—The Modern Method—An Old Argument—Letterpress Varnish—A Cheaper Medium—A Suggestive Recipe—Fire Risks—Gradations of Varnish. Dry Colours.—A Recommendation—An Endless Variety of Materials—Earth Colours—Mineral Colours—Substrates—Toning Earth Colours—Physical Characteristics—Colouring Power—Brilliance—Purity of Tone—Permanence. Dry Colours—Blacks, Whites, Yellows—Lampblack—Process of Manufacture—Calcination—Carbon Black—Acetylene Black—A Simple Test—Lead and Zinc Whites—White Earth Colours—Yellows—Yellow Ochres—Mineral Yellows. Dry Colours—Reds, Browns.—Classification of Reds—Genuine Vermilions—Preparation—Imitation Vermilions—Umber, Raw and Burnt—Sienna, Raw and Burnt. Blues, Greens.—Ultramarine Blue—A Useful Tint—Other Similar Blues—Cobalt Blues—Prussian—Chinese and Bronze Blues—A Test for Purity—Greens—Compound Greens—Mineral Greens. Lakes.—Characteristics—Lake Derivatives—A Point of Importance—Red Lakes—Madder—Cochineal and Carmine—Brazil Wood—Alizarine a Coaltar Derivative—Yellow Lakes—Blue Lakes—Green Lakes. The Grinding of Printing Inks.—Ink-grinding Machinery—Ink-grinding Mill—A Novel Machine—Hand Grinding—Treatment of Gritty Colours—A Question of Proportion—Approximate Calculation—Soap—Saturation—Friction Heat—Consistent Grinding. Ink and Colour Mixing.—A Necessary Acquisition—Ink Mixing Defined—Mixed Green Inks—Mixed Brown Inks—Tints—Ink Mixing—Lithographic Inks—Characteristics of Yellows—Mixing Vermilion—Ultramarine and Other Blues—Bronze, Prussian and Chinese Blues—Working Consistency—Reducing Medium—Letterpress Inks—Gloss Inks—Three-colour Inks—Ink-mixing Machine. The Characteristics of Some Printing Processes.—A Supplementary Discussion—Letterpress Inks—Three-colour Printing—Lithographic Printing Inks—An Important Feature—Suggestive Points—Tinplate Printing. Driers.—A Valuable Auxiliary—Energetic Drying Inks—The Theory of Drying—Liquid Driers—Terebene—Paste Driers—Letterpress Driers—Powder Driers—Turpentine as a Drier. Bronze Powders and Bronzing.—A Brief Justification—Bronze Printing Inks—Bronze Powders—The Process of Manufacture—Preparation of the Leaf—Grinding and Grading—Bronzing Mediums—Requisite Qualities—Wax Varnish. "Things Worth Knowing."—A Record of Notes and Experiences—Index.

(See also Writing Inks, p. 11.)

THREE HUNDRED SHADES AND HOW TO MIX

PAINTS, COLOURS, ETC.—*continued.*

CASEIN. By Robert Scherer. Translated from the German by Chas. Salter. Demy 8vo. Illustrated. 160 pp. Price 7s. 6d. net. (Post free, 7s. 10d. home , 8s. abroad.)

Contents.

Casein: its Origin, Preparation and Properties. Various Methods of Preparing Casein. Composition and Properties of Casein Casein Paints —"Marble-Lime' Colour for Outside Work—Casein Enamel Paint—Casein Façade Paint—Cold-Water Paint in Powder Form—Kistory's Recipe for Casein Paint and Varnish—Pure Casein Paints for Walls, . etc.—Casein Paints for Woodwork and Iron—Casein-Silicate Paints—Milk Paints—Casein-Silicate Paint Recipes—Trojel's Boiled Oil Substitute—Calsomine Wash—Quick-Drying Casein Paint—Boiled Oil Substitute—Ring's Cold-Water Paint—Pormolactin—Waterproof Paint for Playing Cards—Casein Colour Lake—Casein-Cement Paint. The Technics of Casein Painting. Casein Adhesives and Putties —Casein Glue in Plates or Flakes—Jeromin's Casein Adhesive—Hall's Casein Glue—Waterproof Glue—Liquid Casein Glue—Casein and Borax Glue—Solid Casein Adhesive—Casein Solution—Glue Powder—Casein Putties—Washable Cement for Deal Boards—Wenk'a Casein Cement—Casein and Lime Cement —"Pitch Barm"—Casein Stopping—Casein Cement for Stone The Preparation of Plastic Masses from Casein —Imitation Ivory—Anti-Radiation and Anti-Corrosive Composition—Dickmaon's Covering for Floors and Walls—Imitation Linoleum—Imitation Leather—Imitation Bone—Plastic Mass of Keratin and Casein—Insulating Mass—Plastic Casein Masses—Horny Casein Mass—Plastic Mass from Celluloid—Casein Cellulose Composition—Fireproof Cellulose Substitute—Nitrocellulose and Casein Composition—Franquet's Celluloid Substitute—Galalith Uses of Casein in the Textile Industry, for Finishing Colour Printing, etc —Casengum—"Glutin"—Casein Dressing for Linen and Cotton Fabrics—Printing Colour with Metallic Lustre—Process for Softening, Sizing and Loading—Fixing Casein and Other Albuminoids on the Fibre—Fixing Insoluble Colouring Matters—Waterproofing and Softening Dressing—Casein for Mercerising Crêpe—Fixing Zinc White on Cotton with Pormaldehyde—Casein-Magnesia—Casein Medium for Calico Printing—Loading Silk. Casein Foodstuffs —Casein Food—Synthetic Milk—Milk Pood—Emulsifiable Casein —Casein Phosphate for Baking—Making Bread, Low in Carbohydrates, from Flour and Curd —Preparing Soluble Casein Compounds with Citrates—Casein Food Sundry Applications of Casein.

SIMPLE METHODS FOR TESTING PAINTERS' MATERIALS. By A. C. Wright, M.A. (Oxon.), B.Sc. (Lond.). Crown 8vo 160 pp. Price 5s. net. (Post free, 5s. 3d. home ; 5s. 6d. abroad.)

IRON - CORROSION, ANTI - FOULING AND ANTI-CORROSIVE PAINTS. Translated from the German of Louis Edgar Andés. Sixty-two Illustrations. 275 pp. Demy 8vo. Price 10s. 6d. net. (Post free, 10s. 10d. home ; 11s. 3d. abroad.)

Contents.

Iron-rust and its Pormation—Protection from Rusting by Paint—Grounding the Iron with Linseed Oil, etc.—Testing Paints—Use of Tar for Painting on Iron—Anti-corrosive Paints—Linseed Varnish—Chinese Wood Oil—Lead Pigments—Iron Pigments—Artificial Iron Oxides —Carbon—Preparation of Anti-corrosive Paints—Results of Examination of Several Anti-corrosive Paints—Paints for Ship's Bottoms—Anti-fouling Compositions—Various Anti-corrosive and Ship's Paints—Official Standard Specifications for Ironwork Paints—Index.

THE TESTING AND VALUATION OF RAW MATERIALS USED IN PAINT AND COLOUR MANUFACTURE. By M. W. Jones, F.C.S. A Book for the Laboratories of Colour Works. 88 pp. Crown 8vo. Price 5s. net. (Post free, 5s. 3d. home and abroad.)

THE MANUFACTURE AND COMPARATIVE MERITS OF WHITE LEAD AND ZINC WHITE PAINTS By G. Petit, Civil Engineer, etc. Translated from the French. Crown 8vo. 100 pp. Price 4s. net. (Post free, 4s. 3d. home , 4s. 4d. abroad.)

Contents.

Chapters I , The Fundamental Principles of Painting in Oil II., The Different Varieties of White Leads—The Dutch Process—Grinding White Lead in Oil. III., Other Processes of Manufacturing White Lead IV , White Lead Substitutes—Sophistication of White Lead—Analysis of White Lead. V., White Lead Paints—Their Merits and Defects VI., Toxi-

STUDENTS' HANDBOOK OF PAINTS, COLOURS, OILS AND VARNISHES By John Furnell. Crown 8vo. 12 Illustrations. 96 pp. Price 2s. 6d. net. (Post free, 2s. 9d. home and abroad.)

Varnishes and Drying Oils.

OIL CRUSHING, REFINING AND BOILING, THE MANUFACTURE OF LINOLEUM, PRINTING AND LITHOGRAPHIC INKS, AND INDIA-RUBBER SUBSTITUTES. By John Geddes McIntosh. Being Volume I. of the Second, greatly enlarged, English Edition, in three Volumes, of "The Manufacture of Varnishes and Kindred Industries," based on and including the work of Ach. Livache. Demy 8vo. 150 pp. 29 Illustrations. Price 7s 6d. net. (Post free, 7s. 10d. home, 8s. abroad.)

VARNISH MATERIALS AND OIL-VARNISH MAKING.
By J. G. McIntosh. Being Vol. II. of "The Manufacture of Varnishes and Kindred Industries" Demy 8vo. 70 Illustrations 220 pp. Price 10s. 6d. net. (Post free, 10s. 10d home, 11s. 3d. abroad.)

Contents.

Chapter I, Introduction. II, Amber and Amber Oil Varnishes. III, Copal, etc IV., Resins—Assorting, Cleaning and Fusing. V, Asphaltum, Coal-Tar, Pitch, Rubber, etc. VI, Oil-Varnish Making—General Instructions. VII, Copal Oil Varnish VIII., Rosin Oil Varnish —Brunswick Black—Super Black Japan IX, Testing Varnish—Utilisation of Residues.

DRYING OILS, BOILED OIL AND SOLID AND LIQUID DRIERS. By L. E. Andés. Expressly Written for this Series of Special Technical Books, and the Publishers hold the Copyright for English and Foreign Editions. Forty-two Illustrations. 342 pp. Demy 8vo. Price 12s. 6d. net (Post free, 13s. home; 13s. 3d. abroad.)

Contents.

Properties of the Drying Oils; Cause of the Drying Property, Absorption of Oxygen, Behaviour towards Metallic Oxides, etc.—The Properties of and Methods for obtaining the Drying Oils—Production of the Drying Oils by Expression and Extraction, Refining and Bleaching; Oil Cakes and Meal; The Refining and Bleaching of the Drying Oils, The Bleaching of Linseed Oil—The Manufacture of Boiled Oil, The Preparation of Drying Oils for Use in the Grinding of Paints and Artists' Colours and in the Manufacture of Varnishes by Heating over a Fire or by Steam, by the Cold Process, by the Action of Air, and by Means of the Electric Current; The Driers used in Boiling Linseed Oil, The Manufacture of Boiled Oil and the Apparatus therefor, Livache's Process for Preparing a Good Drying Oil and its Practical Application—The Preparation of Varnishes for Letterpress, Lithographic and Copper-plate Printing, for Oilcloth and Waterproof Fabrics, The Manufacture of Thickened Linseed Oil, Burnt Oil, Stand Oil by Fire Heat, Superheated Steam, and by a Current of Air—Behaviour of the Drying Oils and Boiled Oils towards Atmospheric Influences, Water, Acids and Alkalies —Boiled Oil Substitutes—The Manufacture of Solid and Liquid Driers from Linseed Oil and Rosin; Linolic Acid Compounds of the Driers—The Adulteration and Examination of the Drying Oils and Boiled Oil.

Oils, Fats, Waxes, Greases, Petroleum.

LUBRICATING OILS, FATS AND GREASES: Their Origin, Preparation. Properties, Uses and Analyses. A Handbook for Oil Manufacturers, Refiners and Merchants. and the Oil and Fat Industry in General. By George H. Hurst, F.C.S Second Revised and Enlarged Edition. Sixty-five Illustrations. 317 pp Demy 8vo Price 10s. 6d. net. (Post free, 11s. home; 11s. 3d. abroad.)

Contents.

TECHNOLOGY OF PETROLEUM : Oil Fields of the
World—Their History, Geography and Geology—Annual Production and Development—Oil-well Drilling—Transport. By HENRY NEUBERGER and HENRY NOALHAT. Translated from the French by J. G. MCINTOSH. 550 pp. 153 Illustrations. 26 Plates. Super Royal 8vo. Price 21s. net. (Post free, 21s. 9d. home ; 23s. 6d. abroad.)

Contents.
Study of the Petroliferous Strata.
Excavations—Hand Excavation or Hand Digging of Oil Wells.
Methods of Boring.
Accidents—Boring Accidents—Methods of preventing them—Methods of remedying them —Explosives and the use of the "Torpedo" Levigation—Storing and Transport of Petroleum —General Advice—Prospecting, Management and carrying on of Petroleum Boring Operations.
General Data—Customary Formulæ—Memento. Practical Part. General Data bearing on Petroleum—Glossary of Technical Terms used in the Petroleum Industry—Copious Index.

MINERAL WAXES . Their Preparation and Uses By
RUDOLF GREGORIUS. Translated from the German Crown 8vo. 250 pp. 32 Illustrations. Price 6s. net. (Post free, 6s. 4d. home ; 6s. 6d. abroad.)

Contents.
Ozokerite—Ceresine—Paraffin—Refining Paraffin—Mineral Wax—Appliances for Extracting, Distilling and Refining Ozokerite—Uses of Ceresine, Paraffin and Mineral Waxes—Paint and Varnish Removers—Leather and Piston-Rod Greases— Recipes for Silk, Cotton and Linen Dressings—Candles.

THE PRACTICAL COMPOUNDING OF OILS, TAL-LOW AND GREASE FOR LUBRICATION, ETC.
By AN EXPERT OIL REFINER. Second Edition 100 pp. Demy 8vo. Price 7s. 6d. net. (Post free, 7s. 10d. home ; 8s. abroad.)

Contents.
Introductory Remarks on the General Nomenclature of Oils, Tallow and Greases suitable for Lubrication — Hydrocarbon Oils — Animal and Fish Oils — Compound Oils—Vegetable Oils—Lamp Oils—Engine Tallow, Solidified Oils and Petroleum Jelly — Machinery Greases ; Loco and Anti-friction—Clarifying and Utilisation of Waste Fats, Oils, Tank Bottoms, Drainings of Barrels and Drums, Pickings Up, Dregs, etc.—The Fixing and Cleaning of Oil Tanks, etc.—Appendix and General Information.

ANIMAL FATS AND OILS : Their Practical Production,
Purification and Uses for a great Variety of Purposes Their Properties, Falsification and Examination. Translated from the German of LOUIS EDGAR ANDÉS. Sixty-two Illustrations. 240 pp. Second Edition, Revised and Enlarged. Demy 8vo. Price 10s. 6d. net. (Post free, 10s. 10d. home ; 11s. 3d. abroad.)

THE MANUFACTURE OF LUBRICANTS, SHOE POLISHES AND LEATHER DRESSINGS. By
RICHARD BRUNNER. Translated from the Sixth German Edition by CHAS. SALTER. 10 Illustrations. Crown 8vo. 170 pp. Price 7s. 6d. net. (Post free, 7s. 10d. home , 8s. abroad.)

THE OIL MERCHANTS' MANUAL AND OIL TRADE READY RECKONER. Compiled by FRANK F. SHERRIFF.
Second Edition Revised and Enlarged. Demy 8vo. 214 pp. 1904. With Two Sheets of Tables. Price 7s. 6d. net. (Post free, 7s. 10d. home , 8s. 3d. abroad.)

Contents.
Trade Terms and Customs—Tables to Ascertain Value of Oil sold per cwt or ton—Specific Gravity Tables—Percentage Tare Tables—Petroleum Tables—Paraffine and Benzoline Calcu-

VEGETABLE FATS AND OILS: Their Practical Preparation, Purification and Employment for Various Purposes, their Properties, Adulteration and Examination. Translated from the German of LOUIS EDGAR ANDÉS. Ninety-four Illustrations. 340 pp. Second Edition Demy 8vo. Price 10s. 6d. net. (Post free, 11s. home; 11s. 6d. abroad.)

EDIBLE FATS AND OILS: Their Composition, Manufacture and Analysis. By W. H SIMMONS, B.Sc (Lond.), F C S.

[*In preparation*

The Contents will include the Constitution of Oils and Fats; Raw Materials; Bleaching, Deodorising and Refining, Butter, Lard; Margarine, Salad Oils, Chocolate Cream, Analysis of Raw Materials, Statistics.

Essential Oils and Perfumes.

THE CHEMISTRY OF ESSENTIAL OILS AND ARTIFICIAL PERFUMES. By ERNEST J. PARRY, B.Sc. (Lond.), F 1 C., F.C.S Second Edition, Revised and Enlarged. 552 pp. 20 Illustrations. Demy 8vo Price 12s. 6d. net. (Post free, 13s. home, 13s. 6d. abroad.)

Contents.

Chapter 1. **The General Properties of Essential Oils.** 11 **Compounds occurring in Essential Oils**; (I.) The Terpenes—Sesquiterpenes—Olefinic Terpen s and Sesquiterpenes—Pinene—(II.) The Camphor Series—(III) The Geraniol and Citronellol Group—The Geraniol and Citronellol Series—(IV) Benzene Compounds Cymene—Phenols and their Derivatives—Phenols with Nine Carbon Atoms—Phenols with Ten Carbon Atoms—Alcohols—Aldehydes—Ketones—Acids—(V.) Aliphatic Compounds Alcohols—Acids—Aldehydes—Sulphur Compounds—Other Bodies. III **The Preparation of Essential Oils**: Expression—Distillation—Extraction. IV **The Analysis of Essential Oils**: Specific Gravity—Optical Methods (1) Refraction (2) Polarimetry, Melting and Solidifying Points—Boiling Point and Distillation—Quantitative Estimations of Constituents—Aldehydes, Ketones and Oils on which a Direct Determination can be made. V **Systematic Study of the Essential Oils.** VI. **Chemistry of Artificial Perfumes.** Appendix 1. Table on Constants of the more important Essential Oils Appendix II Table of Pharmacopœial Standards. Index

Soaps.

SOAPS. A Practical Manual of the Manufacture of Domestic, Toilet and other Soaps. By GEORGE H. HURST, F.C.S. 2nd edition. 390 pp. 66 Illustrations. Price 12s. 6d. net (Post free, 13s home, 13s. 6d abroad)

Contents.

Introductory—Soap-maker's Alkalies—Soap Fats and Oils—Perfumes—Water as a Soap Material—Soap Machinery—Technology of Soap-making—Glycerine in Soap Lyes—Laying out a Soap Factory—Soap Analysis—Appendices.

TEXTILE SOAPS AND OILS. Handbook on the Preparation, Properties and Analysis of the Soaps and Oils used in Textile Manufacturing, Dyeing and Printing By GEORGE H HURST, F C.S. Crown 8vo. 195 pp. 1904. Price 5s. net. (Post free, 5s. 4d home; 5s. 6d. abroad.)

THE HANDBOOK OF SOAP MANUFACTURE. By WM H. SIMMONS, B.Sc (Lond), F C.S. and H A APPLETON. Demy 8vo. 160 pp. 27 Illustrations. Price 8s 6d net. (Post free, 8s. 10d. home; 9s. abroad.)

Contents.

Definition of Soap.—Properties—Hydrolysis—Detergent Action. Constitution of Oils and Fats, and their Saponification.—Researches of Chevreul and Berthelot—Mixed

Oxide, Soda and Potash. **Raw Materials used in Soap-making.**—Fats and Oils—Waste Fats—Fatty Acids—Less-known Oils and Fats of Limited Use—Various New Fats and Oils Suggested for Soap-making—Rosin—Alkali (Caustic and Carbonated)—Water—Salt Soapstock **Bleaching and Treatment of Raw Materials intended for Soap-making.**—Palm Oil—Cottonseed Oil—Cottonseed " Foots '—Vegetable Oils—Animal Fats—Bone Fat—Rosin **Soap-making.**—Classification of Soaps—Direct combination of Fatty Acids with Alkali—Cold Process Soaps—Saponification under Increased or Diminished Pressure—Soft Soap—Marine Soap—Hydrated Soaps, Smooth and Marbled—Pasting or Saponification—Graining Out—Boiling on Strength—Fitting—Curd Soaps—Curd Mottled—Blue and Grey Mottled Soaps—Milling Base—Yellow Household Soaps—Resting of Pans and Settling of Soap—Utilisation of Nigres—Transparent Soaps—Saponifying Mineral Oil—Electrical Production of Soap. **Treatment of Settled Soap.**—Cleansing—Crutching—Liquoring of Soaps—Filling—Neutralising, Colouring and Perfuming—Disinfectant Soaps—Framing—Slabbing—Barring—Open and Close Piling—Drying—Stamping—Cooling **Toilet, Textile and Miscellaneous Soaps.**—Toilet Soaps—Cold Process Soaps—Settled Boiled Soaps—Remelted Soaps—Milled Soaps—Drying, Milling and Incorporating Colour, Perfumes, or Medicaments—Perfumes—Colouring Matter—Neutralising and Super-fatting Material—Compressing—Cutting—Textile Soaps—Soaps for Woollen, Cotton and Silk Industries—Patent Textile Soaps—Stamping—Medicated Soaps—Ether Soap—Floating Soaps—Shaving Soaps—Miscellaneous Soaps **Soap Perfumes.**—Essential Oils—Source and Preparation—Properties—Artificial and Synthetic Perfumes **Glycerine Manufacture and Purification.**—Treatment of Lyes—Evaporation—Crude Glycerine—Distillation—Distilled and Dynamite Glycerine—Chemically Pure Glycerine—Animal Charcoal for Decolorisation—Glycerine resultant from other methods of Saponification—Yield of Glycerine from Fats and Oils. **Analysis of Raw Materials, Soap and Glycerine** —Fats and Oils—Alkalies and Alkali Salts—Essential Oils—Soap—Lyes—Crude Glycerine **Statistics of the Soap Industry.** Appendix A—**Comparison of Degrees Twaddell, Beaume and Actual Densities.** Appendix B—**Comparison of Different Thermometric Scales.** Appendix C—Table of the Specific Gravities of Solutions of Caustic Soda. Appendix D—Table of Strength of Caustic Potash Solutions at 60° F. **Index.**

Cosmetical Preparations.

COSMETICS : MANUFACTURE, EMPLOYMENT AND TESTING OF ALL COSMETIC MATERIALS AND COSMETIC SPECIALITIES. Translated

from the German of Dr. THEODOR KOLLER. Crown 8vo. 262 pp. Price 5s. net. (Post free, 5s. 4d. home ; 5s. 6d. abroad)

Contents.

Purposes and Uses of, and Ingredients used in the Preparation of Cosmetics—Preparation of Perfumes by Pressure, Distillation, Maceration, Absorption or Enfleurage, and Extraction Methods—Chemical and Animal Products used in the Preparation of Cosmetics—Oils and Fats used in the Preparation of Cosmetics—General Cosmetic Preparations—Mouth Washes and Tooth Pastes—Hair Dyes, Hair Restorers and Depilatories—Cosmetic Adjuncts and Specialities—Colouring Cosmetic Preparations—Antiseptic Washes and Soaps—Toilet and Hygienic Soaps—Secret Preparations for Skin, Complexion, Teeth, Mouth, etc.—Testing and Examining the Materials Employed in the Manufacture of Cosmetics—Index

Glue, Bone Products and Manures.

GLUE AND GLUE TESTING. By SAMUEL RIDEAL, D.SC.

(Lond), F.I.C. Fourteen Engravings. 144 pp. Demy 8vo. Price 10s 6d net (Post free, 10s. 10d. home , 11s. abroad.)

Contents.

Constitution and Properties : Definitions and Sources, Gelatine, Chondrin and Allied Bodies, Physical and Chemical Properties, Classification, Grades and Commercial Varieties—**Raw Materials and Manufacture :** Glue Stock, Lining, Extraction, Washing and Clarifying, Filter Presses, Water Supply, Use of Alkalies, Action of Bacteria and of Antiseptics, Various Processes, Cleansing, Forming, Drying, Crushing, etc., Secondary Products—**Uses of Glue :** Selection and Preparation for Use, Carpentry, Veneering, Paper-Making, Bookbinding, Printing Rollers, Hectographs, Match Manufacture, Sandpaper, etc., Substitutes for other Materials, Artificial Leather and Caoutchouc—**Gelatine :** General Characters, Liquid Gelatine, Photographic Uses, Size, Tanno-, Chrome and Formo-Gelatine, Artificial Silk, Cements, Pneumatic Tyres, Culinary, Meat Extracts, Isinglass, Medicinal and other Uses, Bacteriology—**Glue Testing :** Review of Processes, Chemical Examination, Adulteration, Physical Tests, Valuation of Raw Materials—**Commercial Aspects.**

BONE PRODUCTS AND MANURES: An Account of the most recent Improvements in the Manufacture of Fat, Glue, Animal Charcoal, Size Gelatine and Manures. By THOMAS LAMBERT, Technical and Consulting Chemist. Illustrated by Twenty-one Plans and Diagrams. 162 pp. Demy 8vo. Price 7s. 6d. net. (Post free, 7s. 10d. home; 8s. abroad)

Contents.

Chemical Composition of Bones—Arrangement of Factory—Properties of Glue—Glutin and Chondrin—Skin Glue—Liming of Skins—Washing—Boiling of Skins—Clarification of Glue Liquors—Glue-Boiling and Clarifying House—Specification of a Glue—Size—Uses and Preparation and Composition of Size—Concentrated Size—Properties of Gelatine—Preparation of Skin Gelatine—Drying—Bone Gelatine—Selecting Bones—Crushing—Dissolving—Bleaching—Boiling—Properties of Glutin and Chondrin—Testing of Glues and Gelatines—The Uses of Glue, Gelatine and Size in Various Trades—Soluble and Liquid Glues—Steam and Waterproof Glues—**Manures**—Importation of Food Stuffs—Soils—Germination—Plant Life—**Natural Manures**—Water and Nitrogen in Farmyard Manure—Full Analysis of Farmyard Manure—Action on Crops—Water-Closet System—Sewage Manure—Green Manures—**Artificial Manures**—**Mineral Manures**—Nitrogenous Matters—Shoddy—Hoofs and Horns—Leather Waste—Dried Meat—Dried Blood—Superphosphates—Composition—Manufacture—Common Raw Bones—Degreased Bones—Crude Fat—Refined Fat—Degelatinised Bones—Animal Charcoal—Bone Superphosphates—Guanos—Dried Animal Products—Potash Compounds—Sulphate of Ammonia—Extraction in Zacuo—French and British Gelatines compared—Index.

Chemicals, Waste Products and Agricultural Chemistry.

REISSUE OF **CHEMICAL ESSAYS OF C. W. SCHEELE** First Published in English in 1786. Translated from the Academy of Sciences at Stockholm, with Additions 300 pp. Demy 8vo Price 5s. net. (Post free 5s. 6d. home; 5s 9d abroad.)

Contents.

Memoir C W Scheele and his work (written for this edition by J G McIntosh)—On Fluor Mineral and its Acid—On Fluor Mineral—Chemical Investigation of Fluor Acid, with a View to the Earth which it Yields, by Mr. Wiegler—Additional Information Coocerning Fluor Minerals—On Manganese, Magnesium, or Magnesia Vitrariorum—On Arsenic and its Acid—Remarks upon Salts of Benzoin—On Silex, Clay and Alum—Analysis of the Calculus Vesical—Method of Preparing Mercurius Dulcis Via Humida—Cheaper and more Convenient Method of Preparing Pulvis Algarothi—Experiments upon Molybdæna—Experiments on Plumbago—Method of Preparing a New Green Colour—Of the Decomposition of Neutral Salts by Unslaked Lime and Iron—On the Quantity of Pure Air which is Daily Present in our Atmosphere—On Milk and its Acid—On the Acid of Saccharum Lactis—On the Constituent Parts of Lapis Ponderosus or Tungsten—Experiments and Observations on Ether—Index

THE MANUFACTURE OF ALUM AND THE SULPHATES AND OTHER SALTS OF ALUMINA AND IRON. Their Uses and Applications as Mordants in Dyeing and Calico Printing, and their other Applications in the Arts, Manufactures, Sanitary Engineering, Agriculture and Horticulture. Translated from the French of LUCIEN GESCHWIND. 195 Illustrations. 400 pp. Royal 8vo. Price 12s. 6d. net. (Post free, 13s. home; 13s. 6d abroad.)

AMMONIA AND ITS COMPOUNDS: Their Manufacture and Uses By CAMILLE VINCENT, Professor at the Central School of Arts and Manufactures, Paris. Translated from the French by M. J. SALTER Royal 8vo. 114 pp. Thirty-two Illustrations. Price 5s. net. (Post free, 5s. 4d home; 5s. 6d. abroad)

Contents.

General Considerations: Various Sources of Ammoniacal Products; Human Urine as a Source of Ammonia—**Extraction of Ammoniacal Products from Sewage**—Extraction of Ammonia from Gas Liquor—Manufacture of Ammoniacal Compounds from Bones, Nitrogenous Waste, Beetroot Wash and Peat—Manufacture of

INDUSTRIAL ALCOHOL. A Practical Manual on the Production and Use of Alcohol for Industrial Purposes and for Use as a Heating Agent, as an Illuminant and as a Source of Motive Power. By J. G. M'INTOSH, Lecturer on Manufacture and Applications of Industrial Alcohol at The Polytechnic, Regent Street, London. Demy 8vo 1907. 250 pp With 75 Illustrations and 25 Tables. Price 7s 6d net. (Post free, 7s. 9d home, 8s. abroad.)

Contents.

Alcohol and its Properties.—Ethylic Alcohol—Absolute Alcohol—Adulterations—Properties of Alcohol—Fractional Distillation—Destructive Distillation—Products of Combustion—Alcoholometry—Proof Spirit—Analysis of Alcohol—Table showing Correspondence between the Specific Gravity and Per Cents of Alcohol over and under Proof—Other Alcohol Tables **Continuous Aseptic and Antiseptic Fermentation and Sterilisation in Industrial Alcohol Manufacture. The Manufacture of Industrial Alcohol from Beets.**—Beet Slicing Machines—Extraction of Beet Juice by Maceration, by Diffusion—Fermentation in Beet Distilleries—Plans of Modern Beet Distillery **The Manufacture of Industrial Alcohol from Grain.**—Plan of Modern Grain Distillery. **The Manufacture of Industrial Alcohol from Potatoes. The Manufacture of Industrial Alcohol from Surplus Stocks of Wine,** Spoilt Wine, Wine Marcs, and from Fruit in General. The Manufacture of Alcohol from the Sugar Cane and Sugar Cane Molasses—Plans. **Plant, etc., for the Distillation and Rectification of Industrial Alcohol.**—The Caffey and other "Patent" Stills—Intermittent versus Continuous Rectification—Continuous Distillation—Rectification of Spent Wash. **The Manufacture and Uses of Various Alcohol Derivatives,** Ether, Haloid Ethers, Compound Ethers, Chloroform—Methyl and Amyl Alcohols and their Ethereal Salts, Acetone—Barbet's Ether, Methyl Alcohol and Acetone Rectifying Stills **The Uses of Alcohol in Manufactures,** etc—List of Industries in which Alcohol is used, with Key to Function of Alcohol in each Industry. **The Uses of Alcohol for Lighting, Heating, and Motive Power.**

ANALYSIS OF RESINS AND BALSAMS. Translated from the German of Dr. KARL DIETERICH Demy 8vo 340 pp Price 7s 6d. net. (Post free, 7s. 10d home; 8s. 3d. abroad.)

MANUAL OF AGRICULTURAL CHEMISTRY. By HERBERT INGLE, F.I.C., Late Lecturer on Agricultural Chemistry, the Leeds University, Lecturer in the Victoria University. Second Edition, with additional matter relating to Tropical Agriculture, etc. 438 pp 11 Illustrations. Demy 8vo. Price 7s. 6d. net (Post free, 8s. home, 8s. 6d abroad.)

Contents.

Properties and Characteristics of the Elements.—Hydrogen—Oxygen—Heat of Combustion—Nitrogen—Carbon—Sulphur—Phosphorous—Potassium—Sodium—Fluorine—Magnesium—Iron—Chlorine—Aluminium—Silicon—Borax **The Atmosphere.**—Nitrogen—Oxygen—Argon—Carbon Dioxide—Ammonia—Nitric Acid—Ozone—Solid Matter. **The Soil.**—Classification of Rocks—Quartz—Felspar—Mica—Clay—Sandstones—Shales—Limestones—Calcareous Rocks—Transported Soils. **Formation of Soils.**—By Water, Air, Earth Worms, Vegetation and Bacteria—Sand—Clay—Limestone—Humus—Classification of Soils. **Reactions in Soils.**—Diffusion—Gravitation—Nitrification—Soil Gases—Water of the Soil—Biology of the Soil—Electrolytic Dissociation Theory—Mass Action **Analysis of Soils.**—Sampling—Mechanical and Chemical Analyses—Determination of Silica, Alumina, Ferric Oxide, Total Potash and Phosphoric Acid, Lime, Magnesia, Calcium Carbonate, Sulphuric Acid, Nitrates and Nitrites **Natural Manures.**—Improvement of Soils—Farmyard Manure—Composition of Animal Excreta—Use of Litter, Straw, Peat, Bracken, Leaves, Sawdust, Tanners' Refuse—Fermentation and Preservation of Farmyard Manure **Other Organic Manures.**—Guano—Poultry and Fish Manures—Seaweed—Dried Blood—Bones—Meat Guano—Hair—Soot—Oil cakes **Nitrogenous Manures.**—Sodium Nitrate—Ammonium Sulphate—**Phosphatic Manures**—Tricalcium Phosphate—Coprolites—Phosphorites—Mineral Superphosphates—Basic Slag—**Potash Manures**—Composition of Principal Potash Salts—**Various Manures**—Common Salt—Gypsum—Limestone—Ferrous Sulphate—Gas Lime—Copper Sulphate. **Analysis of Manures.**—Constituents—Determination of Nitrogen—Phosphoric Acid—Potassium—Valuation of Manures from Analysis **Constituents of Plants.**—Carbohydrates—Sugars—Starch—Dextrin—Glycogen—Inulin—Gums—Cellulose—Glucose—Fructose—Cane Sugar—Meletrose—Arabinose—Xylose—Lignose—Pectose—Glycerol—Waxes—Organic Acids and their Salts **Essential Oils and Resins.**—Terpenes—Oxygenated Essential Oils—Essential Oils containing Sulphur—Resins **Nitrogenous Substances.**—Albuminoids—Amides—Alkaloids—Chlorophyll. **The Plant.**—Germination—Roots—Osmotic Pressure—Leaves—Assimilation—Flowers **Crops.**—Cereals—Root Crops—Fodder Crops—Hay—Ventilating Stacks—Silage—Composition of Crops **The Animal.**—Blood—Bones—Fatty Tissue—Muscle—Digestion—Bile—Urine **Foods and Feeding.**—Composition of Oil-cake—Bye-Products as Foods—Digestibility of Foods—Calorific Value of Foods—Feeding Standards—Manurial Value of Foods **Milk and Milk Products.**—Fat—

Milk—Amount of Fat—Determination of Total Solids, Specific Gravity, Proteids, Milk Sugar —Adulteration of Milk—Detection of Preservatives—Butter—Butter Colouring—Cheese— Milk Standards. **Various Products used in Agriculture.**—Arsenious Oxide—Bleaching Powder—Copper Salts—Disinfectants—Fungicides—Iron Sulphate—Mercuric Chloride— Plant Poisons **Appendix.**—Atomic Weights—Hydrometer Scales—Metric System— Solubilities **Tropical Agriculture, etc.**—Composition of Rain Water—Irrigation Water— Earth Worms—Motion of Water in Soil—Analysis of Soils—Green Manuring—Kraal Manure —Bats' Guano—Artificial Manures—The Plant—Rice—Maize—Millet—Cotton—Flax—Castor Seeds—Sunflower—Composition of Various South African Grown Crops—Ash Constituents of Foods—Variations in the Composition of Milk—Butter—Fat—Bordeaux Mixture—Insecticides

THE UTILISATION OF WASTE PRODUCTS. A Treatise on the Rational Utilisation, Recovery and Treatment of Waste Products of all kinds. By Dr. THEODOR KOLLER. Translated from the Second Revised German Edition. Twenty-two Illustrations Demy 8vo. 280 pp. Price 7s. 6d. net. (Post free, 7s 10d home , 8s 3d. abroad.)

THE MANUFACTURE OF CHEMICAL MANURES From the French of J. FRITSCH. With 70 Illustrations and 4 Plates
[*In preparation.*
The Contents will include Superphosphates, Guanos, Nitrate of Soda, Dried Blood Sulphate of Ammonia, Potashes, etc.

Writing Inks and Sealing Waxes.

INK MANUFACTURE : Including Writing, Copying, Lithographic, Marking, Stamping, and Laundry Inks. By SIGMUND LEHNER. Three Illustrations. Crown 8vo 162 pp Translated from the German of the Fifth Edition. Price 5s net. (Post free, 5s 3d home ; 5s 6d abroad.)

SEALING-WAXES, WAFERS AND OTHER ADHESIVES FOR THE HOUSEHOLD, OFFICE, WORKSHOP AND FACTORY. By H. C. STANDAGE. Crown 8vo. 96 pp. Price 5s. net. (Post free, 5s. 3d. home ; 5s 4d. abroad.)

Contents.

Materials Used for Making Sealing-Waxes—The Manufacture of Sealing-Waxes— Wafers—Notes on the Nature of the Materials Used in Making Adhesive Compounds—Cements for Use in the Household—Office Gums, Pastes and Mucilages—Adhesive Compounds for Factory and Workshop Use.

Lead Ores and Compounds.

LEAD AND ITS COMPOUNDS. By THOS. LAMBERT, Technical and Consulting Chemist. Demy 8vo. 226 pp. Forty Illustrations. Price 7s. 6d. net. (Post free, 7s. 10d. home , 8s 3d. abroad)

Contents.

History—Ores of Lead—Geographical Distribution of the Lead Industry—Chemical and Physical Properties of Lead—Alloys of Lead—Compounds of Lead—Dressing of Lead Ores —Smelting of Lead Ores—Smelting in the Scotch or American Ore-hearth—Smelting in the Shaft or Blast Furnace—Condensation of Lead Fume—Desilverisation, or the Separation of Silver from Argentiferous Lead—Cupellation—The Manufacture of Lead Pipes and Sheets—Protoxide of Lead—Litharge and Massicot—Red Lead or Minium—Lead Poisoning —Lead Substitutes—Zinc and its Compounds—Pumice Stone—Drying Oils and Siccatives —Oil of Turpentine Resin—Classification of Mineral Pigments—Analysis of Raw and Finished Products—Tables—Index.

NOTES ON LEAD ORES : Their Distribution and Properties. By JAS. FAIRIE, F.G.S. Crown 8vo. 64 pages. Price 1s. net. (Post free. 1s. 3d. home . 1s. 4d. abroad.)

Industrial Hygiene.

THE RISKS AND DANGERS TO HEALTH OF VARIOUS OCCUPATIONS AND THEIR PREVENTION.

By LEONARD A. PARRY, M D., B.Sc. (Lond.). 196 pp. Demy 8vo. Price 7s. 6d. net. (Post free, 7s. 10d. home ; 8s. abroad.)

Contents.

Occupations which are Accompanied by the Generation and Scattering of Abnormal Quantities of Dust—Trades in which there is Danger of Metallic Poisoning—Certain Chemical Trades—Some Miscellaneous Occupations—Trades in which Various Poisonous Vapours are Inhaled—General Hygienic Considerations—Index.

Industrial Uses of Air, Steam and Water.

DRYING BY MEANS OF AIR AND STEAM.

Explanations, Formulæ, and Tables for Use in Practice. Translated from the German of E. HAUSBRAND. Two folding Diagrams and Thirteen Tables. Crown 8vo. 72 pp. Price 5s. net (Post free, 5s. 3d. home, 5s. 6d. abroad.)

Contents.

British and Metric Systems Compared—Centigrade and Fahr. Thermometers—Estimation of the Maximum Weight of Saturated Aqueous Vapour which can be contained in 1 kilo. of Air at Different Pressure and Temperatures—Calculation of the Necessary Weight and Volume of Air, and of the Least Expenditure of Heat, per Drying Apparatus with Heated Air, at the Atmospheric Pressure: *A*, With the Assumption that the Air is *Completely Saturated* with Vapour both before Entry and after Exit from the Apparatus—*B*, When the Atmospheric Air is Completely Saturated *before entry*, but at its *exit* is only $\frac{2}{3}$, $\frac{1}{3}$ or $\frac{1}{2}$ Saturated —*C*, When the Atmospheric Air is *not* Saturated with Moisture before Entering the Drying Apparatus—Drying Apparatus, in which, in the Drying Chamber, a Pressure is Artificially Created, Higher or Lower than that of the Atmosphere—Drying by Means of Superheated Steam, without Air—Heating Surface, Velocity of the Air Current, Dimensions of the Drying Room, Surface of the Drying Material, Losses of Heat—Index.

(See also " Evaporating, Condensing and Cooling Apparatus," p. 26.)

PURE AIR, OZONE AND WATER.

A Practical Treatise of their Utilisation and Value in Oil, Grease, Soap, Paint, Glue and other Industries By W. B. COWELL. Twelve Illustrations. Crown 8vo. 85 pp. Price 5s. net. (Post free, 5s. 3d. home ; 5s. 6d. abroad.)

Contents.

Atmospheric Air, Lifting of Liquids, Suction Process, Preparing Blown Oils, Preparing Siccative Drying Oils—Compressed Air, Whitewash—Liquid Air, Retrocession—Purification of Water; Water Hardness—Fleshings and Bones—Ozonised Air in the Bleaching and Deodorising of Fats, Glues, etc.; Bleaching Textile Fibres—Appendix ; Air and Gases; Pressure of Air at Various Temperatures, Fuel, Table of Combustibles, Saving of Fuel by Heating Feed Water ; Table of Solubilities of Scale Making Minerals ; British Thermal Units Tables ; Volume of the Flow of Steam into the Atmosphere ; Temperature of Steam—Index.

THE INDUSTRIAL USES OF WATER. COMPOSITION — EFFECTS—TROUBLES — REMEDIES—RESIDUARY WATERS—PURIFICATION—ANALYSIS.

By H. DE LA COUX. Royal 8vo. Translated from the French and Revised by ARTHUR MORRIS. 364 pp. 135 Illustrations. Price 10s. 6d. net. (Post free, 11s. home, 11s. 6d. abroad.)

Contents.

Chemical Action of Water in Nature and in Industrial Use—Composition of Waters—Solubility of Certain Salts in Water Considered from the Industrial Point of View —Effects on the Boiling of Water—Effects of Water in the Industries—Difficulties with Water—Feed Water for Boilers—Water in Dyeworks, Print Works, and Bleach Works—Water in the Textile Industries and in Conditioning—Water in Soap Works—Water in Laundries and Washhouses—Water in Tanning—Water in Preparing Tannin and Dyewood Extracts—Water in Papermaking—Water in Photography—Water in Sugar Refining—Water in Making Ices and Beverages—Water in Cider Making—Water in Brewing—Water in Distilling—Preliminary Treatment and Apparatus—Substances Used for Preliminary Chemical Purification—Commercial Specialties and their Employment—Precipitation of Matters in Suspension in Water —Apparatus for the Preliminary Chemical Purification of Water—Industrial Filters—Indus-

X Rays.

PRACTICAL X RAY WORK. By Frank T. Addyman, B Sc. (Lond.), F.I.C., Member of the Roentgen Society of London; Radiographer to St. George's Hospital, Demonstrator of Physics and Chemistry, and Teacher of Radiography in St. George's Hospital Medical School. Demy 8vo. Twelve Plates from Photographs of X Ray Work. Fifty-two Illustrations. 200 pp. Price 10s. 6d. net. (Post free, 10s. 10d. home, 11s. 3d abroad.)

Contents.

Historical—Work leading up to the Discovery of the X Rays—The Discovery—**Apparatus and its Management**—Electrical Terms—Sources of Electricity—Induction Coils—Electrostatic Machines—Tubes—Air Pumps—Tube Holders and Stereoscopic Apparatus—Fluorescent Screens—**Practical X Ray Work**—Installations—Radioscopy—Radiography—X Rays in Dentistry—X Rays in Chemistry—X Rays in War—Index.

List of Plates.

Frontispiece—Congenital Dislocation of Hip-Joint.—I., Needle in Finger.—II., Needle in Foot —III., Revolver Bullet in Calf and Leg.—IV, A Method of Localisation.—V, Stellate Fracture of Patella showing shadow of "Strapping".—VI., Sarcoma —VII, Six-weeks-old Injury to Elbow showing new Growth of Bone.—VIII., Old Fracture of Tibia and Fibula badly set —IX., Heart Shadow.—X., Fractured Femur showing Grain of Splint.—XI., Barrell's Method of Localisation.

India-Rubber and Gutta Percha.

INDIA-RUBBER AND GUTTA PERCHA. Second English Edition, Revised and Enlarged. Based on the French work of T Seeligmann, G. Lamy Torrilhon and H. Falconnet by John Geddes McIntosh. Royal 8vo. 100 Illustrations 400 pages. Price 12s. 6d. net. (Post free, 13s. home; 13s. 6d. abroad.) [*Just published.*

Contents.

India-Rubber.—Indiarubber, Latex—Definitions—Laticiferous Vessels—Botanical Origin—Habitats—Methods of obtaining the Latex—Methods of Preparing Raw or Crude Indiarubber—Rubber Cultivation in Various Countries—Climatology—Soil—Rational Culture and Acclimatisation of the Different Species of Indiarubber Plants—Classification of the Commercial Species of Raw Rubber—Physical and Chemical Properties of the Latex and of Indiarubber—General Considerations—Mechanical Transformation of Natural Rubber into Washed or Normal Rubber (Purification)—Softening, Cutting, Washing, Drying, Storage—Mechanical Transformation of Normal Rubber into Masticated Rubber—Vulcanisation of Normal Rubber—Chemical and Physical Properties of Vulcanised Rubber—Hardened Rubber or Ebonite—Considerations on Mineralisation and Other Mixtures—Coloration and Dyeing—Analysis of Natural or Normal Rubber and Vulcanised Rubber—Rubber Substitutes—Imitation Rubber—Analysis of Indiarubber.

Gutta Percha.—Definition of Gutta Percha—Botanical Origin—Habitat—Climatology—Soil—Rational Culture—Methods of Collection—Felling and Ringing *versus* Tapping—Extraction of Gutta Percha from Leaves by Toluene, etc.—Classification of the Different Species of Commercial Gutta Percha—Physical and Chemical Properties of Gutta Percha—Mechanical Treatment of Gutta Percha—Methods of Analysing Gutta Percha—Gutta Percha Substitutes.

Leather Trades.

PRACTICAL TREATISE ON THE LEATHER INDUSTRY. By A. M. Villon. Translated by Frank T. Addyman, B.Sc. (Lond.), F.I C., F.C.S.; and Corrected by an Eminent Member of the Trade. 500 pp., royal 8vo. 123 Illustrations. Price 21s net. (Post free, 21s 6d. home, 22s. 6d. abroad.)

Contents.

Preface—Translator's Preface—List of Illustrations.

Part I., **Materials used in Tanning**—Skins Skin and its Structure; Skins used in Tanning; Various Skins and their Uses—Tannin and Tanning Substances Tannin, Barks (Oak), Barks other than Oak; Tanning Woods, Tannin-bearing Leaves, Excrescences, Tan-bearing Fruits; Tan-bearing Roots and Bulbs, Tanning Juices, Tanning Substances used in Various Countries, Tannin Extracts; Estimation of Tannin and Tannin Principles.

Part II., **Tanning**—The Installation of a Tannery: Tan Furnaces, Chimneys, Boilers, etc., Steam Engines—Grinding and Trituration of Tanning Substances Cutting up Bark; Grinding Bark, The Grinding of Tan Woods; Powdering Fruit, Galls and Grains; Notes on the Grinding of Bark—Manufacture of Sole Leather. Soaking, Sweating and Unhairing, Plumping and Colouring, Handling; Tanning; Tanning Elephants' Hides; Drying; Striking or Pinning—Manufacture of Dressing Leather Soaking; Depilation; New Processes for the Depilation of Skins, Tanning; Cow Hides, Horse Hides, Goat Skins, Manu-

THE LEATHER WORKER'S MANUAL. Being a Compendium of Practical Recipes and Working Formulæ for Curriers, Bootmakers, Leather Dressers. Blacking Manufacturers, Saddlers, Fancy Leather Workers. By H. C. STANDAGE. Demy 8vo. 165 pp Price 7s. 6d. net. (Post free, 7s 10d. home ; 8s. abroad.)

Contents.

(See " *Wood Products, Distillates and Extracts*," p. 29).

Books on Pottery, Bricks, Tiles, Glass, etc.

MODERN BRICKMAKING. By ALFRED B SEARLE. Royal 8vo 440 pages 260 Illustrations Price 12s. 6d. net. (Post free, 13s. home; 13s. 6d abroad) *[Just published.*

Contents.

Drying or Steaming—Volatilization—Full Fire—Smoking—Seger Cones—Draught Gauge—
Cooling **Vitrified Bricks for Special Work**—Clinkers and Paving Bricks—Acid-proof
Bricks. **Fire-Bricks and Blocks.**—Materials—Grog—Grinding—Blocks—Drying—Dipped
Fire-bricks—Firing—Silica Bricks—Ganister Bricks—Bauxite and Magnesia Bricks—
Neutral Fire-bricks. **Glazed Bricks.**—Pressing—Dipping—Glazes—Coloured Glazes—Ma-
jolica Glazes—Firing—Salt-glazed Bricks. **Perforated, Radial, and Hollow Bricks.**—
Fireproof Flooring **Moulded and Ornamental Bricks—Drying Raw Clay—Sources of
Difficulty and Loss.**—Improper Materials or Site—Unsuitable Methods of Working—Lack
of Capital—Defective Accounting —**Index.**

THE MANUAL OF PRACTICAL POTTING. Compiled

by Experts, and Edited by CHAS. F. BINNS. Third Edition, Revised
and Enlarged. 200 pp. Demy 8vo Price 17s. 6d. net. (Post free
17s. 10d. home; 18s. 3d. abroad.)

POTTERY DECORATING. A Description of all the Pro-

cesses for Decorating Pottery and Porcelain. By R. HAINBACH.
Translated from the German. Crown 8vo. 250 pp Twenty-two
Illustrations. Price 7s. 6d. net. (Post free, 7s. 10d. home , 8s. abroad.)

Contents.

ARCHITECTURAL POTTERY. Bricks, Tiles, Pipes, Ena-

melled Terra-cottas, Ordinary and Incrusted Quarries, Stoneware
Mosaics, Faiences and Architectural Stoneware. By LEON LEFÈVRE.
Translated from the French by K. H. BIRD, M.A., and W. MOORE
BINNS. With Five Plates 950 Illustrations in the Text, and numerous
estimates. 500 pp, royal 8vo. Price 15s. net. (Post free, 15s. 6d.
home; 16s. 6d. abroad.)

Contents.

F. BINNS. 100 pp. Demy 8vo. Price 12s. 6d. net. (Post free, 12s. 10d. home, 13s. abroad.)

Contents.

Preface—The Chemistry of Pottery — Analysis and Synthesis — Clays and their Components — The Biscuit Oven — Pyrometry — Glazes and their Composition — Colours and Colour-making—Index.

THE ART OF RIVETING GLASS, CHINA AND EARTHENWARE. By J. HOWARTH. Second Edition. Paper Cover. Price 1s. net. (By post, home or abroad, 1s. 1d)

NOTES ON POTTERY CLAYS. The Distribution, Properties, Uses and Analyses of Ball Clays, China Clays and China Stone. By JAS. FAIRIE, F.G.S 132 pp. Crown 8vo. Price 3s. 6d. net. (Post free, 3s 9d. home, 3s. 10d. abroad.)

A Reissue of

THE HISTORY OF THE STAFFORDSHIRE POTTERIES, AND THE RISE AND PROGRESS OF THE MANUFACTURE OF POTTERY AND PORCELAIN. With References to Genuine Specimens, and Notices of Eminent Potters. By SIMEON SHAW. (Originally published in 1829) 265 pp. Demy 8vo. Price 5s. net (Post free, 5s. 4d. home; 5s. 9d. abroad.)

A Reissue of

THE CHEMISTRY OF THE SEVERAL NATURAL AND ARTIFICIAL HETEROGENEOUS COMPOUNDS USED IN MANUFACTURING PORCELAIN, GLASS AND POTTERY. By SIMEON SHAW. (Originally published in 1837.) 750 pp. Royal 8vo. Price 10s. net. (Post free, 10s. 6d. home; 12s. abroad.)

BRITISH POTTERY MARKS. By G. WOOLLISCROFT RHEAD. Demy 8vo. 310 pp. With Fourteen Illustrations in Half-tone and upwards of Twelve-hundred Marks in the Text. Price 7s 6d net. (Post free, 8s. home, 8s. 3d. abroad.) [*Just published.*

Glassware, Glass Staining and Painting.

RECIPES FOR FLINT GLASS MAKING. By a British Glass Master and Mixer. Sixty Recipes Being Leaves from the Mixing Book of several experts in the Flint Glass Trade, containing up-to date recipes and valuable information as to Crystal, Demi-crystal and Coloured Glass in its many varieties. It contains the recipes for cheap metal suited to pressing, blowing, etc., as well as the most costly crystal and ruby. Second Edition. Crown 8vo Price 10s. 6d. net. (Post free, 10s. 9d home; 10s 10d abroad.)

Contents.

Ruby—Ruby from Copper—Flint for using with the Ruby for Coating—A German Metal—Cornelian, or Alabaster—Sapphire Blue—Crysophis—Opal—Turquoise Blue—Gold Colour—Dark Green—Green (common)—Green for Malachite—Blue for Malachite—Black for Malachite—Black—Common Canary Batch—Canary—White Opaque Glass—Sealing-wax Red—Flint—Flint Glass (Crystal and Demi)—Achromatic Glass—Paste Glass—White Enamel—Firestone—Dead White (for moons)—White Agate—Canary—Canary Enamel—Index.

A TREATISE ON THE ART OF GLASS PAINTING.
Prefaced with a Review of Ancient Glass   By ERNEST R SUFFLING.
With One Coloured Plate and Thirty-seven Illustrations   Demy 8vo.
140 pp.   Price 7s. 6d. net   (Post free, 7s. 10d. home; 8s abroad.)

Contents.
A Short History of Stained Glass—Designing Scale Drawings—Cartoons and the Cut Line
—Various Kinds of Glass Cutting for Windows—The Colours and Brushes used in Glass
Painting—Painting on Glass, Dispersed Patterns—Diapered Patterns—Aciding—Firing—
Fret Lead Glazing—Index.

PAINTING ON GLASS AND PORCELAIN AND ENAMEL PAINTING
A Complete Introduction to the
Preparation of all the Colours and Fluxes used for Painting on Porcelain, Enamel, Faïence and Stoneware, the Coloured Pastes and Coloured Glasses, together with a Minute Description of the Firing of
Colours and Enamels.   By FELIX HERMANN, Technical Chemist.   With
Eighteen Illustrations.   300 pp.   Translated from the German second
and enlarged Edition.   Price 10s. 6d net   (Post free, 10s. 10d. home,
11s. abroad.)

Paper Making, Paper Dyeing, and Testing.

THE DYEING OF PAPER PULP.
A Practical Treatise for
the use of Papermakers, Paperstainers Students and others.   By
JULIUS ERFURT, Manager of a Paper Mill.   Translated into English
and Edited with Additions by JULIUS HÜBNER, F C.S., Lecturer on
Papermaking at the Manchester Municipal Technical School   With
Illustrations and **157 patterns of paper dyed in the pulp.**   Royal
8vo, 180 pp.   Price 15s. net.   (Post free, 15s. 6d. home, 16s. 6d. abroad.)

Contents.
**Behaviour of the Paper Fibres during the Process of Dyeing. Theory of the
Mordant—Colour Fixing Mediums (Mordants)—Influence of the Quality of the Water
Used - Inorganic Colours—Organic Colours—Practical Application of the Coal Tar
Colours according to their Properties and their Behaviour towards the Different
Paper Fibres—Dyed Patterns on Various Pulp Mixtures—Dyeing to Shade—Index.**

THE PAPER MILL CHEMIST.
By HENRY P. STEVENS,
M.A., Ph.D., F I.C.   Royal 12mo.   60 Illustrations   300 pp.   Price
7s. 6d. net.   (Post free 7s. 9d. home; 7s 10d. abroad.)

Contents.
Introduction.—Dealing with the Apparatus required in Chemical Work and General
Chemical Manipulation, introducing the subject of Qualitative and Quantitative Analysis.
Fuels.—Analysis of Coal, Coke and other Fuels—Sampling and Testing for Moisture, Ash,
Calorific Value, etc.—Comparative Heating Value of different Fuels and Relative Efficiency
Water.—Analysis for Steam Raising and for Paper Making Purposes generally—Water
Softening and Purification—A List of the more important Water Softening Plant, giving
Power required, Weight, Space Occupied, Out-put and Approximate Cost.   **Raw Materials
and Detection of Adulterants.**—Analysis and Valuation of the more important Chemicals
used in Paper Making, including Lime, Caustic Soda, Sodium Carbonate, Mineral Acids,
Bleach Antichlor, Alum, Rosin and Rosin Size, Glue Gela in and Casein, Starch, China Clay,
Blanc Fixe, Satin White and other Loading Materials, Mineral Colours and Aniline Dyes
Manufacturing Operations.—Rags and the Chemical Control of Rag Boiling—Esparto
Boiling—Wood Boiling—Testing Spent Liquors and Recovered Ash—Experimental Tests
with Raw Fibrous Materials—Boiling in Autoclaves—Bleaching and making up Hand Sheets
—Examination of Sulphite Liquors—Estimation of Moisture in Pulp and Half-stuff—Recom-
mendations of the British Wood Pulp Association   **Finished Products.**—Paper Testing,
including Physical, Chemical and Microscopical Tests. Area, Weight, Thickness, Apparent
Specific Gravity, Bulk or Air Space. Determination of Machine Dir ction, Thickness,
Strength, Stretch, Resistance to Crumpling and Friction, Transparency, Absorbency and
other qualities of Blotting Papers—Determination of the Permeability of Filtering Papers—
Detection and Estimation of Animal and Vegetable Size in Paper—Sizing Qualities of
Paper—Fibrous Constituents—Microscopical Examination of Fibres—The Effect of Beating

Tables—English and Metrical Weights and Measures with Equivalents—Conversion of Grams to Grains and *vice versā*—Equivalent Costs per lb , cwt., and ton—Decimal Equivalents of lbs , qrs , and cwts —Thermometric and Barometric Scales—Atomic Weights and Molecular Weights—Factors for Calculating the Percentage of Substance Sought from the Weight of Substance Found—Table of Solubilities of Substances Treated of in Paper Making—Specific Gravity Tables of such substances as are used in Paper Making, including Sulphuric Acid, Hydrochloric Acid, Bleach, Milk of Lime, Caustic Soda, Carbonate of Soda, etc., giving Percentage Strength with Specific Gravity and Degrees Tw.—Hardness Table for Soap Tests—Dew Point—Wet and Dry Bulb Tables—Properties of Saturated Steam, giving Temperature, Pressure and Volume—List of Different Machines used in the Paper Making Industry, giving Size, Weight, Space Occupied, Power to Drive, Out-put and Approximate Cost—Calculation of Moisture in Pulp—Rag-Boiling Tables, giving Percentages of Lime, Soda and Time required—Loss in Weight in Rags and other Raw Materials during Boiling and Bleaching—Conditions of Buying and Selling as laid down by the Paper Makers' Association—Table of Names and Sizes of Papers—Table for ascertaining the Weight per Ream from the Weight per Sheet—Calculations of Areas and Volumes—Logarithms—Blank pages for Notes

THE TREATMENT OF PAPER FOR SPECIAL PURPOSES. By L. E. ANDÉS. Translated from the German Crown 8vo 48 Illustrations 250 pp. Price 6s. net (Post free, 6s 4d. home; 6s 6d. abroad.)

Contents.

I., **Parchment Paper, Vegetable Parchment.**—The Parchment Paper Machine—Opaque Supple Parchment Paper—Thick Parchment—Krugler's Parchment Paper and Parchment Slates—Double and Triple Osmotic Parchment—Utilising Waste Parchment Paper—Parchmented Linen and Cotton—Parchment Millboard—Imitation Horn and Ivory from Parchment Paper—Imitation Parchment Paper—Artificial Parchment—Testing the Sulphuric Acid II , Papers for Transfer Pictures. III., **Papers for Preservative and Packing Purposes.**—Butter Paper—Wax Paper—Paraffin Paper—Wrapping Paper for Silverware—Waterproof Paper—Anticorrosive Paper IV , Grained Transfer Papers V., Fireproof and Antifalsification Papers VI., **Paper Articles.**—Vulcanised Paper Maché—Paper Bottles—Plastic Articles of Paper—Waterproof Coverings for Walls and Ceilings—Paper Wheels, Roofing and Boats—Paper Barrels—Paper Boxes—Paper Horseshoes VII , Gummed Paper. VIII. Hectograph Papers. IX., **Insecticide Papers.**—Fly Papers—Moth Papers. X., **Chalk and Leather Papers.**—Glacé Chalk Paper—Leather Paper—Imitation Leather. XI., Luminous Papers—Blue-Print Papers—Blotting Papers XII., Metal Papers—Medicated Papers. XIII , Marbled Papers XIV , Tracing and Copying Papers—Iridiscent or Mother of Pearl Papers XV., Photographic Papers—Shellac Paper—Fumigating Papers—Test Papers XVI., **Papers for Cleaning and Polishing Purposes—Glass Paper—**Pumice Paper—Emery Paper. XVII , Lithographic Transfer Papers. XIX., **Sundry Special Papers**—Satin Paper—Enamel Paper—Cork Paper—Split Paper—Electric Paper—Paper Matches—Magic Pictures—Laundry Blue Papers—Blue Paper for Bleachers. XX , Waterproof Papers—Washable Drawing Papers—Washable Card—Washable Coloured Paper—Waterproof Millboard—Sugar Paper. XXI , The Characteristics of Paper—Paper Testing.

Enamelling on Metal.

ENAMELS AND ENAMELLING. For Enamel Makers, Workers in Gold and Silver, and Manufacturers of Objects of Art. By PAUL RANDAU. Translated from the German. With Sixteen Illustrations Demy 8vo 180 pp. Price 10s. 6d. net. (Post free, 10s. 10d. home , 11s. abroad)

THE ART OF ENAMELLING ON METAL. By W. NORMAN BROWN. Twenty-eight Illustrations. Crown 8vo. 60 pp Price 2s. 6d net. (Post free, 2s 9d. home and abroad)

Silk Manufacture.

SILK THROWING AND WASTE SILK SPINNING. By HOLLINS RAYNER. Demy 8vo. 170 pp. 117 Illus. Price 5s. net. (Post free, 5s. 4d home , 5s 6d. abroad)

Contents.

The Silkworm—Cocoon Reeling and Qualities of Silk—Silk Throwing—Silk Wastes—The Preparation of Silk Waste for Degumming—Silk Waste Degumming, Schapping and Dis-

Books on Textile and Dyeing Subjects.

THE FINISHING OF TEXTILE FABRICS (Woollen, Worsted, Union and other Cloths). By ROBERTS BEAUMONT, M Sc., M I Mech.E., Professor of Textile Industries, the University of Leeds; Author of "Colour in Woven Design"; "Woollen and Worsted Cloth Manufacture"; "Woven Fabrics at the World's Fair"; Vice-President of the Jury of Award at the Paris Exhibition, 1900; Inspector of Textile Institutes; Society of Arts Silver Medallist; Honorary Medallist of the City and Guilds of London Institute. With 150 Illustrations of Fibres, Yarns and Fabrics, also Sectional and other Drawings of Finishing Machinery. Demy 8vo, 260 pp. Price 10s 6d. net. (Post free, 10s. 10d. home; 11s. 3d. abroad.) [*Just Published.*

Contents.

1, **Woollen, Worsted and Union Fabrics.**—Sections (1) Woollen Cloths Saxonies and Cheviots—(2) Worsted Fabrics Botany and Crossbred—(3) Fancy and Piece-dye Woollens—(4) Fancy and Piece-dye Worsteds—(5) Union Fabrics· Piece-dyes and Fancies—(6) Whipcords, Buckskins, Venetians, Cords and Twist warp Fancies—(7) Heavy Woollens Box Cloths, Meltons, Pilots—(8) Friezes, Shetlands and Naps—(9) Special Types of Overcoatings—(10) Golf Cloakings—(11) Vestings   II., **Processes of Finishing and their Effects.**—Sections—(12) Qualities of Unfinished Woollens—(13) Worsted Fabrics and Finishing—(14) Preliminary Work—(15) Finishing Processes—(16) Scouring and the Detergents Used—(17) Hydro-extracting—(18) Tentering and Drying—(19) Felting and its Effects—(20) Condition of the Piece in Milling—(21) Potash and Soda Soaps—(22) Effects of Raising—(23) Influence of Textural Conditions on Raising—(24) Theory of Raising and the Twine in the Yarn—(25) Fabric Structure and Raising Surface—(26) Several Kinds of Raising—(27) Lustring Processes—(28) Pressing.   III., **The Process of Scouring: Scouring Machines.**—Sections (29) Impurities in Greasy Pieces—(30) Scouring Machines—(31) The Rope Machine· Scouring Operation—(32) Washing-off—(33) Points in the Use of the Rope Scourer—(34) The Open Scourer Construction—(35) Advantages of the Open Scourer—(36) Scouring Machine with Flanged Rollers—(37) Combined Scouring and Milling Machine.   IV., **Theory of Felting.**—Sections (38) Qualities of Wool in Relation to Felting—(39) Shrinkage Properties of Merino and Cheviot Wools—(40) Felting Contrasts, Merino and Southdown Wools—(41) Utility in Woven Manufactures of Wools of Different Shrinking Qualities—(42) Yarn Structure—(43) Felting Affected by Yarn Composition—(44) Methods of Yarn Construction and Felting—(45) Shrinkage of Fabrics made of Re-manufactured Fibres—(46) Degree of Twine in the Yarn—(47) Folded Yarns and Shrinkage.   V., **Theory of Felting: Fabric Structure.**—Sections (48) Build of the Fabric—(49) Felting Quality of Standard Weaves—(50) Influence of Intersections—(51) Variation in Wefting—(52) Irregular Weaves and Felting—(53) Felting of Two-ply Warp and Weft Fabrics—(54) Relative Shrinkage of Single and Backed Weaves.   VI., **Theory of Felting: Compound Fabrics.**—Sections (55)—Structure of Backed Fabrics and the Felting Quality of the Cloth—(56) Three-ply Weft Fabrics—(57) Yarn Characteristics in Compound Weft Fabrics—(58) Fabrics Compound in the Warp—(59) Felting of Compound Weaves—(60) Double Cloths and Varied Felting—(61) Stitching or Tying of Double and Compound Weaves and the Effects on Milling   VII, **Fulling and Milling Machinery.**—Sections (62) "Fulling" and "Milling"—(63) Routine in the Fulling Stocks and Milling Machine—(64) Construction and Working of the Fuller Stocks—(65) Milling Machines—(66) Routine of Milling—(67) Corrugated Guide Rollers—(68) Machines with Two or More Upper Rollers—(69) Duplex Machines—(70) Machines without Flanged Roller—(71) Mechanical Devices applied to the Spout—(72) Roller Milling Machine with Stampers in the Spout—(73) Principle of Combined Milling Machine and Stocks—(74) Combined Scouring and Milling—(75) Milling without Artificial Compression.   VIII., **The Theory of Raising.**—Sections (76) Treatment of the Cloth—(77) Condition of the Cloth—(78) Dry Raising—(79) Damp and Wet Raising—(80) Raising Determined by the Degree of Felting—(81) Quality of the Material and the Raised Result—(82) Raising and Weave Structure—(83) Quality of the Fibre and Yarn Structure—(84) Raising of Fabrics in which Special or Fancy Yarns are used   IX, **Raising Machinery and the Raising Process.**—Sections (85) Hand Raising—(86) Raising Gig—(87) Operation of the Raising Gig—(88) Two-cylinder Raising Gig—(89) Teazle Raising—(90) Teazles and Card-wire Compared—(91) Card wire Raising Machines—(92) Modern Card Raising Machines—(93) The Horizontal Machine—(94) Rotary Machines   X, **Cutting, Cropping or Shearing.**—Sections—(97) Cropping—(98) The Effects of Cutting—(99) Cutting Machines—(100) The Cross-Cutting Machine—(101) The Continuous Cutting Machine—(102) Setting of the Cutting Parts—(103) Form of the Bar or "Bed" under the Cutters—(104) Machines with Two or More Cylinders—(105) Grinding.   XI, **Lustring Processes and Machinery.**—Sections (106) The Production of Lustre on Woollen and Worsted Fabrics—(107) Steaming and Cooling Machines—(108) Pressing—(109) The Vertical Press—(110) The Rotary Press—(111) Intermittent Pressing Machine.   XII. **Methods of Finishing.**—Sections (112) Routines of Finishing—(113) Woollen

THE CHEMICAL TECHNOLOGY OF TEXTILE

FIBRES: Their Origin, Structure, Preparation, Washing, Bleaching, Dyeing, Printing and Dressing. By Dr. GEORG VON GEORGIEVICS Translated from the German by CHARLES SALTER. 320 pp. Forty-seven Illustrations. Royal 8vo. Price 10s. 6d. net. (Post free, 11s. home ; 11s. 3d. abroad)

POWER-LOOM WEAVING AND YARN NUMBERING,

According to Various Systems, with Conversion Tables. Translated from the German of ANTHON GRUNER. **With Twenty-six Diagrams in Colours.** 150 pp. Crown 8vo. Price 7s 6d. net. (Post free, 7s. 9d home ; 8s abroad.)

TEXTILE RAW MATERIALS AND THEIR CONVERSION INTO YARNS.

(The Study of the Raw Materials and the Technology of the Spinning Process.) By JULIUS ZIPSER. Translated from German by CHARLES SALTER. 302 Illustrations. 500 pp. Demy 8vo. Price 10s. 6d. net. (Post free, 11s. home ; 11s. 6d. abroad.)

GRAMMAR OF TEXTILE DESIGN. By H. NISBET,

Weaving and Designing Master, Bolton Municipal Technical School. Demy 8vo 280 pp. 490 Illustrations and Diagrams Price 6s. net. (Post free, 6s 4d. home ; 6s 6d. abroad.)

Contents.

THE PLAIN WEAVE AND ITS MODIFICATIONS. TWILL AND KINDRED WEAVES.—Classification of Twill Weaves DIAMOND AND KINDRED WEAVES. BEDFORD CORDS. BACKED FABRICS. FUSTIANS. TERRY PILE FABRICS. GAUZE AND LENO FABRICS TISSUE, LAPPET, AND SWIVEL FIGURING , ALSO ONDULE EFFECTS. AND LOOPED FABRICS.

ART NEEDLEWORK AND DESIGN. POINT LACE. A

Manual of Applied Art for Secondary Schools and Continuation Classes. By M. E. WILKINSON. Oblong quarto. With 22 Plates. Bound in Art Linen. Price 3s. 6d. net. (Post free, 3s 10d. home ; 4s. abroad.)

Contents.

Sampler of Lace Stitches—Directions for working Point Lace. tracing Patterns, etc.— List of Materials and Implements required for working Plates I , Simple Lines, Straight and Slanting, and Designs formed from them II , Patterns formed from Lines in previous Lesson. III., Patterns formed from Lines in previous Lesson IV , Simple Curves, and Designs formed from them. V., Simple Leaf form, and Designs formed from it VI , Elementary Geometrical forms, with Definitions VII , Exercises on previous Lessons VIII , Filling of a Square, Oblong and Circle with Lace Stitches. IX., Design for Tie End, based on simple Leaf form X , Lace Butterflies (Freehand) XI Twenty simple Designs evolved from Honiton Braid Leaf. XII , Design for Lace Handkerchief, based on previous Lesson. XIII., Design for Tea-cosy XIV., Freehand Lace Collar XV . Freehand Lace Cuff (to match). XVI., Application of Spray from Lesson XI. XVII , Adaptation of Curves within a Square, for Lace Cushion Centre. XVIII., Conventional Spray for corner of Tea-cloth. XIX , Geometrical form for Rosebowl D Oyley, to be originally filled in XX, Geometrical form for Flower-vase D'Oyley, to be originally filled in. Each Lesson contains Instructions for Working, and application of new Stitches from Sampler

HOME LACE-MAKING. A Handbook for Teachers and

Pupils By M. E. W MILROY. Crown 8vo 64 pp. With 3 Plates and 9 Diagrams. Price 1s. net (Post free, 1s. 3d. home ; 1s. 4d. abroad.)

THE CHEMISTRY OF HAT MANUFACTURING. Lec-

tures delivered before the Hat Manufacturers' Association. By WATSON SMITH, F.C.S , F.I.C. Revised and Edited by ALBERT SHONK. Crown 8vo. 132 pp 16 Illustrations. Price 7s. 6d. net (Post free, 7s. 9d. home ; 7s. 10d. abroad.)

THE TECHNICAL TESTING OF YARNS AND TEXTILE FABRICS.

With Reference to Official Specifications. Translated from the German of Dr. J. HERZFELD. Second Edition. Sixty-nine Illustrations. 200 pp. Demy 8vo. Price 10s. 6d net. (Post free, 10s. 10d. home ; 11s. abroad.)

THEORY AND PRACTICE OF DAMASK WEAVING.

By H. KINZER and K. WALTER. Royal 8vo. Eighteen Folding Plates. Six Illustrations. Translated from the German 110 pp. Price 8s. 6d. net. (Post free, 9s. home ; 9s. 6d. abroad.)

Contents.

The Various Sorts of Damask Fabrics—Drill (Ticking, Handloom-made)—Whole Damask for Tablecloths—Damask with Ground- and Connecting-warp Threads—Furniture Damask—Lampas or Hangings—Church Damasks—The Manufacture of Whole Damask —Damask Arrangement with and without Cross-Shedding—The Altered Cone-arrangement— The Principle of the Corner Lifting Cord—The Roller Principle—The Combination of the Jacquard with the so-called Damask Machine—The Special Damask Machine—The Combination of Two Tyings.

FAULTS IN THE MANUFACTURE OF WOOLLEN GOODS AND THEIR PREVENTION. By NICOLAS

REISER. Translated from the Second German Edition. Crown 8vo. Sixty-three Illustrations. 170 pp. Price 5s. net. (Post free, 5s. 4d. home ; 5s. 6d abroad)

Contents.

Improperly Chosen Raw Material or Improper Mixtures—Wrong Treatment of the Material in Washing, Carbonisation, Drying, Dyeing and Spinning—Improper Spacing of the Goods in the Loom—Wrong Placing of Colours—Wrong Weight or Width of the Goods —Breaking of Warp and Weft Threads—Presence of Doubles, Singles, Thick, Loose, and too Hard Twisted Threads as well as Tangles, Thick Knots and the Like—Errors in Cross-weaving—Inequalities, i.e., Bands and Stripes—Dirty Borders—Defective Selvedges— Holes and Buttons—Rubbed Places—Creases—Spots—Loose and Bad Colours—Badly Dyed Selvedges—Hard Goods—Brittle Goods—Uneven Goods—Removal of Bands, Stripes, Creases and Spots.

SPINNING AND WEAVING CALCULATIONS, especially

relating to Woollens. From the German of N. REISER. Thirty-four Illustrations. Tables. 160 pp. Demy 8vo. 1904 Price 10s. 6d. net. (Post free, 10s. 10d. home ; 11s. abroad)

Contents.

Calculating the Raw Material—Proportion of Different Grades of Wool to Furnish a Mixture at a Given Price—Quantity to Produce a Given Length—Yarn Calculations—Yarn Number—Working Calculations—Calculating the Reed Count—Cost of Weaving, etc

WATERPROOFING OF FABRICS. By Dr. S. MIERZINSKI.

Crown 8vo 104 pp. 29 Illus Price 5s. net. (Post free, 5s. 3d. home , 5s. 4d. abroad.)

Contents.

Introduction—Preliminary Treatment of the Fabric—Waterproofing with Acetate of Alumina—Impregnation of the Fabric—Drying—Waterproofing with Paraffin—Waterproofing with Ammonium Cuprate—Waterproofing with Metallic Oxides—Coloured Waterproof Fabrics—Waterproofing with Gelatine, Tannin, Caseinate of Lime and other Bodies—Manufacture of Tarpaulin—British Waterproofing Patents—Index

HOW TO MAKE A WOOLLEN MILL PAY. By JOHN

MACKIE. Crown 8vo. 76 pp. Price 3s. 6d. net. (Post free, 3s 9d. home ; 3s 10d. abroad)

Contents.

Blends, Piles, or Mixtures of Clean Scoured Wools—Dyed Wool Book—The Order Book —Pattern Duplicate Books—Management and Oversight—Constant Inspection of Mill Departments—Importance of Delivering Goods to Time, Shade, Strength, etc —Plums.

(For " Textile Soaps and Oils " see p. 7.)

Dyeing, Colour Printing, Matching and Dye-stuffs.

THE COLOUR PRINTING OF CARPET YARNS. Manual

for Colour Chemists and Textile Printers By DAVID PATERSON, F.C.S. Seventeen Illustrations. 136 pp. Demy 8vo. Price 7s. 6d. net. (Post free, 7s. 10d. home ; 8s abroad)

Contents.

Structure and Constitution of Wool Fibre—Yarn Scouring—Scouring Materials—Water for Scouring—Bleaching Carpet Yarns—Colour Making for Yarn Printing—Colour Printing

THE SCIENCE OF COLOUR MIXING. A Manual intended for the use of Dyers, Calico Printers and Colour Chemists. By DAVID PATERSON, F C.S. Forty-one Illustrations, **Five Coloured Plates, and Four Plates showing Eleven Dyed Specimens of Fabrics.** 132 pp. Demy 8vo. Price 7s. 6d. net. (Post free, 7s. 10d home , 8s abroad.)

Contents.

Colour a Sensation; Colours of Illuminated Bodies, Colours of Opaque and Transparent Bodies, Surface Colour—Analysis of Light, Spectrum, Homogeneous Colours, Ready Method of Obtaining a Spectrum—Examination of Solar Spectrum, The Spectroscope and Its Construction; Colourists' Use of the Spectroscope—Colour by Absorption, Solutions and Dyed Fabrics, Dichroic Coloured Fabrics in Gaslight—Colour Primaries of the Scientist *versus* the Dyer and Artist, Colour Mixing by Rotation and Lye Dyeing, Hue, Purity, Brightness, Tints, Shades, Scales, Tones, Sad and Sombre Colours—Colour Mixing: Pure and Impure Greens, Orange and Violets; Large Variety of Shades from few Colours, Consideration of the Practical Primaries Red, Yellow and Blue—Secondary Colours, Nomeoclature of Violet and Purple Group, Tints and Shades of Violet Changes in Artificial Light —Tertiary Shades, Broken Hues, Absorption Spectra of Tertiary Shades—Appendix Four Plates with Dyed Specimens Illustrating Text—Index.

DYERS' MATERIALS: An Introduction to the Examination, Evaluation and Application of the most important Substances used in Dyeing, Printing, Bleaching and Finishing By PAUL HEERMAN, Ph D Translated from the German by A C. WRIGHT, M.A (Oxon), B.Sc (Lond.) Twenty-four Illustrations. Crown 8vo. 150 pp. Price 5s. net. (Post free, 5s. 4d. home , 5s. 6d. abroad)

COLOUR MATCHING ON TEXTILES. A Manual intended for the use of Students of Colour Chemistry, Dyeing and Textile Printing. By DAVID PATERSON, F.C.S Coloured Frontispiece. Twenty-nine Illustrations and **Fourteen Specimens of Dyed Fabrics** Demy 8vo. 132 pp. Price 7s. 6d. net. (Post free, 7s. 10d home ; 8s. abroad)

COLOUR: A HANDBOOK OF THE THEORY OF COLOUR. By GEORGE H. HURST, F.C.S. **With Ten Coloured Plates** and Seventy-two Illustrations. 160 pp. Demy 8vo. Price 7s. 6d. net (Post free, 7s. 10d. home , 8s. abroad.)

Contents.

Colour and Its Production—Cause of Colour in Coloured Bodies—Colour Phenomena and Theories—The Physiology of Light—Contrast—Colour in Decoration and Design—Measurement of Colour.

Reissue of

THE ART OF DYEING WOOL, SILK AND COTTON. Translated from the French of M. HELLOT, M MACQUER and M. LE PILBUR D'APLIGNY First Published in English in 1789. Six Plates Demy 8vo. 446 pp Price 5s. net. (Post free, 5s. 6d. home; 6s. abroad.)

Contents.

Part I , The Art of Dyeing Wool and Woollen Cloth, Stuffs, Yarn, Worsted, etc. Part II., The Art of Dyeing Silk. Part III , The Art of Dyeing Cotton and Linen Thread, together with the Method of Stamping Silks, Cottons, etc.

THE CHEMISTRY OF DYE-STUFFS By Dr. GEORG VON GEORGIEVICS. Translated from the Second German Edition. 412 pp. Demy 8vo Price 10s 6d net (Post free, 11s home , 11s. 6d. abroad.)

THE DYEING OF COTTON FABRICS A Practical Handbook for the Dyer and Student By FRANKLIN BEECH, Practical Colourist and Chemist. 272 pp. Forty-four Illustrations of Bleaching and Dyeing Machinery Demy 8vo. Price 7s 6d net. (Post free, 7s 10d home ; 8s. abroad.)

THE DYEING OF WOOLLEN FABRICS. By FRANKLIN BEECH, Practical Colourist and Chemist. Thirty-three Illustrations. Demy 8vo 228 pp Price 7s 6d net (Post free 7s 10d home

Bleaching and Bleaching Agents.

A PRACTICAL TREATISE ON THE BLEACHING OF LINEN AND COTTON YARN AND FABRICS. By L. TAILFER, Chemical and Mechanical Engineer. Translated from the French by JOHN GEDDES McINTOSH. Demy 8vo. 303 pp. Twenty Illus. Price 12s. 6d. net. (Post free, 13s home, 13s. 6d abroad.)

MODERN BLEACHING AGENTS AND DETERGENTS.

By Professor MAX BOTTLER. Translated from the German Crown 8vo. 16 Illustrations 160 pages Price 5s. net. (Post free, 5s. 3d. home; 5s 6d. abroad.) *[Just published.*

Contents.

Contents of " Modern Bleaching Agents and Detergents "—
continued.

Behaviour of Oxygenol toward Dyed Fabrics. **Sodium Peroxide as a Detergent.**--Sodium Peroxide Soap. **Sundry New Detergents and Cleansing Agents.**—Tetrapol—Lavado—Novol—Weiss's Benzine Washing Preparation—Hexol—Steinberg's Detergent Oil—Ozonite—Ozonal—Quillola—Gruner's Washing Powder—Eureka Washing Powder—Detergent Soaps that Liberate Oxygen—Klein's Detergent Soap—Detergent for Sensitive Colours—Poltzow's Detergent Soap — Wolzendorff's Cyanide and Photographer's Ink — Detergent Liquids—Hummel's Detergent Liquid—Detergent Paste—Blanchissine—Henkel's Persil—Reinol, Triol, Tetra-Isol, Benzin-Isol, Terpin-Isol, Isobenzine Soap and Iso Soap

Cotton Spinning and Combing.

COTTON SPINNING (First Year). By THOMAS THORNLEY, Spinning Master, Bolton Technical School. 160 pp. Eighty-four Illustrations. Crown 8vo. Second Impression. Price 3s. net. (Post free, 3s. 4d. home , 3s. 6d. abroad.)

COTTON SPINNING (Intermediate, or Second Year). By THOMAS THORNLEY. Second Impression. 180 pp. Seventy Illustrations Crown 8vo Price 5s. net. (Post free, 5s. 4d. home ; 5s. 6d. abroad)

COTTON SPINNING (Honours, or Third Year). By THOMAS THORNLEY. 216 pp Seventy-four Illustrations. Crown 8vo Second Edition. Price 5s. net (Post free, 5s. 4d. home , 5s. 6d abroad.)

COTTON COMBING MACHINES. By THOS. THORNLEY, Spinning Master, Technical School, Bolton. Demy 8vo. 117 Illustrations 300 pp Price 7s 6d net. (Post free, 8s. home ; 8s. 6d. abroad.)

Flax, Hemp and Jute Spinning.

MODERN FLAX, HEMP AND JUTE SPINNING AND TWISTING. A Practical Handbook for the use of Flax, Hemp and Jute Spinners, Thread, Twine and Rope Makers. By HERBERT R. CARTER, Mill Manager, Textile Expert and Engineer, Examiner in Flax Spinning to the City and Guilds of London Institute. Demy 8vo. 1907. With 92 Illustrations. 200 pp. Price 7s. 6d net. (Post free, 7s 9d. home ; 8s. abroad.)

FIBRES USED IN TEXTILE AND ALLIED INDUS-TRIES. By C. AINSWORTH MITCHELL, B.A. (Oxon.), F.I.C., and R. M. PRIDEAUX, F.I.C. With 66 Illustrations specially drawn direct from the Fibres. Demy 8vo. 200 pp. Price 7s. 6d net (Post free, 7s. 9d. home , 8s. abroad.) *[Just published.*

Contents.

Classification, General Characteristics, and Microscopical Examination of Fibres—Stegmata—Chemical Examination—Ultimate Fibres—Methyl Value—Moisture in Fibres. **Wool.**—Nature of Wool—Commercial Varieties—Characteristics of Good Wool—Merino—Microscopical Appearance—Mould in Wool—Felting Property—Curl of Wool—Chemical Composition—Action of Reagents on Wool—Chlorinised Wool—Detection of Dyed Fibres in Wool—Conditioning of Wool **Vicuna—Camel Hair—Alpaca—Llama Hair—Mohair—Cashmere—Goats' Hair—Cow Hair—Horse Hair—Deer Hair—Reindeer Hair—Rabbits' Hair—Cats' Hair—Dogs' Hair—Kangaroos' Hair—Human Hair. Silk.**—Origin of Silk—Reeling—Waste Silk—History—Commercial Varieties of Thread—Size of Yarns—Wild Silks—Microscopical Characteristics—Colour of Silk—Size of Fibres—Strength and Elasticity—Specific Gravity—Chemical Composition—Fibroin—Sericin—Hydrolysis of Silk Proteins—Action of Chemical Agents—Absorption of Tannin—Weighting—Differentiation and Separation from other Fibres **Cotton.**—Origin—History—Commercial Varieties—Structure of the Fibre—Cell Walls—Dimensions of Fibre—Chemical Composition—Cellulose—Action of Reagents—Nitrated Cotton—Examination of Bleached Fabrics—Absorption of Tannin—Absorption of Gases—Absorption of Dyestuffs—"Animalizing " of Cotton—Sized Cotton—Polished Cotton—Mould in Cotton—Waterproofed Cotton. **Mercerised Cotton.**—History—Structural Alteration of Fibres—Affinity for Dyestuffs—Chemical Changes in Mercerisation—Effect upon Strength of Fibre—Measurement of Shrinkage—Reactions and Tests for Mercer-

and Elasticity—Covering Power—Specific Gravity—Water—Microscopical Appearance—Reactions and Chemical Tests. **Linen and Ramie**—**Linen**—Source—Varieties of Commercial Flax—Retting of Flax—Lustrous Linen—Use of Linen as a Textile—Characteristics of the Fibre—Structure—Action of Reagents—Physical Properties—Composition—Flax Wax **Ramie**—Source—Preparation—History—Properties—Composition **Jute and other Fibres.**—**Jute**—Source—Commercial Varieties—Properties—Microscopical Appearance—Chemical Composition—The Cellulose of Jute—Lignocelluloses—Chemical Reactions. **Hemp.**—Source—History—Varieties—Properties—Microscopical Appearance—Chemical Composition **Sisal Hemp.**—Properties—Microscopical Characteristics—Chemical Composition **Pita Fibre. Manila Hemp.**—Characteristics—**Musa Paradisiaca Fibre. Banana Fibre. Andansonia Fibre.**—Differentiation of Jute: Manila and Andansonia **Sanseviera Fibre (Bowstring Hemp)**—Source **Sunn Hemp—Gambo Hemp—New Zealand Flax—Mauritius Hemp—Yercum Fibre—Pine Apple Fibre. Brush Fibres.**—Cocoanut Fibre (Coir)—Characteristics—Ixtle Fibre—Piassava—Brazilian Piassava—African Piassava **Vegetable Downs and Upholstery Fibres.**—Bombax Cottons—Kapok—Ochroma Down—Kumbi or Galgul—Vegetable Silk—Asclepias Cotton—Calotropis Down—Beaumantia Down—Other Vegetable Silks—Vegetable Wool—Tillandsia Fibre—Vegetable Horsehair. **Index.**

Collieries and Mines.

RECOVERY WORK AFTER PIT FIRES. By ROBERT LAMPRECHT, Mining Engineer and Manager Translated from the German. Illustrated by Six large Plates, containing Seventy-six Illustrations. 175 pp., demy 8vo Price 10s 6d. net. (Post free, 10s. 10d. home; 11s. abroad.)

VENTILATION IN MINES. By ROBERT WABNER, Mining Engineer. Translated from the German. Royal 8vo. Thirty Plates and Twenty-two Illustrations. 240 pp. Price 10s. 6d. net. (Post free, 11s. home; 11s. 3d abroad.)

HAULAGE AND WINDING APPLIANCES USED IN MINES. By CARL VOLK. Translated from the German. Royal 8vo. With Six Plates and 148 Illustrations 150 pp. Price 8s. 6d. net. (Post free, 9s. home; 9s 3d. abroad.)

Contents.

Haulage Appliances—Ropes—Haulage Tubs and Tracks—Cages and Winding Appliances—Winding Engines for Vertical Shafts—Winding without Ropes—Haulage in Levels and Inclines—The Working of Underground Engines—Machinery for Downhill Haulage.

THE ELECTRICAL EQUIPMENT OF COLLIERIES. By W. GALLOWAY DUNCAN, Electrical and Mechanical Engineer, Member of the Institution of Mining Engineers, Head of the Government School of Engineering, Dacca, India; and DAVID PENMAN, Certificated Colliery Manager, Lecturer in Mining to Fife County Committee. Demy 8vo. 310 pp. 155 Illustrations and Diagrams. Price 10s. 6d. net. (Post free, 11s. home; 11s. 3d. abroad.)

Contents.

General Principles, Magnetism, Units, Cells, etc.—Dynamos and Motors—Transmission and Distribution of Power—Prime Movers—Lighting by Electricity—Initial Outlay and Working Cost of Electrical Installations—Electricity Applied to Coalcutting—Electric Haulage, Winding, and Locomotives—Electric Pumps and Pumping—Electric-Power Drills and Underground Coal Conveyers—Typical Colliery Electrical Installations—Miscellaneous Applications of the Electric Current—Comparison of the Different Modes of Transmitting Power—Dangers Occurring from the Use of Electricity in Collieries—APPENDIX: Questions suitable for students preparing for colliery managers' examinations—INDEX.

Dental Metallurgy.

DENTAL METALLURGY: MANUAL FOR STUDENTS AND DENTISTS. By A. B. GRIFFITHS, Ph.D. Demy 8vo. Thirty-six Illustrations. 200 pp Price 7s. 6d. net. (Post free, 7s. 10d. home, 8s. abroad.)

Contents.

Introduction—Physical Properties of the Metals—Action of Certain Agents on Metals—Alloys—Action of Oral Bacteria on Alloys—Theory and Varieties of Blowpipes—Fluxes—

Engineering, Smoke Prevention and Metallurgy.

THE PREVENTION OF SMOKE. Combined with the Economical Combustion of Fuel. By W. C. POPPLEWELL, M.Sc., A M.Inst., C.E, Consulting Engineer. Forty-six Illustrations 190 pp. Demy 8vo Price 7s. 6d. net. (Post free, 7s. 10d. home, 8s. 3d. abroad)

Contents.
Fuel and Combustion— Hand Firing in Boiler Furnaces—Stoking by Mechanical Means—Powdered Fuel—Gaseous Fuel—Efficiency and Smoke Tests of Boilers—Some Standard Smoke Trials—The Legal Aspect of the Smoke Question—The Best Means to be adopted for the Prevention of Smoke—Index

GAS AND COAL DUST FIRING. A Critical Review of the Various Appliances Patented in Germany for this purpose since 1885. By ALBERT PUTSCH. 130 pp. Demy 8vo. Translated from the German. With 103 Illustrations. Price 5s. net (Post free, 5s 4d. home, 5s. 6d. abroad.)

Contents.
Generators—Generators Employing Steam—Stirring and Feed Regulating Appliances—Direct Generators—Burners—Regenerators and Recuperators—Glass Smelting Furnaces—Metallurgical Furnaces—Pottery Furnace—Coal Dust Firing—Index

THE HARDENING AND TEMPERING OF STEEL IN THEORY AND PRACTICE. By FRIDOLIN REISER. Translated from the German of the Third Edition. Crown 8vo. 120 pp Price 5s. net. (Post free, 5s. 3d home, 5s. 4d. abroad.)

Contents.
Steel—Chemical and Physical Properties of Steel, and their Casual Connection—Classification of Steel according to Use—Testing the Quality of Steel — Steel-Hardening—Investigation of the Causes of Failure in Hardening—Regeneration of Steel Spoilt in the Furnace—Welding Steel—Index.

SIDEROLOGY. THE SCIENCE OF IRON (The Constitution of Iron Alloys and Slags) Translated from German of HANNS FREIHERR V. JUPTNER 350 pp. Demy 8vo Eleven Plates and Ten Illustrations. Price 10s 6d. net (Post free, 11s. home; 11s 6d. abroad)

Contents.
The Theory of Solution.—Solutions—Molten Alloys—Varieties of Solutions—Osmotic Pressure—Relation between Osmotic Pressure and other Properties of Solutions—Osmotic Pressure and Molecular Weight of the Dissolved Substance—Solutions of Gases—Solid Solutions—Solubility—Diffusion—Electrical Conductivity—Constitution of Electrolytes and Metals—Thermal Expansion. **Micrography.**—Microstructure—The Micrographic Constituents of Iron—Relation between Micrographical Composition, Carbon-Content, and Thermal Treatment of Iron Alloys—The Microstructure of Slags. **Chemical Composition of the Alloys of Iron.**—Constituents of Iron Alloys—Carbon—Constituents of the Iron Alloys, Carbon—Opinions and Researches on Combined Carbon—Opinions and Researches on Combined Carbon—Applying the Curves of Solution deduced from the Curves of Recalescence to the Determination of the Chemical Composition of the Carbon present in Iron Alloys—The Constituents of Iron—Iron—The Constituents of Iron Alloys—Manganese—Remaining Constituents of Iron Alloys—A Silicon—Gases. **The Chemical Composition of Slag.**—Silicate Slags—Calculating the Composition of Silicate Slags—Phosphate Slags—Oxide Slags—Appendix—Index.

EVAPORATING, CONDENSING AND COOLING APPARATUS. Explanations, Formulæ and Tables for Use in Practice. By E HAUSBRAND, Engineer Translated by A C. WRIGHT, M.A. (Oxon.), B Sc (Lond.). With Twenty-one Illustrations and Seventy-six Tables 400 pp Demy 8vo. Price 10s. 6d. net. (Post free, 11s. home, 11s. 6d. abroad.)

Contents.
ReCoefficient of Transmission of Heat, k/, and the Mean Temperature Difference, $\theta/$in—Parallel and Opposite Currents—Apparatus for Heating with Direct Fire—The Injection of Saturated Steam—Superheated Steam—Evaporation by Means of Hot Liquids—The Trans-

from which Extra Steam is Taken—The Weight of Water which must be Evaporated from 100 Kilos. of Liquor in order its Original Percentage of Dry Materials from 1-25 per cent up to 20-70 per cent—The Relative Proportion of the Heating Surfaces in the Elements of the Multiple Evaporator and their Actual Dimensions—The Pressure Exerted by Currents of Steam and Gas upon Floating Drops of Water—The Motion of Floating Drops of Water upon which Press Currents of Steam—The Splashing of Evaporating Liquids—The Diameter of Pipes for Steam, Alcohol, Vapour and Air—The Diameter of Water Pipes—The Loss of Heat from Apparatus and Pipes to the Surrounding Air, and Means for Preventing the Loss—Condensers—Heating Liquids by Means of Steam—The Cooling of Liquids—The Volumes to be Exhausted from Condensers by the Air-pumps—A Few Remarks on Air-pumps and the Vacua they Produce—The Volumetric Efficiency of Air-pumps—The Volumes of Air which must be Exhausted from a Vessel in order to Reduce its Original Pressure to a Certain Lower Pressure—Index.

Sanitary Plumbing, Electric Wiring, Metal Work, etc.

EXTERNAL PLUMBING WORK. A Treatise on Lead Work for Roofs. By JOHN W. HART, R.P.C. 180 Illustrations 272 pp. Demy 8vo. Second Edition Revised. Price 7s. 6d net. (Post free, 7s. 10d. home, 8s. abroad.)

HINTS TO PLUMBERS ON JOINT WIPING, PIPE BENDING AND LEAD BURNING. Third Edition, Revised and Corrected. By JOHN W. HART, R.P.C. 184 Illustrations. 313 pp. Demy 8vo. Price 7s. 6d net. (Post free, 8s home; 8s. 6d. abroad)

Contents.

Pipe Bending — Pipe Bending (continued) — Pipe Bending (continued) — Square Pipe Bendings—Half-circular Elbows—Curved Bends on Square Pipe—Bossed Bends—Curved Plinth Bends—Rain-water Shoes on Square Pipe—Curved and Angle Bends—Square Pipe Fixings—Joint-wiping—Substitutes for Wiped Joints—Preparing Wiped Joints—Joint Fixings—Plumbing Irons—Joint Fixings—Use of "Touch" in Soldering—Underhand Joints—Blown and Copper Bit Joints—Branch Joints—Branch Joints (continued)—Block Joints—Block Joints (continued)—Block Fixings—Astragal Joints—Pipe Fixings—Large Branch Joints—Large Underhand Joints—Solders—Autogenous Soldering or Lead Burning—Index

SANITARY PLUMBING AND DRAINAGE. By JOHN W. HART. Demy 8vo. With 208 Illustrations. 250 pp. 1904. Price 7s. 6d net. (Post free, 7s. 10d home, 8s. abroad.)

ELECTRIC WIRING AND FITTING FOR PLUMBERS AND GASFITTERS. By SYDNEY F. WALKER, R.N., M.I.E.E, M.I Min E., A M.Inst.C.E., etc., etc. Crown 8vo. 150 pp With Illustrations and Tables. Price 5s. net. (Post free, 5s. 3d. home; 5s. 6d. abroad.)

Contents.

Chapter I., **Electrical Terms Used.**—Pressure and Current—The Volt—Ampère—Electrical Resistance—Earth—Continuous and Alternating Currents—The Electric Circuit—Leakage—Heating of Conductors—Size and Forms of Conductors—The Kilowatt—Loss of Pressure—Arrangement of Conductors—Looping In—The Three Wire System—Switches—Fuses—Circuit—Breakers II, **The insulation of Wires, Their Protection, Fixing, etc.**—Conductors Insulated with Paper and Similar Materials—Sparking between Conductors—Dialite Insulation—Flexible Cords—Concentric Conductors—Twin Conductors—Three-Core Cables—Fireproof Insulation for Conductors—Jointing—T Joints—Covering T Joints in Vulcanized Rubber Cables III, **Fixing the Wiring and Cables.**—Laying Out the Route—The Protection of the Wires and Cables—Wood Casing—Metallic Conduits—Non-Metallic Conductors—Fixing the Conduits and Running Wires in Them—Drawing Wires into Tubes—To Avoid Shock. IV., **Lamps.**—The Incandescent Lamp—Lamp Holders—Lamp Fittings—The Nernst Lamp V, **Switches, Fuses, Distribution Boards, etc** —The Electricity Meter—Prepayment Meters.

THE PRINCIPLES AND PRACTICE OF DIPPING, BURNISHING, LACQUERING AND BRONZING BRASS WARE. By W. NORMAN BROWN. 35 pp. Crown 8vo. Price 2s. net. (Post free, 2s. 3d. home and abroad.)

A HANDBOOK ON JAPANNING AND ENAMELLING
FOR CYCLES, BEDSTEADS, TINWARE, ETC. By
WILLIAM NORMAN BROWN. 52 pp. and Illustrations. Crown 8vo.
Price 2s. net. (Post free, 2s. 3d. home and abroad.)

THE PRINCIPLES OF HOT WATER SUPPLY. By
JOHN W. HART, R.P.C. With 129 Illustrations. 177 pp., demy 8vo.
Price 7s. 6d. net. (Post free, 7s. 10d. home; 8s. abroad.)

House Decorating and Painting.

THREE HUNDRED SHADES AND HOW TO MIX
THEM. For Architects, Painters and Decorators. By A.
DESAINT, Artistic Interior Decorator of Paris The book contains 100
folio Plates, measuring 12 in. by 7 in., each Plate containing specimens
of three artistic shades. These shades are all numbered, and their
composition and particulars for mixing are fully given at the beginning
of the book. Each Plate is interleaved with grease-proof paper, and
the volume is very artistically bound in art and linen with the Shield
of the Painters' Guild impressed on the cover in gold and silver. Price
21s. net. (Post free, 21s. 6d. home; 22s. 6d. abroad.)

HOUSE DECORATING AND PAINTING. By W.
NORMAN BROWN. Eighty-eight Illustrations 150 pp. Crown 8vo.
Price 3s. 6d. net. (Post free, 3s. 9d. home and abroad)

A HISTORY OF DECORATIVE ART. By W. NORMAN
BROWN. Thirty-nine Illustrations. 96 pp. Crown 8vo. Price 1s. net.
(Post free, 1s. 3d home and abroad.)

WORKSHOP WRINKLES for Decorators, Painters, Paper-
hangers and Others. By W. N. BROWN. Crown 8vo. 128 pp. Second
Edition. Price 2s. 6d. net. (Post free, 2s. 9d. home; 2s. 10d abroad.)

Brewing and Botanical.

HOPS IN THEIR BOTANICAL, AGRICULTURAL
AND TECHNICAL ASPECT, AND AS AN ARTICLE
OF COMMERCE. By EMMANUEL GROSS, Professor at
the Higher Agricultural College, Tetschen-Liebwerd. Translated
from the German. Seventy-eight Illustrations. 340 pp. Demy 8vo.
Price 10s. 6d. net. (Post free, 11s home; 11s. 6d. abroad.)

Contents.

HISTORY OF THE HOP—THE HOP PLANT—Introductory—The Roots—The Stem—
and Leaves—Inflorescence and Flower. Inflorescence and Flower of the Male Hop, Inflorescence and Flower of the Female Hop—The Fruit and its Glandular Structure The
Fruit and Seed—Propagation and Selection of the Hop—Varieties of the Hop (a) Red Hops;
(b) Green Hops; (c) Pale Green Hops—Classification according to the Period of Ripening:
Early August Hops; Medium Early Hops; Late Hops—Injuries to Growth—Leaves Turning
Yellow, Summer or Sunbrand, Cones Dropping Off, Honey Dew, Damage from Wind, Hail
and Rain, Vegetable Enemies of the Hop: Animal Enemies of the Hop—Beneficial Insects on
Hops—CULTIVATION—The Requirements of the Hop in Respect of Climate, Soil and
Situation Climate; Soil, Situation—Selection of Variety and Cuttings—Planting a Hop
Garden Drainage; Preparing the Ground, Marking-out for Planting; Planting, Cultivation
and Cropping of the Hop Garden in the First Year—Work to be Performed Annually in the
Hop Garden Working the Ground; Cutting, The Non-cutting System, The Proper Per-
formance of the Operation of Cutting: Method of Cutting: Close Cutting, Ordinary Cutting,
The Long Cut, The Topping Cut, Proper Season for Cutting Autumn Cutting, Spring
Cutting; Manuring; Training the Hop Plant Poled Gardens, Frame Training, Principal
Types of Frames Pruning, Cropping, Topping, and Leaf Stripping the Hop Plant; Picking,
Drying and Bagging—Principal and Subsidiary Utilisation of Hops and Hop Gardens—Life
of a Hop Garden; Subsequent Cropping—Cost of Production, Yield and Selling Prices.

Wood Products, Timber and Wood Waste.

WOOD PRODUCTS: DISTILLATES AND EXTRACTS.

By P. DUMESNY, Chemical Engineer, Expert before the Lyons Commercial Tribunal, Member of the International Association of Leather Chemists; and J NOYER. Translated from the French by DONALD GRANT. Royal 8vo. 320 pp. 103 Illustrations and Numerous Tables. Price 10s. 6d. net. (Post free, 11s. home, 11s. 6d. abroad.)

Contents.

Part I., Wood Distillation—Principal Products from the Carbonisation of Wood—Acetates—Secondary Products of the Distillation of Wood—Acetone—Analysis of Raw Materials and Finished Products—Appendix—The Destructive Distillation of Olive Oil Residuals. Part II, Manufacture and Testing of Tan Wood Extracts and their Utilisation in Modern Tanneries—Plant and Equipment for Treating Chestnut Wood —Analysis of Tanning Substances—The Official Method of the International Association of Leather Chemists, with Supplementary Notes.

TIMBER: A Comprehensive Study of Wood in all its Aspects

(Commercial and Botanical), showing the Different Applications and Uses of Timber in Various Trades, etc. Translated from the French of PAUL CHARPENTIER. Royal 8vo. 437 pp. 178 Illustrations. Price 12s. 6d. net. (Post free, 13s. home; 14s. abroad.)

Contents.

Physical and Chemical Properties of Timber—Composition of the Vegetable Bodies —Chief Elements—M. Premy's Researches—Elementary Organs of Plants and especially of Forests—Different Parts of Wood Anatomically and Chemically Considered—General Properties of Wood—Description of the Different Kinds of Wood—Principal Essences with Caducous Leaves—Coniferous Resinous Trees—Division of the Useful Varieties of Timber in the Different Countries of the Globe—European Timber—African Timber—Asiatic Timber—American Timber—Timber of Oceania—Forests—General Notes as to Forests, their Influence—Opinions as to Sylviculture—Improvement of Forests—Unwooding and Rewooding —Preservation of Forests—Exploitation of Forests—Damage caused to Forests—Different Alterations—The Preservation of Timber—Generalities—Causes and Progress of Deterioration—History of Different Proposed Processes—Dessication—Superficial Carbonisation of Timber—Processes by Immersion—Generalities as to Antiseptics Employed—Injection Processes in Closed Vessels—The Boucherie System, Based upon the Displacement of the Sap—Processes for Making Timber Uninflammable—Appfications of Timber—Generalities —Working Timber—Paving—Timber for Mines—Railway Traverses—Accessory Products— Gums—Works of M. Premy—Resins—Barks—Tan—Application of Cork—The Application of Wood to Art and Dyeing—Different Applications of Wood—Hard Wood—Distillation of Wood—Pyroligneous Acid—Oil of Wood—Distillation of Resins—Index.

THE UTILISATION OF WOOD WASTE. Translated from

the German of ERNST HUBBARD. Crown 8vo. 192 pp. Fifty Illustrations. Price 5s. net. (Post free, 5s. 4d. home; 5s 6d abroad.)

Building and Architecture.

THE PREVENTION OF DAMPNESS IN BUILDINGS;

with Remarks on the Causes, Nature and Effects of Saline, Efflorescences and Dry-rot, for Architects, Builders, Overseers, Plasterers, Painters and House Owners. By ADOLF WILHELM KEIM. Translated from the German of the second revised Edition by M. J. SALTER, F.I.C., F.C.S. Eight Coloured Plates and Thirteen Illustrations. Crown 8vo. 115 pp. Price 5s. net. (Post free, 5s. 3d. home; 5s. 4d. abroad.)

HANDBOOK OF TECHNICAL TERMS USED IN ARCHITECTURE AND BUILDING, AND THEIR ALLIED TRADES AND SUBJECTS. By AUGUSTINE C. PASSMORE.

The Preserving of Foods and Sweetmeats.

THE MANUFACTURE OF PRESERVED FOODS AND SWEETMEATS. By A. HAUSNER. With Twenty-eight Illustrations. Translated from the German of the third enlarged Edition. Crown 8vo. 225 pp. Price 7s. 6d. net. (Post free, 7s. 9d. home, 7s 10d abroad.)

Contents.

RECIPES FOR THE PRESERVING OF FRUIT, VEGETABLES AND MEAT. By E. WAGNER. Translated from the German. Crown 8vo. 125 pp. With 14 Illustrations. Price 5s net. (Post free, 5s. 3d home, 5s. 4d. abroad.)

Contents.

FOODS AND DRUGS. Volume I., Chemistry and Analysis of Foods and Drugs. Volume II., Law Relating to Foods and Drugs. By E. J. PARRY, B.Sc. (Lond.). [*In preparation*

Dyeing Fancy Goods.

THE ART OF DYEING AND STAINING MARBLE, ARTIFICIAL STONE, BONE, HORN, IVORY AND WOOD, AND OF IMITATING ALL SORTS OF WOOD. A Practical Handbook for the Use of Joiners, Turners, Manufacturers of Fancy Goods, Stick and Umbrella Makers, Comb Makers, etc. Translated from the German of D. H. Soxhlet.

Celluloid.

CELLULOID: Its Raw Material, Manufacture, Properties and Uses. A Handbook for Manufacturers of Celluloid and Celluloid Articles, and all Industries using Celluloid; also for Dentists and Teeth Specialists. By Dr. Fr. BOCKMANN, Technical Chemist. Translated from the Third Revised German Edition. Crown 8vo. 120 pp. With 49 Illustrations. Price 5s. net. (Post free, 5s 3d. home; 5s 4d. abroad)

Contents.

Chapters I., **Raw Materials for the Manufacture of Celluloid**. Cellulose and Pyroxylin—Gun-cotton—Properties of Gun-cotton—Special Gun cottons for Celluloid Manufacture—Nitrating Centrifugalisers—Collodion Wool—Methods of Preparing Collodion Wool—Camphor—Japanese (Formosa) Camphor, O dinary Camphor—Borneo Camphor (Borneol), Sumatra Camphor, Camphol, Baros Camphor)—Properties of Camphor—Artificial Camphor—Camphor Substitutes. II., **The Manufacture of Celluloid**, Manufacturing Camphor by the Aid of Heat and Pressure—Manufacture of Celluloid by Dissolving Gun-cotton in an Alcoholic Solution of Camphor—Preparing Celluloid by the Cold Process—Preparation with an Ethereal Solution of Camphor—Preparation with a Solution of Camphor and Wood Spirit. III., **The Employment of Pyroxylin for Artificial Silk**: Denitrating and Colouring Pyroxylin — Uninflammable Celluloid — Celluloid and Cork Composition—Incombustible Celluloid Substitute — Xylonite or Fibrolithoid. IV., **Properties of Celluloid**. V., **Testing Celluloid**. VI., **Application and Treatment of Celluloid**: Caoutchouc Industry — Making Celluloid Ornaments — Working by the Cold Process — Working by the Warm Process—Celluloid Combs—Celluloid as a Basis for Artificial Teeth — Stained Celluloid Sheets as a Substitute for Glass — Celluloid, Printing Blocks and Stamps—Collapsible Seamless Vessels of Celluloid—Making Celluloid Balls—Celluloid Posters—Pressing Hollow Celluloid Articles—Casting Celluloid Articles—Method for Producing Designs on Plates or Sheets of Celluloid, Xylonite, etc—Imitation Tortoiseshell—Metallic Incrustations—Imitation Florentine Mosaic—Celluloid Collars and Cuffs—Phonograph Cylinder Composition—Making Umbrella and Stick Handles of Celluloid — Celluloid Dolls—Celluloid for Ships' Bottoms—Celluloid Pens—Colouring Finished Celluloid Articles—Printing on Celluloid—Employment of Celluloid (and Pyroxylin) in Lacquer Varnishes—Index

Lithography, Printing and Engraving.

PRACTICAL LITHOGRAPHY. By ALFRED SEYMOUR. Demy 8vo. With Frontispiece and 33 Illus. 120 pp. Price 5s. net. (Post free, 5s. 4d. home; 5s. 6d. abroad.)

Contents.

Stones—Transfer Inks—Transfer Papers—Transfer Printing—Litho Press—Press Work—Machine Printing—Colour Printing—Substitutes for Lithographic Stones—Tin Plate Printing and Decoration—Photo-Lithography.

PRINTERS' AND STATIONERS' READY RECKONER AND COMPENDIUM. Compiled by VICTOR GRAHAM Crown 8vo. 112 pp. 1904. Price 3s. 6d. net. (Post free, 3s. 9d. home, 3s. 10d. abroad.)

Contents.

Price of Paper per Sheet, Quire, Ream and Lb—Cost of 100 to 1000 Sheets at various Sizes and Prices per Ream—Cost of Cards—Quantity Table—Sizes and Weights of Paper, Cards, etc.—Notes on Account Books—Discount Tables—Sizes of spaces — Leads to a lb.—Dictionary—Measure for Bookwork—Correcting Proofs, etc

ENGRAVING FOR ILLUSTRATION. HISTORICAL AND PRACTICAL NOTES. By J. KIRKBRIDE. 72 pp. Two Plates and 6 Illustrations. Crown 8vo. Price 2s. 6d. net. (Post free, 2s. 9d. home; 2s. 10d. abroad.)

TINPLATE PRINTING. By ALFRED SEYMOUR. Crown 8vo. *[In preparation.*

Bookbinding.

PRACTICAL BOOKBINDING. By PAUL ADAM. Translated

THE TECHNOLOGY OF SUGAR : Practical Treatise on the Modern Methods of Manufacture of Sugar from the Sugar Cane and Sugar Beet. By JOHN GEDDES MCINTOSH. Second Revised and Enlarged Edition. Demy 8vo. Fully Illustrated. 436 pp Seventy-six Tables. 1906. Price 10s. 6d net. (Post free, 11s. home ; 11s. 6d. abroad)

(See " Evaporating, Condensing, etc., Apparatus " p. 26.)

Libraries and Bibliography.

CLASSIFIED GUIDE TO TECHNICAL AND COM-MERCIAL BOOKS. Compiled by EDGAR GREENWOOD. Demy 8vo 224 pp. 1904 Being a Subject-list of the Principal British and American Books in print ; giving Title, Author, Size, Date, Publisher and Price. Price 5s. net. (Post free, 5s. 4d. home , 5s. 6d. abroad)

HANDBOOK TO THE TECHNICAL AND ART SCHOOLS AND COLLEGES OF THE UNITED KINGDOM. Containing particulars of nearly 1,000 Techni-cal, Commercial and Art Schools throughout the United Kingdom. With full particulars of the courses of instruction, names of principals, secretaries, etc. Demy 8vo 150 pp. Price 3s. 6d. net. (Post free, 3s 10d. home , 4s. abroad.)

THE LIBRARIES, MUSEUMS AND ART GALLERIES YEAR BOOK, 1910-11. Being the Third Edition of Green-wood's "British Library Year Book" Edited by ALEX. J. PHILIP. Demy 8vo 286 pp. Price 5s. net. (Post free, 5s 4d. home ; 5s. 6d. abroad) *[Just published*

Contents.
Preface—Introduction—Chronological List of Adoptions of the Libraries Acts—Public Libraries Assessed for the Payment of Rates—Special Collections of Books in Libraries, Museums and Art Galleries—Alphabetical Index to Librarians, Curators and Assistants—Architects who have Designed Public Libraries—Libraries, Museums and Art Galleries in the United Kingdom—Women Librarians Occupying Chief Positions—Women Assistants—Methods of Charging or of Issuing Books—Classifications in Use—Public Libraries Opening on Sundays—Public Libraries Opening on Bank Holidays—Public Libraries in which Betting News is Obliterated—Public Libraries Publishing Magazines, Bulletins, etc

THE PLUMBING, HEATING AND LIGHTING ANNUAL FOR 1911. The Trade Reference Book for Plumbers Sanitary, Heating and Lighting Engineers, Builders' Mer-chants, Contractors and Architects. Quarto Bound in cloth and gilt lettered (Published in December, 1910.) Price 3s. net. (Post free, 3s. 4d home , 3s. 8d abroad)

SCOTT, GREENWOOD & SON,
Technical Book and Trade Journal Publishers,
8 BROADWAY, LUDGATE HILL,
LONDON, E.C.

Telegraphic Address, " Printeries, London "   Telephone, Bank 5403.

January, 1911.

CPSIA information can be obtained
at www.ICGtesting.com
Printed in the USA
LVOW04s1556131217
559595LV00013B/502/P